BUS

RAISING TEENAGERS

The Best Resources To Help Yours Succeed

John Ganz, Ed.D.
Editor

A Resource Pathways Guidebook

Seattle, Washington

✓

Published by Resource Pathways, Inc.
22525 S.E. 64th Place, Suite 253
Issaquah, WA 98027

Editor: John J. Ganz, Ed.D.

Managing Editor:
        Lisle Steelsmith, M.A.

Associate Editors and Researchers:
        Lillias Bever, Lucy Campos, Lesa Haakenson, Pam Mauseth,
        Maureen McLaughlin-Crawford, Susan O'Brien,
        David C. Osborn, Shannon Tucker

Book Design and Production:
        Sandra Harner and Kelly Rush,
        Laing Communications Inc., Redmond, Washington

Printing: Hignell Book Printing, Winnipeg, Manitoba, Canada

Publisher's Cataloging-in-Publication

Raising teenagers : the best resources to help yours
        succeed / John J. Ganz, editor. -- 1st ed.
            p. cm.
            Includes bibliographical references and index.
            ISBN: 1-892148-04-8

        1. Adolescent psychology--Bibliography. 2.
    Parent and teenager--Bibliography. 3. Teenagers--
    Family relationships--Bibliography.   I. Ganz, John
    J.

    Z7204.A3R35 1998   016.649'125
                                    QBI98-1544

Printed in Canada.

CONTENTS

INTRODUCTION

I

THE TEENAGER, A TALE OF TWO EXTREMES

Preface

"It was the best of times, it was the worst of times, it was the age of wisdom, it was the age of foolishness, it was the epoch of belief, it was the epoch of incredulity, it was the season of Light, it was the season of Darkness, it was the spring of hope, it was the winter of despair, we had everything before us, we had nothing before us . . . "

—Charles Dickens

Adolescence has been referred to as a time of stretching and strutting, and a time of storm and stress. Young people passing through adolescence become caught between childhood and adulthood. Our society asks its youth to take on adult responsibilities, such as driving, voting, and serving in the armed forces, yet often treats adolescents as if they are still children. Confused, these future parents, politicians, teachers, workers then proceed to act as children one minute, while the next minute they solve problems that even adults have difficulty with.

Yes, it's a confusing and frustrating time for young people, as well as for parents. Yet, it is also a time of great energy, potential adventure, risk-taking, and accomplishment. It's a time of mood swings, great insight, and enormous hormonal surges. This is a period of extremes. There is no middle ground, no meeting half-way, no making decisions at half-speed. Adolescents often see life as black or white, good or evil, their way or their parents' way. And parents must watch while their children try on the vestiges of young adulthood, while at the same time reject what their parents stand for.

Adolescence has been described by others as a developmental disturbance, as a departure from normalcy, and as a syndrome. Parents, watching their adolescent deal with the ups and downs, struggle and strife of the teenage years, remember that period, and are thankful they themselves survived those days. Yet, life has changed a great deal since parents traveled the path of adolescence toward adulthood. There is a different kind of stress adolescents deal with today. Concepts, foundations, and institutions, such as parenting practices, the family, the community, and religion have evolved, as have the rules for coping and succeeding in our society.

At times parenting an adolescent can seem like negotiating a mine field . . . only the mine field is moving, unpredictably. For past generations of parents, it at least seemed as if the mines were placed in fairly predictable places and patterns. Today's world, however, is marked with fluidity and constant change. The dangers are as real as ever, but the rules have changed on us. The concerns parents face about teenage sexual behavior are not just about pregnancy, but about dying of a sexually transmitted disease. Diseases and conditions once considered part of the adult world, such as alcoholism and depression, are now killers of our young people. Truly the stakes are higher for this generation. We're no longer dealing with problems that were once likened to threats of nuclear war, in which the problems were real, but they remained distant and abstract to most of us. We now must actually deal with harsh realities—teen suicides at epidemic proportions, young women and men struggling with eating disorders and potential death, the increase in gang involvement, and random delinquent behavior that has taken on a violent nature. Yes, parenting in the later part of the 20th century is difficult and different than it was for our parents.

The flip side of this is the experience of our children as they negotiate that mine field. It looks different to them than it does to adults. Adolescents have a ground's-eye view of this time of their lives. They deal intimately with the varied expectations of families, peers, and society. They have to learn how to survive in the day-to-day world of peer challenges and understand the inherent problems with "taking the easy way out." They must sort through mixed messages about success, make decisions between instant pleasure and long-term fulfillment, and handle racism, gender disparities, and ageism. Much has been written about adolescent angst, but by adults. Of course, adults **were** adolescents once. But the raw challenges of being an adolescent today are best illustrated through their music, art, poetry, and their graffiti as teens struggle to endure adolescence. Through these media, adults can then behold those sweet and bittersweet battle scars adolescents exhibit as they bounce between fresh discovery and trauma.

Parents, on the other hand, work from a standpoint of looking at "the big picture." There, from their bird's-eye view, parents perch constantly on guard for the dangers that lie in their adolescent's path as they navigate the minefield. Will their child fall victim to the blasts along the way or will they come out of the experience only witnessing others' struggles? Certainly, parents have traversed this time. No doubt they remember the temptations and the decisions they had to choose between, surely they remember the highs and the lows. But now embroiled with adult responsibilities and rights, parents often get frustrated at their teenager's inability to see beyond their narcissistic framework. Parents get annoyed and often believe that adolescent problems are not that great in the scheme of things. If teens just made correct choices, like the wise ones their parents advise them to make, things will work out okay.

From the ground's-eye view of the adolescent to the bird's-eye view of their parents, we must also acknowledge the satellite's-view from society. Social institutions charged with the care and guidance of our children have undergone great change as well. The institutions of marriage and parenting have seen an evolution within the last generation which has left them almost unrecognizable. For good or bad, the concept of the long-term, heterosexual, two-parent marriage as the socially acceptable paradigm has been replaced with blended family structures, same sex marriages and parents, and single parent households. The extended family has been replaced with a mobile and modified nuclear family, religion has lost its influence on many individuals and families, and in some communities, for some adolescents, the family has been replaced by the gang.

Logically, the impact of this evolution on young people during adolescence has been significant.

In addition, the institution of education has and is undergoing changes as well, and the role of the school has become cloudy. Schools are being challenged to become the hub of community service and activity as they were in the early years of our country. The school has redefined itself as a place where social, medical, mental health, as well as academic services are available to the community. Yet, in other places, schools are mandated to increase standardized test scores and academic performance of its students. These opposing missions for schools highlight our ambivalence concerning the role of the school in our society. Although these changes have not been necessarily bad, the societal distrust, the questioning of these institutional changes, and the resulting stress cannot be discounted.

Parents want their children to emerge from adolescence as integrated and effective adults ready to take on society's tasks and responsibilities. But what do adolescents want from their parents? What qualities do they identify as admirable traits in their parents? This question was posed to students of a Seattle high school. The students, ranging from 14 to 18 years of age, responded by describing these qualities that they deemed were worthy adult characteristics—show of compassion, giving space to grow and develop, having standards and guidance, exhibiting honesty and trust, possessing the ability to communicate, appreciating individuality while allowing for differences, taking an interest in others, and not having a pre-determined idea of what constitutes an adolescent. As parents will agree, these are pretty compelling qualities coming from kids who have been identified as victims of a syndrome, this developmental disturbance we call adolescence.

Sometimes we create sweeping generalizations about the dysfunctional characteristics attributed to adolescence, implying these struggles will happen to all adolescents. This is a mistake. For all the pitfalls, minefields, dangers, and risks out there in adolescent land, it's easy but inaccurate to conclude that all teens will manifest expressions of adolescent angst. Parents may find it refreshing to hear that their child (and themselves) may not experience adolescence as an on-going trauma. They may find that their child actually likes them, and wants to spend time with them . . . on occasion. During adolescence, it is difficult to predict whether or not a teenager will struggle with the many pitfalls experienced by their peers. Parents may find that this time of storm and stress only rears its ugly head periodically or episodically. Certainly this time of life is chockfull of phase-like characteristics. Thus, the issues and behaviors that worry parents may only occasionally impact their child or be manifested chronically.

Our purpose in creating this guidebook is to help you find your way to those resources that can answer your questions and concerns. This guidebook will identify resources that:

- Help you **understand adolescents,** and how they change and grow physically, cognitively, emotionally, and psychologically. We have also identified resources that highlight specific problems faced by either **teenage boys** or **teenage girls**.

- Help you deal with a **teenager's relationships.** Here parents will find resources that offer tips for improving **family dynamics** and dealing with the daily trials and tribulations of living with a teenager. Also included are resources that focus solely on ways to improve communication. Still other resources describe the role of a teen's peers, how to circumvent problems arising from their **peer group's influence**, and ways you can continue the bond between yourself and your teen as they seem to move away from you.

- Help you handle **critical issues and concerns** that your family may be affected by. Resources that are identified highlight specific problems such as:

  Substance Abuse: ways to prevent its occurrence; how to determine if your teen is using or abusing drugs, alcohol, and other substances; advice on how to confront and intervene if you detect a problem; treatment options; and post-treatment aftercare once the abuse problem has been addressed and your teen must face daily events again

Sexuality and Pregnancy: how to clarify and determine your own values in terms of teenage sexual behavior; advice on how to discuss romance, love, emotional involvement, and sexuality issues; how to educate your teen about AIDS; how to prevent your teen from becoming pregnant or infected by STDs; and what to do if your teen does become pregnant and must decide whether to parent, choose adoption, or decide on abortion

Eating Disorders: how to determine whether or not your child has an eating disorder; advice on when to confront, intervene, or back away if you think they do; treatment options; and how to deal with the emotional, psychological, and physical effects afterwards

Delinquent Behavior and Gangs: ways of becoming familiar with the various identifiers which determine whether or not your teen is involved with delinquency or gang involvement, such as specific hand signs and gestures, clothing, graffiti, jewelry, language, symbols, and more; intervention options; helping other family members cope with an adolescent's gang involvement; and community-wide approaches

Depression and Suicide: recognizing the warning signs; when to determine whether or not the depression is a serious concern warranting professional assistance; understanding the link between depression and other adolescent problems such as alcohol, drugs, divorce, eating disorders, etc.; how to take action while dealing with your child's despair; handling suicide threats; medication, counseling, and hospitalization options; how to help your teen and family recover after the crisis so they can successfully renavigate daily problems and adolescent issues

Divorce and Death: understanding loss and how teens perceive divorce and death; how to help a teen cope with this loss; and ways to assist them as they grieve and struggle to deal with the normal stresses involved with adolescence

As a child enters and travels through adolescence, their family travels through adolescence as well. As a parent, you may find your child telling you everything that happens to them and their friends, even things you'd rather not know. Or you may find your child divulging very little, often responding in monosyllabic words or sounds. In any case, you and the rest of your family will ride this roller coaster along with your teenager . . . the nervous anxiety of a first date, the school dances and the triumphant football games, the constant interplay between their fear of failure and their world-conquering confidence, the secrets and gossip, the drama and the melodrama, the late nights waiting up, the mornings when they still have yet to arrive, the emergency room visits, and sadly, the funerals.

There will be times when, as a parent, your heart will be moved watching your teenager read a story snuggled up, side-by-side with their 5 year old brother or sister. You'll be amazed at their compassion when they bring home a friend who has nowhere else to go for the night. And you'll be reminded that they are still a child as they bring home a stray dog promising they will take care of it and be responsible. You know at the time, of course, that the dog will become yours. Distractions such as cars, trips to the mall, movies, drive-ins, boyfriends and girlfriends, dances and concerts, road trips, jobs, college, and so on and so on will fill up their lives and yours.

HOW WE'VE ORGANIZED THIS BOOK

During the course of our ongoing research, we've identified the best resources to use to understand the various challenges involved with parenting a teenager. Within our guidebook's four main sections—**Sections II, III, IV, and V**—we introduce each topic granting parents an overall perspective of the subject matter and enough specific background information so they will feel confident during their quest for answers. We then provide our recommendations for the "best resources" for each of these subject areas. We always recommend several resources for each subject area, so you'll have the freedom to choose resources that are convenient for you to find and that meet your specific requirements. Recommended resources can be found directly following the introduction to each section and are noted by the following icon:

 **Recommended For:**

All resources pertaining to a given topic (Understanding Adolescents, Parent-Teen Relationships, Critical Issues & Concerns, and General Overview) will be found within that topic's section and are arranged in order by their Overall Star Rating (1–4 Stars), so that the best resources are always listed first. Use the resources which are best suited for your specific concerns, and which can help you understand and manage aspects of parenting that relate to your family's specific needs.

For those who want to focus on specific parenting topics, we've grouped a number of outstanding resources together in **Section VI—**

"Terrific Resources for Selected Topics." Use this section to find unusual resources that focus on specific concerns that arise during the teenage years. Topics range from how to improve parent-teen communication to ways to "let go" of your teenager. You will also find our recommendations for specific resources that discuss a mother's or father's influence on a daughter's eating habits, videotapes that offer advice on how to deal with sexuality and substance abuse, and much more. Also included in this section are recommended resources that address the needs, beliefs, and practices of families with a Christian perspective. We would encourage you to peruse the specific topic recommendations we make in Sections II, III, IV, and IV as well.

Finally, we've also provided a variety of indices in **Section VII** which list **all** the resources reviewed in this guidebook. Using these indices, parents interested in one resource they've heard about can easily find our full-page review of that particular resource. The resources can be found alphabetically by title, author, publisher, or media type; they are also listed by subject area for each of the book's four topics and are then arranged by their Overall Star Rating (best resources are listed first).

In **Section VIII** at the end of this guidebook, we've also included a helpful listing of support organizations and other groups you may want to contact for more information and parent support.

Conventions Used

Throughout this guidebook, we've defined important terms as follows:

- **"Adolescent"** or **"Teenager"** includes the age span that occurs between the time a child enters puberty (anywhere from 10 years old onward) and the time they enter into adulthood (anywhere from 18 years old onward)

- **"Puberty"** refers to the time period in which marked changes occur in a child's emotional, psychological, social, and cognitive growth, as well as an acceleration of their physical development including the ability to sexually reproduce

- **"Parent"** or **"parents"** refers to biological parents, stepparents, adoptive parents, foster parents, or any other guardians responsible for the care and safety of a child

Adolescence . . . it's the best of times, and the worst of times. As a parent, you'd better be prepared because ready or not, here it comes. But remember, you are not alone. Find comfort in knowing that other parents and teenagers have struggled, have found new ways to communicate, and have discovered the great possibilities and hidden treasures that can arise during these years. Good luck to you and your quest for support and guidance. May your journey be enlightening and prove rewarding!

MEET RESOURCE PATHWAYS

In this Information Age, we all want to take advantage of the many sources of information available to help us make important decisions or deal with major events we experience. Unfortunately, we don't always know where to find these sources of information. Often, we don't know very much about their quality, value, or relevance. In addition, many times we don't know much about the issues we're facing, and as a result don't really know where to begin our learning process.

Resource Pathways' guidebooks solve the problem of "information overload" faced by those who want to learn about a topic of critical importance in their life. Those interested in doing such research typically:

- Don't know what resources are available, particularly those outside traditional print media.

- Don't know where to find most of those resources, particularly since most bookstores stock only a limited selection.

- Can't assess the quality or focus of those resources before spending time and money first finding, then evaluating, and perhaps buying them.

- Don't understand which resources will be particularly useful for each dimension of a multi-dimensional issue. For each aspect of the challenge we're trying to deal with, certain resources will be very helpful, while others may be completely worthless.

This guidebook will help you overcome these hurdles. In this guidebook, you will find that:

- Virtually all available quality resources are reviewed, including those from "high-technology" media like the Internet or CD-ROMs.

- We make a reasoned judgment about the quality of each resource, and decide whether or not a resource should be recommended (roughly 1 in 4 are recommended).

- We define and explain the different issues typically encountered in easy-to-read chapter introductions, and classify each resource we review according to its primary focus.

- Information on where to buy or how to access each resource is provided, including ISBN numbers for obscure print media, direct order numbers for publishers, and URL "addresses" for sites on the Internet's World Wide Web.

After you have used this guidebook to learn which sources of information are best suited to you, you can then acquire or access those resources knowing that your time and money will be well spent.

Our Quality Standards

Those who turn to Resource Pathways guidebooks find the **best** sources of information on critical issues having an important impact on their lives. To ensure that we merit the trust placed in our recommendations, we've developed a proven set of quality standards:

- We are independent from the publishers of products we review; we do not accept advertising or compensation of any kind from those companies.

- We employ Editors and Advisory Councils of independent professionals with many years of experience in each subject area we cover. These professionals help ensure that we are kept abreast of developments in the field, and that our evaluations meet their standards for accuracy and relevance.

- We review new products and editions as they become available, so that our guidebooks include the most up-to-date information about products available in various media. We revisit websites on the Internet and the online services frequently, to keep up with changes in those offerings as they are introduced.

We put a great deal of time and effort into reviewing and evaluating each resource carefully. Here's what that process includes:

- **Printed Guidebooks:** For these resources, we read the book from cover to cover, identify the particular focus taken by each author, and make a judgment about how the book's contents could be best applied. Our judgment about the relative quality of each source is based upon useful content, breadth, depth, readability, organization, and style. We make every effort to ensure that the latest editions of books are reviewed, and that no out-of-print resources are included.

- **Internet Websites & Online Services:** We review websites and online services that have any significant amount of original material related to the subject. Our reviews include judgments about the site's graphic and navigation design, as well as the usefulness of material provided relative to that available in other media. We revisit sites frequently to stay abreast of changes and improvements.

- **CD-ROM & Software:** We carefully review each facet of each CD, including all branches and multimedia options, and thoroughly test software applications available on disk. Our reviews include judgments about the "cost/benefit" of multimedia additions, as well as the usefulness of the content provided relative to the same offering in other media by the same publisher. We note technical problems in loading or using programs provided.

- **Videotapes & Audiotapes:** We listen to and view each tape from beginning to end. We then make our judgement based on how well the tape covers its topic (breadth and depth), its organization, and production quality.

Because our mission is to help you find your way through this "forest" of information, we also provide you with our recommendations on which resources are best to help you each step of the way (roughly 25% of the resources we review are recommended). In making these recommendations, we have attempted to err on the side of providing too many choices rather than too few. Our recommendations are based upon our judgment of value, not only relative to alternatives in the same media, but against **all** available resources regardless of media.

PUBLISHER'S NOTE

In our reviews of websites, we include the current "address" of the website home page or specific page within a website, to facilitate direct access on the Internet. The nature of the Internet's World Wide Web is, of course, dynamic; this means that many website/page "addresses" change over time. If you find that an address is outdated, the recommended solution is simple; just delete the last expression within the address and hit the "Enter" or "Return" key again.

Here's an example:

http://www.sourcepath.com/cguide/bookorder.html

If this is an outdated address, try this instead:

http://www.sourcepath.com/cguide

This will simply point your browser to a file "further up" in the website's file directory. In most cases, you can follow this procedure until you find yourself at the website's home page (indicated by the phrase ending in ".com" or ".edu" or ".gov," etc.). Usually, you can then find your way back to the specific information (or page) that you were interested in.

II

UNDERSTANDING ADOLESCENTS

INTRODUCTION

The age of adolescence is one marked by change. Other ways to describe this period might include growth, maturation, and experimentation. Some of these changes are quite obvious, while others are subtle, yet powerful. Adolescents experience enormous growth physically, emotionally, cognitively, socially, and psychologically. They also experience changes in their relationships, as well as different consequences for their behavior within the various environments they interact.

Perhaps the most visible area of change centers on an adolescent's physical growth. Their internal and external transition physically from childhood to adulthood is enormous and influential. As adults can remember, the physical changes of puberty also bring with it everything good, but everything stressful, about becoming a man or a woman. Body changes influence how adolescents are treated, and how they understand and view themselves. Young women find themselves vulnerable to the narrow societal view of what constitutes desirable physical beauty, while young men find themselves trying to understand why they view girls differently . . . all of a sudden. These mysteries of biology visit themselves on both genders.

The less visible changes tend to be in the emotional, psychological, and cognitive realms. Changes in their thoughts and feelings, while not as tangible as physical changes, are nonetheless forerunners to understanding adolescent behavior. Although the desired outcome for all of these aspects of growth is an integrated, effective person, adolescents often experience these aspects competing against one another. "I know drugs are not good for my body, but I don't want my friends to think I'm a nerd." The result can be a fragmented relationship between these areas of growth instead of helping to create an integrated package.

Physical Changes

Changes in body shape and function are received by teenagers with curiosity, guilt, fear, and excitement. Of course, the adults around them receive these changes with some fear as well. For instance, it is still difficult for many parents to have those "how-babies-are-made" conversations with their teens. The fact that these conversations are needed at an earlier age doesn't make it any easier for parents. Yet, these conversations have evolved to discussions of how to engage in sexual behavior in safe ways. Yes, the world is changing. Not many of us were shown how to use a condom by our parents, but the risks today make it necessary for adults to be more proactive than past generations.

Not all physical changes during adolescence instill fear in parents. Boys begin to shave, as do girls. Issues of complexion can reach crisis proportions. Disproportionately sized appendages, those inches gained in height and girth, and the emergence of body hair all add to the adolescent's heightened sense of inadequacy. Given the dynamics of adolescence, how teenagers view themselves is often determined by how they are viewed by others. As a result, these immense changes in their physical appearance feed an adolescent's volatile and constant self-appraisal process, greatly influencing their developing ego and identity.

Emotional Changes

Adolescent emotionality is often extreme, and greatly dependent on external forces. Adolescents tend to live in the present, and their emotions reflect the most pressing adolescent need—acceptance. Yet, in today's society we find an ever-expanding permission for expression of emotions. Sexuality in the lives of teens is a driving force behind their emotions, psychological self-appraisal, and behavior. The range of experiences in this area span from a first kiss to an adolescent's awareness and expression of sexual orientation. All of a sudden, love and acceptance take on broader meanings than they did in the past.

This emotional roller coaster of adolescence is compounded by family, religious, and societal values. Add to this the experimental and risk-taking nature of adolescence, and we have emotional angst of enormous potential! The challenge for teens during this time is to find emotional balance. The journey between these extremes of emotionality, however, is infinitely fatiguing. Life, at the high point or the low point, is exhausting. Finding ways of mitigating these extremes then becomes a task of adolescence. But it is also an opportunity for adults to model balanced emotional behavior during this time of a teenager's development.

Cognitive Changes

The here-and-now aspect of an adolescent's emotions often comes into conflict with their cognitive growth, as an adolescent transitions from the concrete thinking of a child to the abstract thinking capabilities of an adult. Their ability to project issues into the future, connect their behavior with consequences, accept responsibility for themselves, and understand complex issues such as universality and death, are all normal developmental tasks of adolescence. Though the external actions of the adolescent often attract the greater share of attention, their inner evaluations are the work of the future. If the desired outcome for an adolescent's growth is an integrated and effective person, then coordinating the thinking and feeling aspects of this growth with their actions is extremely important.

Although this may seem like an inevitable process, other factors intercede and influence these changes. The world today demands that adults should be able to think independently, work cooperatively with others, and make complex decisions. In addition, our adolescents will have to survive in an increasingly technical and global world. These demands necessitate a different way of thinking than in past generations. Expanding our sense of self is a primary example. We often view adolescents as individuals narrowly preoccupied with themselves. In the past, adolescents had to be able to deal with family, local peers, and work environments. These arenas tended to be familiar and stable. However, nowadays adolescents must contend with a very different type of family system, extended peer groups and media heroes, and work environments that no longer reward tasks involving individualized linear thinking.

Our world has indeed become smaller. The amount of information available to us and its immediate accessibility have created a need to think differently. The excess of this stimuli has put demands on our individual and collective psyche, and the increase of technical advancements of communication have broken down geographic, cultural, ethnic, and trade barriers. What does this all mean for an adolescent?

Adolescent cognition will be challenged to deal with a post-industrial and highly technical world. This means that cognitively, they must learn how to think globally and view themselves as global culture. This is an overwhelming thought. For just as an adolescent struggles for individual identity, we then ask them to see themselves as part of a larger whole. As they struggle to understand why their complexion disintegrates just before a big date, they must also try to understand why certain parts of the world experience famine. And just when they struggle to come to terms with their body and its newly developed functions, they have to acknowledge that they can't get a job because of the collapse of economic markets in foreign countries.

Freud talked about subconscious aggression, Glasser talked about responsibility, and Adler talked about logical consequences. Now theorists and parents must try to understand the growth issues encountered by an adolescent in a world and time that is quite different than previously acknowledged or addressed.

As a parent, you might be thinking that this is all fine and good, but how does it help me Friday night when this creature, who was my child, is on her way out of the door to join a Mash Pit dressed in clothes you didn't know she owned? Obviously, there are layers to understanding the adolescent psyche. The practical day to day issues of cognition, emotionality, and behavior have a great deal more to do with the physical, hormonal, and basic adolescent need to be accepted than does the global economy. Our greatest task as adults may be in creating and maintaining an environment for our adolescents that allows for the growth of abstract thinking, independent decision-making, safer risk-taking and experimentation, healthy development of their ego and sense of self, as well as fostering emotional safety.

Understanding the various facets of adolescent growth and development would seem to be all that parents might need to have under their belt to survive this tumultuous period. Yet, there are two other factors that add further complications. Inherent differences between raising adolescent boys and adolescent girls create additional challenges as parents strive to successfully navigate adolescence.

Adolescent Boys

When we think of adolescent boys we often conjure up thoughts of aggression, reckless behavior, "acting out" behavior, and "posing" behaviors. Yet, this is also the group that sits opposite girls in the classroom, hugs the walls at dances, and still knows the camp songs—even if they won't sing them. Being an adolescent boy is no easy task. Girls tend to mature faster than they do and this only serves to reinforce the daunting inadequacies boys already feel. Society also taunts boys as they wrestle with leaving boyhood behind and embrace impending manhood. They are constantly challenged to be "a man" in our society, yet they aren't permitted to drive until they're 16 or drink until they are 21 years of age.

Many adolescent development specialists view the task of teenage boys in our society as seeking their identity first before they seek intimacy. Societal messages of what constitutes a "man" begin early in a child's life and leave no room for question. Expressing one's emotions and sensitivity are viewed as a sign of weakness, and adolescent boys all know that the weak don't survive during adolescence. So teenage boys spend a great deal of their time and energy seeking an identity that will serve them well with the most important judges in their life . . . their peers.

In addition, recent studies support the proposition that growing up as an adolescent boy is an extremely fragile time. Society, on the one hand, paints a picture of what a man should be like. However, when these same young men become involved in relationships with young women, many times these societal standards create internal havoc. On one hand, boys are expected to maintain a strong exterior, yet on the other hand, they are expected to divulge their deepest most heartfelt emotions to the opposite sex. This all translates into personal confusion at a time when an adolescent is, of course, seeking to be an integrated individual.

Many variables interact as boys traverse their adolescence, not the least of which include role models, family dynamics, ethnic culture, gender identity, religion, and the body they are born with. Certainly these are generalities, but parents need to consider all factors which influence their adolescent's motives and behavior.

Adolescent Girls

The transformation into an adolescent may appear more dramatic for a girl than for a boy. Certainly a girl's physiological maturation along with the visible signs of physical changes causes a huge, if not catastrophic, impact on and in the lives of teenage girls.

Further complicating these changes is the quandary girls often face between looking good and being smart. Girls are not universally encouraged to be smart in this society. Though some of the ground rules for girls and women are evolving in society, adolescent girls are still caught in the midst of society's mixed messages. Contradictory messages of "you can do anything" coupled with images of what constitutes a desirable woman only serve to confuse adolescent girls. And to compound this confusion even further, adolescent girls tend to establish intimacy with others first before they even begin to tackle identity.

In light of all these different expectations, it's no wonder it may be tougher for girls to traverse adolescence healthfully. The outcomes aren't very defined, and the underlying messages are clouded. The pitfalls for girls emanate from their vacillating attempts to satisfy these differing expectations—trying to be a desirable woman as defined through society's eyes, while pursuing society's desired outcome of an adolescent, being an effective person. Adolescent girls feel pressured to accomplish it all, and in trying, they often find many of the potholes on their journey to adulthood.

As parents can see, there is an enormous amount of change and growth happening during adolescence, and this process is happening at many levels simultaneously. Perhaps at no other period or stage in our lives do we have to deal with and assimilate this level of growth. A time of storm and stress, developmental disturbance, a syndrome . . . all of these descriptions seem to fall short in explaining the dynamics at work here. Aren't we glad we only have to experience adolescence once?

In this section, we have included resources that focus on how adolescents grow and develop. We have divided these resources into the following categories to help focus your search for answers:

Use these resources to gain an understanding of the various developmental changes that your adolescent will undergo. By recognizing these changes, and appreciating some of the tasks of adolescence, parents will be in a better position to deal with the ups and downs of their seemingly irrational, yet highly captivating child. These resources can offer parents a wonderful overview of how their adolescent develops into a young man or a young woman, along with advice on how parents can make that a positive experience for all.

To understand adolescent growth and behavior within the context of a family's dynamics, we also recommend parents read the full-page reviews of resources we recommend in **Section III—"Parent-Teen Relationships."** Here, parents will find general discussions of why adolescents and teenagers think, feel, and behave the way they do, coupled with specific ways to deal with daily family problems and inability to communicate with one another.

Teenage Boys

★★★★

Overall Rating
★★★★
New, inspiring, bold insight into the lives and development of adolescent boys

Design, Ease Of Use
★★★★
Effective language; well-organized; comprehensive index; detailed table of contents

1–4 Stars; N/R = Not Rated

Media:
Print

Price:
$24.95

Principal Subject:
Understanding Adolescents

ISBN:
0874779197

Edition:
1998

Publisher:
Jeremy P. Tarcher/Putnam (Penguin Putnam)

Author:
Michael Gurian

About The Author: (From Cover Notes)
Gurian is a father, therapist, educator, and author of seven previous books. He has served as a consultant to families, therapists, school districts, youth organizations, churches, the media, and other groups. Gurian's work reflects the diverse cultures in which he has lived.

A FINE YOUNG MAN
What Parents, Mentors, And Educators Can Do To Shape Adolescent Boys Into Exceptional Men

 Recommended For:
Understanding Adolescents

Description:
The premise of this book states that, "We do not understand adolescent-male development, and therefore are unable to give our adolescent males the kind of love they need to become fully responsible, loving, and wise men." Gurian dedicates ten chapters and four major sections to pointing out current problems and advocating new ways of dealing with adolescent boys. He brings in past experiences and shares specific activities in which he suggests parents should immerse their child. The second part of the book describes adolescence, divided by age range (9–13, 14–17, 18–21); each stage is discusses with information on what's happening and how parents can influence emotional development. The third and fourth sections deal with education and "refinement." Gurian combines "medical science, psychology, anthropology, and personal observation" throughout his book. He states that the final qualities of a properly raised boy is the "core of manhood"—compassion, honor, responsibility, and enterprise.

Evaluation:
This book is a heartwarming resource with a charming goal. The all-too-familiar parental cry of "what's wrong with my kid?" is answered by a gentle voice, saying "they're not yet complete." This book successfully shares ways that parents can assist in the "completion" of their adolescent boy. Gurian demonstrates an amazingly complete knowledge of male development, which he has gained from his observation of cultures in the U.S., along with those of Turkey, Germany, Israel, the Southern Ute Reservation, and scholarly studies of 20 other cultures. Applications of this book, then, are worldwide, and are not limited to American boys. The words of advice and encouragement are undeniably new, but make a great deal of sense in their essential simplicity. The only difficulties some may have with this book are 1) its length (298 pages), and 2) some chapters require a bit more thought than the typically busy person is able to dedicate. For inspiring, thought-provoking, accurate insight, though, this is the book.

Where To Find/Buy:
Bookstores and libraries.

Teenage Boys

REAL BOYS
Rescuing Our Sons From The Myths Of Boyhood

★★★★

 **Recommended For:**
Understanding Adolescents

Description:

Real Boys describes conventional expectations about masculinity which expect boys to be "little men," toughening them up by helping them deny their fears and suppress the gentler sides of their natures. Pollack uses the voices of real boys and their parents to counteract these old stereotypes. Claiming that boys are in many ways as empathic and intuitive as girls, he discusses many issues facing boys today, such as drugs and alcohol, depression, divorce, violence, and love and sexuality. Pollack believes that by internalizing their fears, boys develop outer shells that hide feelings of loneliness and isolation. Part One describes how boys relate and the common myths/stereotypes associated with boys. Part Two offers ways to connect with boys: the importance of mothers and fathers, the changes of adolescence, and the role of schools, friendships, and sports in helping to develop happy, well-adjusted young men. Part Three deals with more serious issues of the unwritten "Boy Code:" depression, suicide and violence in young men feeling alienated from themselves, and Part Four presents ways to stay connected with boys.

Evaluation:

Based on the author's 20 years of work with men and boys, this extraordinary book examines how boys are raised to be men in our society. Pollack illuminates the ways in which we damage boys' self-esteem by expecting them to deny their fears and pain in order to "act like a man." Boys, he believes, then become ashamed of their vulnerability, learning to mask their emotions. As a society, Pollack says, we tear boys away from their mothers at an early age, push them out into the world, and tell them to be strong. As a result they lose self-confidence and suffer a crisis of identity. This ultimately keeps boys from becoming fulfilled men with lives rich with love and support. Pollack provides excellent how-tos and advice in this "must-have" 447 page book to help parents reevaluate how they can teach "connection" as the new model. He also describes how boys themselves can guide us, so parents and teachers can learn to respond to the real needs of boys, and thus help prepare them for life's major and minor stresses.

Where To Find/Buy:

Bookstores and libraries. An audiotape version (1998) of this book is also available for $18.00 (ISBN No. 0375402918)

Overall Rating
★★★★
Insightful, well-researched; highly recommended for anyone who works with boys

Design, Ease Of Use
★★★★
Each chapter divided into small essays; bold subheadings and numerous quotations

1–4 Stars; N/R = Not Rated

Media:
Print

Price:
$24.00

Principal Subject:
Understanding Adolescents

ISBN:
0375501312

Edition:
1998

Publisher:
Random House

Author:
William Pollack, Ph.D.

**About The Author:
(From Cover Notes)**
This clinical psychologist is co-director of the Center for Men at McLean Hospital/ Harvard Medical School, assistant clinical professor of psychiatry at Harvard Medical School, and founding member and Fellow of the Society of Men and Masculinity of the A.P.A.

II. Understanding Adolescents

★★★

Overall Rating
★★★
Hope-inspiring, this resource offers a new "gameplan" for the parents of boys

Design, Ease Of Use
★★★
TOC rather ambiguous, excellent index; easy-to-read w/numerous charts, exercises, etc.

1–4 Stars; N/R = Not Rated

Media:
Print

Price:
$12.95

Principal Subject:
Understanding Adolescents

ISBN:
0890878110

Edition:
2nd (1996)

Publisher:
Celestial Arts

Author:
Don Elium & Jeanne Elium

About The Author:
(From Cover Notes)
Don Elium is a marriage, family, and child counselor in private practice. As a transpersonal educator and workshop leader, Jeanne Elium challenges parents to put aside stereotypes and gender roles in order to see their child through a wider lens. They both conduct seminars.

Teenage Boys

RAISING A SON
Parents And The Making Of A Healthy Man

Description:

The authors of *Raising A Son* (a husband-wife duo) take an in-depth look at the way parents raise their boys. Specifically, the authors believe that parents aren't really raising their sons—rather, they claim that society has taken over the job. They believe that, due to increased focus on the individual and an increased human call for people to "find themselves," parents have relinquished control of their boys. Their call is for a large-scale change of thought and behavior. There are a great deal of quotes interspersed throughout the book to illustrate the authors' points, ranging from the words of Mark Twain to Don Elium's own unpublished song lyrics. The 3 sections of this 307 page book include "The Puzzle of Being Male," ways to parent as a team, and an age-by-age description of male development ("Cradle to Career") divided into four stages to explain how males progress through each stage. New to this 2nd edition is a section on Attention Deficit Hyperactivity Disorder. There is also a comprehensive index.

Evaluation:

The Eliums have written a book that successfully paves the path for changing stereotypes about parenting boys. Both parents should read this book, if possible, as it presents a perfect balance of mother and father, resulting in an astounding combination of feeling and logic. Specific recommendations include such advice as taking a firm stance with a boy in terms of consequences, but flexing parental expectations based on his age. They advocate an authoritarian style of parenting which combines kindness, understanding, and compassion—three adjectives that don't typically describe authoritarian parenting. Although it is a bit lengthy, this book is a heartwarming tale of what we, as a society, have done wrong, and what we can do to correct it. The only caution is directed at the parent wanting a quick-reference book to help them discipline or change their teenage boy. This is not the book for you. It is, however, a calm, insightful look into a new role for parents in the lives of their boys.

Where To Find/Buy:

Bookstores, libraries, or order direct by calling 1-800-841-BOOK, or contacting Celestial Arts at P. O. Box 7123, Berkeley, CA 94707.

Teenage Boys

BOYS TO MEN
Maps For The Journey

Description:

Boys To Men is a compilation of short essays. Each essay contains ideas, thoughts, and reflections on the author's experiences—as well as those of others. The underlying premise of the book, the point that Mr. Williams embraces, is that the roads of life are best traveled with maps. These "maps" are the experiences of others, combined with one's own values, thoughts, and goals. Thus, he creates a sort of interdependence among people; in his mind, we rely on each other to make it to the next step, or follow a new path. He uses a certain degree of humor where appropriate, and writes in the first person. Williams's personal history has a large influence on his writing; his father died when Williams was young, he was raised by his mother, and he's been down some not-so-easy roads. A few ideas and sentences contain deeper meanings and allusions, so the reader must be careful to look beyond the surface. There are three major sections.

Evaluation:

Many times it feels as if the author is speaking directly to a teenage boy. Therefore, parents might be well served passing this book on to their children, for Williams uses language that teens can easily relate to. He manages to consistently return to his underlying theme—that life is a journey of maps—without sounding redundant. He advises boys to absorb the good around them, to use only high-quality "maps," and that if they have a good "selection," they can pick the best path. He stresses the importance of honor, recognizing that honor is an ideal. All too often, he believes, boys are true to their peer group rather than themselves. To be truly honorable, though, he believes that men need to be true to themselves. Written in a rather poetic fashion with the weave of a good storyteller, this book must be read cover-to-cover to fully gain the author's perspectives. This is a good book for teenage boys, but if a father and a son have a workable bond, or wish a father-son friendship, both would benefit from reading this book.

Where To Find/Buy:

Bookstores and libraries.

Overall Rating
★★
A calm, intriguing book that speaks directly to the reader; simplistic insight

Design, Ease Of Use
★★
Vague chapter titles; should be read cover-to-cover; modern language, non-academic

1–4 Stars; N/R = Not Rated

Media:
Print

Price:
$10.95

Principal Subject:
Understanding Adolescents

ISBN:
038548688X

Edition:
1996

Publisher:
Main Street Books (Doubleday/Bantam Doubleday Dell Publishing Group)

Author:
GregAlan Williams

**About The Author:
(From Cover Notes)**
An Emmy Award-winning actor and author, Williams is best known for his roles on "Baywatch" and "Baywatch Nights." A speaker at high schools and universities, and an HIV/AIDS spokesperson for the American Red Cross, he is the author of two other books.

II. Understanding Adolescents

Overall Rating
★★
Good primer on growing up male, but with little constructive advice

Design, Ease Of Use
★★
(Dime store) novel-like style; chapters are separate essays which can be randomly read

1–4 Stars; N/R = Not Rated

Media:
Print

Price:
$22.00

Principal Subject:
Understanding Adolescents

ISBN:
0807023167

Edition:
1998

Publisher:
Beacon Press

Author:
Geoffrey Canada

About The Author:
(From Cover Notes)
Canada is president of the Rheedlen Centers for Children and Families in New York City. He is the recipient of the 1995 Heinz Foundation Award, and a *Parents* magazine Award for his work in child advocacy, and he is the author of *Fist Stick Knife Gun*.

Teenage Boys

REACHING UP FOR MANHOOD
Transforming The Lives Of Boys In America

Description:
The author wrote this 160 page book to address what he believes is becoming a crisis in our country: our "false sense of security . . . about how our boys are faring." Boys lives are becoming impossibly intertwined with stories of violence and immoral behavior. Drawing on stories from his own childhood in New York, the author discusses his topics of concern: learning to heal from old hurts; structuring risk so that boys don't need to engage in dangerous activities; teaching boys that their self-worth isn't tied in to what they buy; issues of fatherhood in a culture that teaches teenagers how to be sexual without responsibility; providing a clear message on drug use; providing examples of faith; the importance of hard work; and the need for mentors in young men's lives. Each chapter includes vignettes from the author's life and a discussion on what things have changed and remained the same. Canada stresses the importance of mentoring and allowing boys to express their fear and hurt in helping them grow up to be happy well-adjusted adults.

Evaluation:
Reading much like a novel, this book is so simple in its narrative that at times it is easy to forget the message. Canada discusses his boyhood with candor, providing insight on how boys are pushed into harmful lifestyle choices. He pleads with parents to understand the ways young men are becoming disconnected from their feelings and emotions. Although he focuses on his own experiences with inner city boys, his message is universal: boys need to be guided through their adolescence with love, faith, and a harbor to express their fears and concerns without feeling ashamed of them. He believes fathers and sons must establish and nurture bonds that teach the truly important facets of what it means to be a man. Otherwise, in becoming "real men," they will lose the qualities that enable them to make connections in their own lives. Although some of the language may be objectionable, this resource affords parents an excellent look at how we raise boys. Unfortunately, Canada's advice on how to solve this problem is rather mundane relying on adult male connections, mentors, who themselves may have been raised disconnectedly.

Where To Find/Buy:
Bookstores and libraries.

Teenage Boys

STRONG MOTHERS, STRONG SONS

Description:

Strong Mothers, Strong Sons is a 321 page adolescent development guide. There are thirteen chapters, which discuss everything from a boy's young days to his late teens. Some chapters focus entirely on communication; other chapters discuss puberty, sex, drugs & alcohol, boys & violence, and homosexuality. For mothers who feel they are "softening" their sons by being a strong presence, the last chapter is dedicated entirely to the dilemma of sensitivity and strength. Each chapter contains subheadings. The author offers general discussions on the topics, offering bits and pieces of advice essentially from the viewpoint of the adolescent boy (as well as the author). At the end of each chapter, the advice is recapped in a section called "Memos for Moms." In this section, the reader is told exactly what to do—with advice to mothers such as "include him in all family discussions" and "always discuss love and commitment when discussing sex, so he associates the two." There is an index, as well as a reference notes section.

Evaluation:

This guidebook for mothers is based on the premise that mothers and sons have been socially separated, that moms raise daughters, and fathers raise sons. Caron believes that boys need strong mothers, and that mothers need to speak freely with their boys, and encourage (or discourage) a wide range of behaviors. Some readers may question some of the author's statements, such as "seldom does a boy want to get emotionally involved with a girl." She also believes that the drinking age should be 18 or 19, her reasoning being that after high school, kids are adults and should be treated accordingly. These types of statements may make this book a bit questionable to some. The major problem though is that this book really doesn't offer anything new. It also seems to place the entire burden of raising sons on the shoulders of the mothers; Caron seems to have forgotten that parenting is (ideally) a two-person job. This book perhaps will be of some value in encouraging single moms to foster closer communications with their sons.

Where To Find/Buy:

Bookstores and libraries.

Overall Rating

★

Some good information; a few statements without factual base; helpful for single moms

Design, Ease Of Use

★★★

Concise chapters; each chapter contains summary of recommendations to mothers

---

1–4 Stars; N/R = Not Rated

Media:
Print

Price:
$14.00

Principal Subject:
Understanding Adolescents

ISBN:
0060976489

Edition:
1994

Publisher:
HarperPerennial
(HarperCollins Publishers)

Author:
Ann F. Caron, Ed.D.

About The Author:
(From Cover Notes)
Caron is a psychologist and parenting expert and author of *Don't Stop Loving Me: A Reassuring Guide for Mothers of Adolescent Daughters*. She is a frequent lecturer and workshop leader. She is the mother of four sons and two daughters.

II. Understanding Adolescents

Teenage Girls

ALL THAT SHE CAN BE
Helping Your Daughter Maintain Her Self Esteem

Overall Rating
★★★★
Practical advice aimed at developing, maintaining, or restoring girls' self-esteem

Design, Ease Of Use
★★★★
Easily accessible, bold subheadings with bulleted information

1–4 Stars; N/R = Not Rated

Media:
Print

Price:
$11.00

Principal Subject:
Understanding Adolescents

ISBN:
0671885545

Edition:
1994

Publisher:
Fireside (Simon & Schuster)

Author:
Dr. Carol J. Eagle and Carol Colman

About The Author:
(From Cover Notes)
Eagle is head of Child and Adolescent Psychology at Montefiore Medical Center/ Einstein College of Medicine, and is Associate Professor of Psychiatry at Einstein College. Colman is a freelance writer and coauthor of several books.

 Recommended For:
Understanding Adolescents

Description:
The principal author (Eagle) of this 252 page book believes that different rates of adolescent development psychologically impact girls. She wrote this book to help parents "better understand [their] daughter's adolescence so [they] can be a more compassionate and effective parent." This book then offers solutions on how parents can help their girls develop and maintain their self-esteem throughout adolescence. It includes chapters on how to approach the following: assessing whether a girl is at risk; intellectual and emotional development issues; the family dynamic; the adolescent girl's changing body; obsession with appearances and looks; peers and friendship; academics; dating and sexuality; self-destructive behaviors; and divorce and stepfamilies. The authors stress the importance of parental communication. Parents need to be advocates, helping to build their daughter's vital self-esteem and strength during the adolescent years when girls traditionally lose their personal identities and feelings of self-worth. This book includes an index, bibliography, and a list of resources.

Evaluation:
All That She Can Be is an excellent blending of facts and advice. The authors draw from several studies, case histories, and various research to help parents learn how to understand the importance of being advocates for their girls during the critical time of adolescence. Delving into research on why girls begin to slide academically during these years, Eagle and Colman examine everything from how body image, societal images, and teacher interaction help to shape girls' perceptions of who they are and what is expected from them. The chapter on family dynamics is especially helpful. It highlights relationship styles between mothers and daughters, fathers and daughters, and siblings, including advice on how to maximize the healthy benefits that positive family interaction can have on a girl's development. Designed specifically for parents of young adolescents, this is an excellent resource for parents of girls of any age who are intent on restoring their daughter's self-confidence and ability to tackle new challenges.

Where To Find/Buy:
Bookstores and libraries.

II. Understanding Adolescents

Teenage Girls

DON'T STOP LOVING ME
A Reassuring Guide For Mothers Of Adolescent Daughters

 Recommended For:
Understanding Adolescents

Description:
Detailing the psychological development of adolescent girls, this 228 page book aims to provide support for mothers of adolescent girls. Chapters cover the following topics: the physiological, emotional and physical changes of adolescence, the adolescent mind, dilemmas of trust, the father's influence, limits and demands, female body image, alcohol and drugs, the generation gap, and ways to build a new appreciation of each other. The author combines her research in the field of female adolescent psychology along with her experience as a lecturer on the subject of mother-daughter relationships to inform mothers about their daughters' experiences and needs during adolescence. Each chapter includes personal histories of mothers and daughters, questions for the mother to ask herself and her daughter, and "memos for moms," consisting of a list of helpful reminders and inspirational sayings to help a mother when dealing with her daughter. A chapter-by-chapter notes section is included as well as an index.

Evaluation:
This book advises mothers to view adolescence as a healthy challenge in which daughters need to develop an identity separate from their family, especially their moms. It gives mothers real tools for weathering the seemingly constant storm of disapproval they face, providing tips for understanding that their daughter's behavior is a natural process. Caron states the importance of a mother acknowledging her daughter's feelings; she also supports moms by saying they need to state their feelings too and their desire for respect. Caron discusses positive parenting by examining the behavior of well-liked mothers, their ability to forgive, their means of dealing with disagreement, their high expectations for their daughters' behavior (curfews, guidelines for homework and household chores, and other expectations), and more; sexuality is covered well, but specific issues (alcohol, drugs, eating disorders, etc.) are treated quite briefly, and other resources are needed to supplement this one. Caron's advice is solid and her support of mothers makes this book a gem for all who read it.

Where To Find/Buy:
Bookstores and libraries.

Overall Rating
★★★
Excellent resource for mothers of girls, providing great insight and sensible advice

Design, Ease Of Use
★★★★
Great layout; bold subheadings, chapter contents outlined; void of jargon, user-friendly

1–4 Stars; N/R = Not Rated

Media:
Print

Price:
$13.00

Principal Subject:
Understanding Adolescents

ISBN:
0060974028

Edition:
1991

Publisher:
HarperPerennial
(HarperCollins Publishers)

Author:
Ann F. Caron, Ed.D.

About The Author:
(From Cover Notes)
Ann F. Caron has a doctorate in education and developmental psychology. She lectures and conducts workshops for mothers of adolescent daughters. She lives in Connecticut with her husband and the youngest of their six children, a daughter in college.

Teenage Girls

RAISING A DAUGHTER
Parents And The Awakening Of A Healthy Woman

Description:

This 377 page reference is the authors' companion to their other guide on *Raising A Son*. Aimed at parents of adolescent girls, it discusses what it means to be female in a male-oriented society, along with ways to develop healthy relationships between mothers and daughters, and fathers and daughters. Divided into 3 parts, the authors' discussion focuses on ways to validate the "female experience" in our society. Sifting through the often conflicting messages girls receive regarding their bodies, minds, and health, the Eliums discuss these issues, going step-by-step through each stage of a female's development, from birth to the age of 29. Each chapter includes personal asides from the authors on how various situations impacted their marriage and parenting, quotes from parents and daughters, and exercises for effective parenting. Also included within each chapter is a suggested reading list for further resources. This book also includes an index.

Evaluation:

Upon reading this book, the authors hope parents will see their daughters as they really are, leaving assumptions behind. Girls, they say, seek ways of relating that "use power with others, rather than power over others." Using personal narratives and quotes from daughter-parent pairs, the Eliums do a fine job discussing the problems girls face in a society that often sends them conflicting messages as they grow up. Among the good advice offered: help girls develop a sense of strength, power, and physical competence; help them learn that anger is a healthy component of emotions; encourage them in "non-girl" endeavors, and more. Of particular use is Part 3, which focuses on different age groups of girls. Here valuable information is provided on girls' needs, their developmental tasks, their "inner guidance system" (feelings, intuition, etc.), "fences" (behaviors, consequences), sexuality, and more. Citing various developmental theorists (Steiner, Dreikurs, and others), this is an excellent overall resource for parents of girls.

Where To Find/Buy:

Bookstores, libraries, or order direct by calling 1-800-841-BOOK.

★★★

Overall Rating
★★★
Excellent resource, providing compassionate down-to-earth advice

Design, Ease Of Use
★★★
Well-organized; quotes in italics; indented/bold subheadings; best read cover-to-cover

1–4 Stars; N/R = Not Rated

Media:
Print

Price:
$12.95

Principal Subject:
Understanding Adolescents

ISBN:
0890877084

Edition:
1994

Publisher:
Celestial Arts

Author:
Jeanne Elium and Don Elium

About The Author:
(From Cover Notes)
Jeanne and Don Elium are the parents of a son and a daughter. Jeanne is an author, a former instructor, women's counselor, and elementary school teacher. Don is a marriage, family, and child counselor in private practice, as well as a professional author and speaker.

Teenage Girls

ALTERED LOVES
Mothers And Daughters During Adolescence

Description:

The author draws on her academic background and research to explore the complex and powerful nature of mother-daughter relationships. Her 276 page book incorporates recent psychological studies from Harvard Medical School, the University of Texas at Austin, and other schools, along with the author's interviews of 65 mother and daughter pairs from the U.S. and Great Britain. The author's premise is that the mother-daughter bond is far from being severed in adolescence as is often believed. "A model of adolescent development involving separation and conflict was either inadequate or inappropriate." Instead, she believes the mother-daughter relationship undergoes a transformation that deepens their attachment into adulthood. Chapters focus on the following topics: a definition of adolescence and puberty; traditional and feminist views of adolescence; the battle for recognition, adolescent identity, sexuality, independence and intimacy; friends and peers; and risk, discipline and growth.

Evaluation:

Apter does an excellent job of sifting through traditional and feminist views of mother-daughter relationships. She then counters these arguments using her research and interviews of mothers and daughters to illustrate her belief that strife between them can be seen as a tool for a daughter to gain confidence in her own opinions and views. "Mothers and daughters continue to quarrel because neither gives up on the other." Apter believes that because there is great intimacy in the mother-daughter bond, there are higher stakes and victory is more important. She provides sound and compelling reasoning for her views, citing studies and facts for each topic covered. Stories from the interviewed mothers and daughters give Apter's findings credence and depth, although the text tends toward the academic at times. Written primarily for mothers, this book is an excellent resource for any woman who will most likely see themselves reflected in the mother-daughter struggles illustrated throughout the book.

Where To Find/Buy:

Bookstores and libraries.

Overall Rating
★★★
Describes how the mother-daughter bond changes, but is not severed in adolescence

Design, Ease Of Use
★★
Subheadings w/in chapters; unclear TOC, index needed; heavy dense text at times

1–4 Stars; N/R = Not Rated

Media:
Print

Price:
$10.00

Principal Subject:
Understanding Adolescents

ISBN:
0449906310

Edition:
1990

Publisher:
Fawcett Columbine (Ballantine Books/Random House)

Author:
Terri Apter

About The Author:
(From Cover Notes)
Apter is a research fellow at Clare Hall, Cambridge. She is the author of *Why Women Don't Have Wives: Professional Success and Motherhood*. She lives with her husband and two teenage daughters in Cambridge, England.

★★★

Overall Rating
★★★
Insightful observations (mostly classroom oriented) on mixed messages girls receive

Design, Ease Of Use
★★
Should be read all the way through, no index, vague TOC

1–4 Stars; N/R = Not Rated

Media:
Print

Price:
$14.00

Principal Subject:
Understanding Adolescents

ISBN:
0385425767

Edition:
1994

Publisher:
Anchor Book (Doubleday/ Bantam Doubleday Dell Publishing Group)

Author:
Peggy Orenstein

About The Author:
(From Cover Notes)
Orenstein, former managing editor of *Mother Jones* magazine, and founding member of the award-winning *7 Days* magazine, is an author whose works have appeared in publications, such as *The New York Times Magazine, Vogue, Glamour, The New Yorker,* and others.

Teenage Girls

SCHOOL GIRLS
Young Women, Self-Esteem, And The Confidence Gap

Description:

This 335 page book details a year the author spent at two radically different middle schools—Audubon, an inner city middle school, and Weston, a suburban middle school. Orenstein interviewed girls at both schools along with some of their parents. She chronicles their vastly different life experiences at the two sites, discussing the challenges for all of them in their quest to reach adulthood. Part One describes her experience at Weston. Issues of gender bias (in terms of teachers' approaches toward boys and girls), the "confidence gap" between boys and girls, issues of sexuality and promiscuity, sexual harassment, and harmful manifestations of low self-esteem (self-mutilation, bingeing, and purging) are all examined. At Audubon, Orenstein describes girls who were deemed "unteachable" and "lost," girls faced with the split loyalty of drop-out friends, and girls confronting the harmful reality of life in their urban environment. Part Three provides an example of a gender-fair classroom in action.

Evaluation:

Orenstein provides disturbing information and insight into how girls are being undermined in school. She details classroom practices that reinforce certain values, such as overlooking a girl's input, reinforcing passive "good student" behavior, and more. For example, in compiling a time capsule at Weston, boys bring pictures of computers and the latest technologies, girls bring cosmetics and photos of fashion models. School for these young women is clearly a side issue. Boys are tacitly encouraged to speak their minds and be boisterous, while girls who behave in a similar fashion are labeled as problem children who need to modify their behavior. Orenstein does a fine job of illustrating the epidemic of young girls who lose their way and its traceable roots. The sample gender-fair classroom shows how change is evolving, but parents of girls and boys should be aware of the uphill battle required to change our perceptions of girls. Orenstein's keen insight into classroom dynamics and honest portrayal of what life is like for girls should be required reading for parents and teachers everywhere.

Where To Find/Buy:

Bookstores and libraries.

Teenage Girls

PROMISCUITIES
The Secret Struggle For Womanhood

★★

Description:

Written by the author of *The Beauty Myth*, this 286 page book details a "group of girls' sexual coming of age in a particular set of circumstances in late-twentieth-century urban America . . . how we grew . . . how it felt." Using a confessional format, it is Wolf's attempt to "elucidate the emotional truths that emerge from a particular generation's erotic memory." Through tracing the history of the women's feminist and sexual revolutions, and revealing various women's stories, Wolf examines why the teenage girl is cast as a victim of culture and sexuality, instead of as a sexual creator. She also presents an inquiry into the nature of female passion and the value our culture places on it. Through her own story and others' stories, she examines adolescent desires, and the reasons why they have endured a "long history of active censorship" and been driven underground in our culture. Chapter titles (21 in all) include: "Girlfriends," "Sluts," "First Base: Hierarchy," "More Skipped Homework: Our Pleasure," "A Virus," "The Technically White Dress," and more. A bibliography and an index are also given.

Evaluation:

Wolf unflinchingly examines adolescent girls' desires, lesbian tendencies, and various other "taboo" subjects using her personal history and those of others, along with examples of how other societies treat a young woman's coming of age with reverence. Her statement that "In our world, 'Demonstrate that you are a woman' means simply 'Take off your clothes'," will most likely hit a nerve with many parents concerned about our society being sexually saturated. For example, Wolf discusses the dilemma of how girls, on the one hand, are afraid to be labeled promiscuous, yet, on the other hand, are fully aware of the media's messages on how they should dress and act. Wolf believes girls are never able to be fully in control of their own sexuality. They miss out on rituals that let them test their autonomy, so as to leave their childhood behind. In effect, our culture determines that "the power to define our entering womanhood was bestowed upon boys and men." This book is not for the faint of heart, but will prove to be excellent reading for those interested in taking a direct look at the sexuality and sensuality of adolescent girls.

Where To Find/Buy:

Bookstores and libraries.

Overall Rating
★★
Focused on the subversion of female sexuality; frank and graphic

Design, Ease Of Use
★★
Must be read cover-to-cover; at times rather densely packed with author's treatise

---

1–4 Stars; N/R = Not Rated

Media:
Print

Price:
$13.95

Principal Subject:
Understanding Adolescents

ISBN:
0449907643

Edition:
1997

Publisher:
Fawcett Columbine (The Ballantine Publishing Group/ Random House)

Author:
Naomi Wolf

About The Author:
(From Cover Notes)
Wolf has also written *Fire With Fire* and *The Beauty Myth*. Her essays appear regularly in *The New Republic, The New York Times, The Washington Post, Glamour, Ms.,* and other publications. She lectures widely, and has taught at George Washington University.

★★

Overall Rating
★★
Solid information particular to teenage girls, written with authority

Design, Ease Of Use
★★
Too wordy at times; lack of index, but detailed TOC; suggested resource list would help

1–4 Stars; N/R = Not Rated

Media:
Print

Price:
$17.95

Principal Subject:
Understanding Adolescents

ISBN:
0824513568

Edition:
1994

Publisher:
The Crossroad Publishing Company

Author:
Lauren K. Ayers, Ph.D.

About The Author:
(From Cover Notes)
Ayers is a practicing psychologist, a registered school psychologist, a licensed secondary school teacher, and a psychologist for the TV show "Family Matters." She was a former college dorm director and a Girl Scout leader. She is the mother of three daughters.

Teenage Girls

TEENAGE GIRLS
A Parent's Survival Manual

Description:

This 320 page book is a reference manual for parents facing the challenge of raising a teenage girl age 11 to 19. The book discusses, in 6 sections, teen girls' thoughts, how to change a daughter, how to deal with problems and crises that arise, various emergencies parents may face, and a chapter on parental support. Chapter One, "Inside Her Head," discusses thought processes of teenage girls (newfound abilities, power, ignorance, wonder, appearance, and peer influence). Chapter Two provides specific advice and pointers on "changing a daughter," such as how to avoid power struggles and be optimistic. The next three chapters overview problems (shyness, driving, selfishness, etc.), crises (bad language, smoking, violence, sexuality/homosexuality, etc.), and emergencies (antisocial behaviors, self regulation problems, threats to personal safety such as rape and suicide, etc.). The final chapter is intended to help preserve parents' sanity by offering ways they can take care of themselves in the midst of their daughter's changes.

Evaluation:

Teenage girls grow up with different assumptions and expectations placed on them by society, as illustrated in this guide. There are also biological and familial discrepancies amongst boys and girls. This resource is valuable for its singular focus—the development and care of teenage girls. Ayers covers an enormous amount of territory in this densely packed manual. At times her chapter introductions are too wordy, but the sections within are relatively straightforward. Over 30 problems are discussed, such as personal hygiene, sourness, discourtesy, chore avoidance, sexual involvement, and others. Similarly, over 20 crises and 15 emergencies are presented. Obviously, none of these problems, crises, or emergencies are discussed at length, however. One major downfall of this resource is its lack of an index and list of suggested resources, given the limited amount of information included about each topic. Although the language rambles at times, the information is solid. Parents will find this book provides a basic overview of teenage girls' behavior. But other resources provide a clearer description of their development and particular needs.

Where To Find/Buy:
Bookstores and libraries.

Teenage Girls

REVIVING OPHELIA
Saving The Selves Of Adolescent Girls

Description:

This 15 chapter, 304 page book gives detailed portraits of adolescent girls encountered by the author in her clinical practice. Also sprinkled throughout are some of the author's own personal relationships and experiences when she was younger. Pipher reflects on the changes in American culture ("girl-poisoning culture") and how it has affected adolescent girls. She believes that adolescent girls face "a problem with no name" and when trying to solve it, they look to what's wrong with themselves or their family, instead of looking within a broader cultural context. As a result of the debates she hopes to create by writing this book, Pipher suggests "we can work together to build a culture that is less complicated and more nurturing, less violent and sexualized and more growth-producing." She discusses adolescent girls and their families (mothers, fathers, divorce), depression, "worshiping the gods of thinness," drugs and alcohol, and sex and violence. A list of recommended readings is provided at the back of the book.

Evaluation:

Pipher has given many interesting stories about adolescent girls facing various problems and situations in her book. When presented with problems in a book like this, one almost always anticipates answers. However, this book is more of an evaluation of the state of adolescent girls in America, than it is a book on parenting teenage girls. The problems and issues adolescent girls face are clearly represented, but the author does not delve into fixing the problems; she only presents light and very general treatment on how to begin to resolve problems. Frequently, Pipher offers no concrete advice about the girls' and their families' problems, thus leaving the reader, after having read well-illustrated stories about these girls, in a fog. If the book's purpose is to present a collection of the author's case studies involving adolescent girls, the purpose has been fulfilled. However, most parents will come away empty, not finding the solutions that the book's subtitle, *Saving The Selves Of Adolescent Girls*, implies might be found.

Where To Find/Buy:

Bookstores and libraries. An audiotape version (1996) of this book is also available for $16.99 (ISBN No. 0553476947)

Overall Rating
★★
Many interesting stories, but few conclusions of substance

Design, Ease Of Use
★
Free-flowing collection of stories; no real internal structure; ample index, vague TOC

1–4 Stars; N/R = Not Rated

Media:
Print

Price:
$24.95

Principal Subject:
Understanding Adolescents

ISBN:
0399139443

Edition:
1994

Publisher:
Grosset/Putnam Book (G. P. Putnam's Sons/The Putnam Berkley Group)

Author:
Mary Pipher, Ph.D.

**About The Author:
(From Cover Notes)**
Pipher, Ph.D., is a clinical psychologist in private practice in Lincoln, Nebraska. She teaches part-time at the University of Nebraska and Nebraska Wesleyan University. Pipher is also a commentator for Nebraska Public Radio.

II. Understanding Adolescents

★★★★

Overall Rating
★★★★
Excellent overall resource, character studies extremely personal and helpful

Design, Ease Of Use
★★★★
Well-organized; detailed table of contents and index makes information easy to access

1–4 Stars; N/R = Not Rated

Media:
Print

Price:
$24.95

Principal Subject:
Understanding Adolescents

ISBN:
0525939709

Edition:
1997

Publisher:
Dutton Book (Penguin Group/Penguin Putnam)

Author:
Ava L. Siegler, Ph.D.

About The Author:
(From Cover Notes)
Siegler is the mother of two grown sons, and the director of the Institute For Child, Adolescent & Family Studies in New York City. She maintains a private practice, lectures frequently, and writes a monthly column on parenting for *Child* magazine.

ESSENTIAL GUIDE TO THE NEW ADOLESCENCE (THE)
How To Raise An Emotionally Healthy Teenager

 Recommended For:
Understanding Adolescents

Description:
The author views adolescence as a series of necessary developmental steps on the path to independence. The book's first part discusses the formation and transformation of adolescence, examining the changes that take place, and the impact these changes have on the whole family. The second part of this 271 page book illustrates the lives of five teens, highlighting their experiences and transformation into adulthood, while illustrating the five key experiences that generally shape an adolescent's response: anxiety, depression, rebellion, withdrawal, and overattachment. The author believes all of these reactions are normal. But they can become abnormal, if they are too intense, are prolonged, or interfere with the adolescent's ability to master the five developmental tasks needed for adolescent development, which she defines as: separating from old ties, developing new attachments, establishing a mature sexual identity and sexual life, formulating new ideas and ideals, and consolidating character.

Evaluation:
This insightful book successfully combines facts with warm advice, focusing on the challenges and decisions faced by adolescents, and the ensuing changes parents must make to accommodate this growth. By assigning names and faces to her facts, Siegler creates an emotional and human impact that makes the book more digestible. Her compassion for her subjects is apparent throughout the book. She offers liberal doses of moral support alongside reasonable and helpful insights about how to recognize the difference between normal adolescent responses and cries for help that demand immediate attention. Chapter 4, "Talking with Your Adolescent," is particularly helpful, advocating the use of the four Cs to connect with one's teen: compassion, communication, comprehension, and competence; the author provides numerous examples. A wonderful appendix is devoted to finding outside help, from finding a therapist to debunking five of the most common mental health myths. This book is an excellent general reference for parents.

Where To Find/Buy:
Bookstores and libraries.

General Overview

UNDERSTANDING THE ADOLESCENT

★★★★

 Recommended For:
Understanding Adolescents

Description:

Based on the premise that adolescence is a "healthy and natural process," Orvin writes a book for parents that focuses on both teenage and parental psychological and social growth. Divided into 4 major sections, this 192 page book consists of 10 chapters. Chapters in Section 1, "Adolescents, Families, and Parents," discuss adolescent struggles in diverse family environments (single parent, stepfamilies, competent, dysfunctional, etc.), general guidelines to help parents and teens treat each other with respect, communicating with adolescents, and setting limits for adolescents. Section 2 focuses on the changes adolescents go through. Within this section, Chapter 5 describes "behaviors within normal limits," Chapter 6 deals with personal identity, and Chapter 7 addresses biological changes and sexual identity. Section 3 deals with problems in adolescence, and includes chapters on "destructive" risk-taking and "serious problems" like abuse and eating disorders. Section 4 explains the transition to adulthood.

Evaluation:

Orvin explains, without passing judgement, that while all teens are different and parental values are different, there are teen behaviors that fall "within normal limits," and others that don't. The structure of this book is a strength; each chapter contains guidelines and a conclusion. An especially strong chapter is Chapter 4 on setting limits. Orvin gives parents "Some Rules About Setting Rules" that include "Rules should have value . . . a purpose . . . be limited in number," etc. Each of these rules is fully explained with examples. Many sections like this are valuable for any parents, not just those with teens. Also, subsections are never more than a few paragraphs, making this book easy to read and skim. Orvin recognizes that there are no perfect parents or teens, but gives checkpoints to enhance parents' relationships and skills. He practices what he preaches, and it's obvious he encourages and cares about parents and teens. Containing many useful guidelines, this resource will be worthwhile reading for any parent.

Where To Find/Buy:
Bookstores and libraries.

Overall Rating
★★★★
Refreshing approach focuses on parents understanding teens and themselves

Design, Ease Of Use
★★★★
Easy to read with bullets, subheadings, tips, cartoons, TOC, index, references

1–4 Stars; N/R = Not Rated

Media:
Print

Price:
$21.95

Principal Subject:
Understanding Adolescents

ISBN:
0880486511

Edition:
1995

Publisher:
American Psychiatric Press

Author:
George H. Orvin, M.D.

About The Author:
(From Cover Notes)
A psychiatrist, Orvin has worked with adolescents and their families for 30+ years. He is a lecturer, a consultant for youth and family service agencies, and is a founder and chairman of the board of New Hope (residential treatment centers for emotionally disturbed teens).

★★★

Overall Rating
★★★
A good general guide to understanding a teen's motivations

Design, Ease Of Use
★★★★
Chapter subheadings well organized; easy to read and access

1–4 Stars; N/R = Not Rated

Media:
Print

Price:
$11.95

Principal Subject:
Understanding Adolescents

ISBN:
096249450X

Edition:
1996

Publisher:
Silvercat Publications

Author:
Elizabeth Caldwell

About The Author:
(From Cover Notes)
Caldwell raised her son as a single mother.

General Overview

TEENAGERS!
A Bewildered Parent's Guide

 Recommended For:
Understanding Adolescents

Description:

Caldwell relies upon her experience as a single mother of a teenaged son to help explain the importance of parenting teenagers in today's world. Believing that parent-teen conflicts revolve around six principles (authority, direction, choices, freedom, communication, relationships), Caldwell describes what teens are doing and why. Her 174 page book is divided into 14 chapters that discuss these six principles along with: manipulation ("But you let Jenny do it!"), privacy (their bedrooms, personal time, etc.), "teenage playrooms" (teens' freedom to make choices), mistakes, and testing. A chapter is also included on what to do if parents suspect or discover that their teen is using drugs. She also includes a chapter offering parting advice, such as "successful parents learn humility," are consistent, are definitive, are willing to discipline, and more. Throughout the book, positive and negative examples are provided to illustrate the ways in which teens "act out" and come to terms with their maturation processes.

Evaluation:

Teenagers! provides many examples of how to handle the daily struggle of living with teens. Based on observations and first-hand experiences with teens, the author describes what teenagers need from their parents as they learn to become responsible. Caldwell makes recommendations that have worked with her teenager and others she has observed; she also asked for teen feedback during the writing of this book. The chapters on "Testing the Waters" and "Mistakes" are particularly well done. She views "testing the waters" as a teenager's way of exploring boundaries and finding their independence in a relatively safe environment. She believes that teens experiment with their reality, developing a strategy for testing rules, and restrictions. The chapter on "mistakes" includes her advice for parents ("only sweat the big stuff") along with reasons why teenagers make mistakes (poor judgment, lack of knowledge, inattention). Not to be considered an end-all, this book provides good anecdotes and sound reasoning.

Where To Find/Buy:

Bookstores, libraries, or order direct by calling (619) 299-6774.

General Overview

A TRIBE APART
A Journey Into the Heart Of American Adolescence

Description:

The eight adolescents chosen for this book ran the gamut from those entering middle school to those who are seniors in high school. Hersch chose different age groups in order to highlight the maturation process that takes place between early adolescence and adulthood. She tracked their development over a 3 year time frame, focusing on "regular kids" in order to reveal the major differences between what kids face today as a matter of course compared to what teenagers dealt with a generation ago. By immersing herself in their "culture," attending school and free time activities with her subjects, Hersch attempts to bring each person's life into sharp focus. Her observations include times adolescents wrestle with the challenges facing them, issues of sexuality, the temptation of drugs and delinquency, and seeking their own path. Hersch hopes that by trying to understand and empathize with these kids, we can help kids in our own circles of influence and bridge the distance between us, "one kid at a time."

Evaluation:

This book should be read by anyone who cares about kids. Hersch offers an insiders' look into the lives of eight adolescents who are different ages, come from different socioeconomic backgrounds, and who have vastly different goals and aspirations. From school assemblies of nominal importance, to a 14 year old girl's uncertainty of whether she is ready for sex, Hersch highlights the struggle kids endure. She believes that parents have forgotten how much adolescents need adults to set limits and take an active interest in their well-being. In so doing, our society has created a culture of people who are looking to their peers instead to help them steer the treacherous path to adulthood—kids who have learned to take care of themselves and decipher the many mixed messages they receive in their own ways. In the words of one of Mrs. Hersch's subjects, "Kids and grown-ups do not have to be strangers. Aloneness makes adolescents a tribe apart." Her 391 page resource offers a bridge toward understanding one another.

Where To Find/Buy:

Bookstores and libraries.

Overall Rating
★★★
Compassionate, loving look at what it takes to grow up in today's world

Design, Ease Of Use
★★★
Reads like a novel, hard to put down; table of contents obscure, but index is detailed

1–4 Stars; N/R = Not Rated

Media:
Print

Price:
$25.00

Principal Subject:
Understanding Adolescents

ISBN:
0449907678

Edition:
1998

Publisher:
Fawcett Columbine (Ballantine Publishing Group)

Author:
Patricia Hersch

**About The Author:
(From Cover Notes)**
Hersch has been published in *The Washington Post, McCall's, Family Therapy Networker, The Baltimore Sun, New Age Journal,* and other newspapers and magazines. She has conducted an ethnographic study of homeless adolescents in San Francisco and New York.

Overall Rating
★★★
A useful tool for the parent dealing with a child's anger, with a Christian perspective

Design, Ease Of Use
★★★
Four broad sections; relevant anecdotes and case studies; logically presented; no index

1–4 Stars; N/R = Not Rated

Media:
Print

Price:
$12.99

Principal Subject:
Understanding Adolescents

ISBN:
0785280022

Edition:
1995

Publisher:
Thomas Nelson Publishers

Author:
Dr. Wm. Lee Carter

About The Author:
(From Cover Notes)
Carter is a licensed psychologist with Child Psychiatry Associates in Waco, Texas. He provides psychological counseling and consultation to children, teens, and their families. He and his wife have three daughters, two of which are teenagers.

General Overview

ANGRY TEENAGER (THE)
Why Teens Get So Angry, And How Parents Can Help Them Grow Through It

Description:
Carter's goal in writing this book is to help parents understand their child's anger. He counsels parents on how to either successfully diffuse their child's anger or use it positively. The book is divided into four main sections, which deal with aspects of anger. Part One explains the reasons why some teenagers become angry; the chapters also address self-esteem and communication issues. Next, Carter addresses the "masks of teenage anger"—the different faces that can be worn to cover up this emotion, including aggression, depression, and passive-aggressive behavior. Part III addresses things parents/peers do to fuel anger. Different warnings are offered, as well as explanations for why teenagers get out of control. The last part offers parents advice on what they can do to solve the problem. Concepts and actions such as family unity, forgiveness, boundary-setting, and dispute resolution are discussed and advocated. An afterword emphasizes that if parents understand their teen's emotions, family harmony is possible.

Evaluation:
Whether displayed in actions, words, or body language, adolescents do get angry. This book does an excellent job of answering parents' questions of "why?" and "what can I do?" Using examples from his personal experience as a child psychiatrist, Carter's book will likely hit home with most readers. It is important to note, however, that this book's usefulness is limited. Although it advises parents how to deal with the anger displayed (or hidden) by their child, in certain situations (substance abuse, depression, etc.), the teenager might be better served by professional counseling. Also, what may be normal and healthy bouts of irritation expressed by a teen, may be blown out of proportion by the parent who follows the advice given in this resource blindly. This book deals in-depth with a difficult issue, and it brings to light some valuable tools and information to help the confused parent. But parents need to use the author's advice wisely, while taking into consideration their child's own situation.

Where To Find/Buy:
Bookstores and libraries.

General Overview

ALL GROWN UP AND NO PLACE TO GO
Teenagers In Crisis

★★★

Description:
Elkind's underlying premise is that society and parents force adolescents to grow up too soon, foisting responsibility on them without providing them safe places to develop and grow. There are three main parts to this book. Part One—"Needed: A Time to Grow"—includes issues that adolescents universally encounter— puberty and peer pressure; the discussion focuses on the social climate that is unique to today's teenager and the roles played by technology and a relaxed parenting style and lack of authority structure. Part Two discusses the vanishing of "markers" such as clothing, activity, information, image, and authority, that once illuminated an adolescent's growing maturity. The changing family structure (single parents, blended families, divorce, teenage mothers) is discussed, as is the current state of our education system (class size, curriculum, school size, teachers). The third part "Stress and Its Aftermath" discusses the effect of stresses in the post-modern world on different personality types and offers solutions on how to help teenagers cope with their stress at home and at school.

Evaluation:
Thoughtful and compassionate, this book unabashedly advocates for teenagers. Writing in an essay style with examples from real conversations with teens, Elkind makes a strong case for reevaluating how we, as a society, are raising our children. He effectively discusses the difference between what teenagers need to grow up in today's society and what they are actually getting from it. The chapter on vanishing markers is especially helpful. It discusses milestones of development which used to represent new stages of growth and maturity. For example, the switch from knee-length pants to long pants used to be a sign that a young person had "arrived" and was no longer a child. Today's clothing standards, however, have more to do with fashion trends and fads, signifying nothing more than personal taste and monetary concerns. Parents concerned with how to preserve their youth in a post-modern world will find this to be an excellent resource for understanding the universal challenges facing young people today.

Where To Find/Buy:
Bookstores and libraries.

Overall Rating
★★★
Combines facts and compassion to discuss teenage development in today's society

Design, Ease Of Use
★★
Essay format, best read cover-to-cover; student examples help break up the text

1–4 Stars; N/R = Not Rated

Media:
Print

Price:
$14.00

Principal Subject:
Understanding Adolescents

ISBN:
0201483858

Edition:
2nd (1998)

Publisher:
Addison-Wesley

Author:
David Elkind, Ph.D.

About The Author:
(From Cover Notes)
Elkind, author of *The Hurried Child*, is a professor of child development at Tufts University. A specialist in adolescent psychology, he cohosts the Lifetime TV series *Kids These Days*. Elkind for many years wrote a column on teenagers for *Parents* magazine.

II. Understanding Adolescents

Overall Rating
★★
Good research and background for professionals, but advice for parents is a bit outdated

Design, Ease Of Use
★★★
Detailed, straightforward TOC; comprehensive index; a bit wordy at times

1–4 Stars; N/R = Not Rated

Media:
Print

Price:
$13.95

Principal Subject:
Understanding Adolescents

ISBN:
0878223541

Edition:
1995

Publisher:
Research Press

Author:
Ann Vernon, Ph.D., N.C.C., L.M.H.C. & Radhi H. Al-Mabuk, Ph.D.

About The Author:
(From Cover Notes)
Vernon is professor of the counselor education program at the University of Northern Iowa. She specializes in working with children, adolescents, and their parents. Al-Mabuk is assistant professor of education at UNI in the Department of Educational Psychology.

General Overview

WHAT GROWING UP IS ALL ABOUT
A Parent's Guide To Child And Adolescent Development

Description:
Describing developmental stages from the preschool years through mid-adolescence, Vernon and Al-Mabuk attempt to explain what happens from the perspective of the child. The authors believe that if parents understand what to expect at each stage of development, difficulties which arise will be less surprising. The basic goal of this book is to provide parents with a reference point, to check whether their child is behaving normally compared to others of the child's same developmental stage. In addition to their discussions of these four major developmental stages, the authors describe different practices of discipline and communication, explaining why some methods are good, while others are ineffective or detrimental. The first chapter is dedicated to dispelling rumors of parenting, as well as talking about different parenting styles. Within each section on development, the authors explain the physical, intellectual, self, social, and emotional development. Each chapter then ends with a brief conclusion.

Evaluation:
The authors state that this book is intended for professionals, so they can then offer parents guidelines to determine whether or not their child is normal, and receive comfort knowing "it's just a phase." Like other resources, this book follows the logic that "tried-and-true" parenting practices work. However, some of the situations they use as examples seem straight out of an 80s TV sitcom. This book does offer many of the same solutions as others of its type, such as: communicate openly, stick with a discipline plan, explain calmly how you feel about a situation, and inform kids of the consequences of their behavior, and so on. In addition, the book's most valuable advice includes things not to do in terms of discipline and communication. But the recommendations for effective parenting are a bit weak and simplistic. For example, there are no specific recommendations for what to do if the author's first piece of advice backfires. Therefore, following only the advice on these pages may leave the parent frustrated and feeling helpless.

Where To Find/Buy:
Bookstores, libraries, or order direct by contacting Research Press at 2612 North Mattis Avenue, Champaign, IL 61821.

General Overview

HOW TO PREPARE FOR ADOLESCENCE

Description:

Dobson, president and founder of the Focus on the Family corporation, presents his views on how parents can prepare for adolescence in this 1 hour 39 minute videotape. This two part presentation is incorporated as Parts Four and Five of the "Focus on the Family" series. During the tape's segment "The Origins of Self-Doubt," Dobson discloses his two recommendations—parents should postpone adolescence until kids "get there," and then consciously prepare them for what to expect. He suggests that a parent should take their adolescent child away over a weekend, and describe on a one-on-one basis the following self-doubts that adolescents will experience: feelings of inferiority (feel ugly, feel dumb, feel unloved), feelings of conformity, the meaning of love, strains between the generations, a search for their identity, and the meaning of puberty. Dobson believes that parents can't head off these feelings, and that kids will profit from addressing them if given direct parental counsel. He offers some biblical citations to support his views.

Evaluation:

The tape has a much dated feel (of the early 1980s), but Dobson followers will most likely appreciate his directives on how to deal with adolescence knowing that "rebellion is necessary and perhaps healthy." He emphasizes flaws in how our society approaches adolescence through its perpetuation of the Barbie ideal and inappropriate Saturday cartoons. He also reflects on how our value system, which rewards physical attractiveness and intelligence (two areas he feels are unearned), unknowingly undermines adolescents' feelings of confidence. Dobson's presentation of adolescent development differs from other resources in that he not only sheds light on what generally happens to adolescents, but he also suggests that parents meet that development head on with their child. As he states, many parents discuss "the birds and the bees," but rarely, until a crisis occurs, do they discuss the feelings of self-doubt that plague a young adult. Good for a basic prompter for parent-teen discussions, nonetheless, parents will benefit from more in-depth resources that discuss and offer parental advice on adolescent development.

Where To Find/Buy:

Bookstores, libraries, and videotape dealers.

Overall Rating
★★
Basic presentation of adolescent "self-doubts" with emphasis on parent-teen discussions

Design, Ease Of Use
★★
Seminar footage, with dated feel from the early 1980s; humorous, but rambles at times

1–4 Stars; N/R = Not Rated

Media:
Videotape

Price:
$29.98

Principal Subject:
Understanding Adolescents

ISBN:
6302482941

Edition:
1985

Publisher:
WORD

Author:
Dr. James C. Dobson, Ph.D.

About The Author:
(From Cover Notes)
Dobson is founder and president of Focus on the Family, a nonprofit corporation dedicated to the preservation of the home. For 14 years, he was associate clinical professor of pediatrics at U.S.C., and for 17 years, he served on the attending staff of Children's Hospital of L.A.

Overall Rating
★★
Good for understanding stages of moral development, but full attention is required

Design, Ease Of Use
★★
Heavy with psych jargon at times; good parent-teen interaction examples

1–4 Stars; N/R = Not Rated

Media:
Print

Price:
$13.95

Principal Subject:
Understanding Adolescents

ISBN:
055337429X

Edition:
1994

Publisher:
Bantam Books (Bantam Doubleday Dell Publishing Group)

Author:
Dr. Thomas Lickona

About The Author:
(From Cover Notes)
Dr. Lickona is a developmental psychologist and Professor of Education at the State University of New York at Cortland. A past president of the Association for Moral Education, he now serves on the board of directors of the Character Education Partnership.

General Overview

RAISING GOOD CHILDREN
From Birth Through The Teenage Years

Description:
As the title suggests, this book is designed to help parents instill a high sense of morality in their children, starting at birth and continuing through young adulthood. There are four major sections of this book. Part 1 explains 10 "big ideas" or themes that comprise the author's "moral development approach" (respect, teach by example, teach by telling, and more). Part 2 then highlights ways to lay the foundation for children's moral development. Here, the author explains the five stages of moral development, as he sees them, and what parents can do to ensure that the child successfully "completes" each stage. Parts 3 and 4 discuss, respectively, how to help children through "stages of moral reasoning," and how to converse with children while dealing with some critical issues such as sex, drugs and drinking, TV's influence, etc. The book relies heavily on statistics, all of which are cited. Parenting dos and don'ts are interspersed in various chapters. A comprehensive index and four appendices conclude this 447 page book.

Evaluation:
This book relies heavily on Lickona's experience as a developmental psychologist and the work of Kohlberg, Piaget, and others. Although the language is rather complicated at times, this book breaks down the stages of moral development in an engaging manner with plenty of parent-child examples. Parents should recognize, however, that 90% of Dr. Lickona's references are dated prior to 1980. Also, although children's moral development from birth to preschool age encompasses a quarter of the book, the author weaves his 10 themes throughout the rest stating that these are "principles that are important whether you're dealing with a 4-year-old or a 14-year-old." A complete reading of this text is necessary making it awkward for those parents wanting immediate help for a particular issue. We highly recommend Part 4 for all parents seeking alternate ways to converse with their child. Conversation openers, questions to invite discussions, and more are offered here. Parents wanting tips on how to challenge kids' stage of reasoning, or how to "go with the flow" of their current stage will find this interesting reading.

Where To Find/Buy:
Bookstores and libraries.

General Overview

STEPPING INTO ADULTHOOD
Discover The Most Significant Event In Your Child's Life

Description:

Discussing his unique perspective as a Christian minister who converted from the Jewish faith, Brodsky studies the "Rite of Passage," and its importance in the journey from childhood to adulthood. He believes that parents are given to children by God to be their guides through life. The first part of this 157 page book is devoted to the author's personal story of how he adopted the Christian faith and what led him to focus on the Bar Mitzvah, or Rite of Passage, as a means of transformation for adolescents. Part Two details the adolescent's "Journey Into Adulthood." Here, Brodsky cites Scriptural passages and presents the author's personal experience and testimonials of parents and young adults. He advises parents to be present for their children, listen to them, hear their cries for help, and celebrate the "Rite of Passage." The book includes a bibliography, a phone list of international suicide/help lines, and information on Joy International, the author's foundation.

Evaluation:

Advocating a Christian rite of passage, similar in meaning to the Jewish Bar Mitzvah, Brodsky quotes scripture and illustrates his beliefs using testimony from parents and youth in his ministry. He draws on his Jewish history and Christian faith to espouse his belief that young people today need to have direction and guidance on their path to adulthood. In today's often violent world, Brodsky believes that kids should realize that becoming an adult is a powerful moment, and a cause for celebration. As they step into adulthood, adolescents need to know that there are people who have gone before them who will continue to guide them and celebrate their growth. The chapter on planning the right celebration is helpful. Brodsky examines several widely accepted rites of passage that he believes celebrate the wrong things (hunting, sex, gangs, etc.), then asks parents to reflect on what coming of age means to them. This guide may offer Christian parents advice and support to help their children step into adulthood with confidence and pride in themselves.

Where To Find/Buy:

Bookstores, libraries, or order direct by contacting Joy International at (303) 766-2650 or (toll free) at 1-888-JOY-4-ALL.

Overall Rating
★★
Christian approach to understanding an adolescent's coming-of-age or "Rite of Passage"

Design, Ease Of Use
★★
Book is best when read as a whole, but it is easily read

1–4 Stars; N/R = Not Rated

Media:
Print

Price:
$10.00

Principal Subject:
Understanding Adolescents

ISBN:
0965674924

Edition:
1997

Publisher:
ACW Press

Author:
Jeff Brodsky

About The Author:
(From Cover Notes)
Brodsky has been in full-time ministry to children, youth, and families for the past 18 years, and is the founder of Joy International (begun in 1981). He is married and lives in Colorado. He has three children.

II. Understanding Adolescents

Overall Rating
★★
General reference, treats most subjects in a light, brief manner

Design, Ease Of Use
★
Confusing layout—2 upside down books; no index to help guide parents to cross-references

1–4 Stars; N/R = Not Rated

Media:
Print

Price:
$11.95

Principal Subject:
Understanding Adolescents

ISBN:
1863510885

Edition:
1992

Publisher:
Sally Milner Publishing Pty Ltd

Author:
Dr. Charmaine Saunders

About The Author:
(From Cover Notes)
Saunders is an author, counselor, teacher, and columnist. She has written two other books about stress and writes a weekly column for a West Australian newspaper, as well as regular articles for magazines and other publications.

General Overview

TEENAGE STRESS
A Guide For Teenagers, A Guide For Parents

Description:

This book is written as two books in one, 168 pages for the teenagers' guide and 72 pages for the parents' guide; the type is flipped upside down to distinguish the two parts. The book written for teenagers includes a discussion of stressors in life, with tips on how to deal with them. The major headings (home, school, sexuality, emotions, work and employment, health, personal growth) are each the subject of one of the book's 11 chapters; Chapter 9—"The A to Z of Stress"—is only included in the teenagers' guide. This chapter contains a dictionary of potential stressors for teens (AIDS, divorce, illness, loss, marriage, etc.). The chapter on personal growth explores aspects of personal development (religion, spirituality, positive thinking, creative visualization, inner peace, personal power). The book for parents discusses the major stressors facing teens today, giving parents insight on how they affect teens and how parents can diminish the impact of stressors on their children.

Evaluation:

The author's experience as a teacher and counselor is exhibited in this book as she grants parents a very general overview of the many sources of stress facing teenagers today. Her approach is compassionate and she displays a true affection for adolescents. Unfortunately though, the author merely identifies arenas that produce stress providing basic information on how to reduce its impact on adolescents. For example, the section on "sexual activity" contains almost one page of advice (compared to four pages on how to help kids with homework) consisting of four bulleted tips and the acknowledgment that "how you as parents handle the training of your children can make all the difference." The layout is annoying, in that the two guides are upside down from each other, and the advice is quite simplistic many times. The book is concise, listing the common stressors and providing parents and children with positive ways to deal with them, but the author's discussions are too brief to be of any real help for parents.

Where To Find/Buy:

Bookstores and libraries.

PARENT-TEEN RELATIONSHIPS

III

INTRODUCTION

As with children and adults of all ages, relationships are at the heart of any issue surrounding adolescence. Relationships also tend to be the greatest and most consistent source of stress for teenagers. Their relationships come in different configurations and are given various levels of importance, yet they are still the central point of focus for adolescents.

One of the contradictions so apparent at this age is the adolescent's growing narcissism, which is coupled with the adolescent's desperate need to be accepted and needed. Relationships, then, are the venue where these conflicting aspects of adolescence play themselves out. Generally, teenagers steer away from their relationship with their families and the influence of their parents. Though this often is a cause for concern and a source of immense stress for parents, family, and adolescents, it is nevertheless a normal part of life's development. The constant pushing away from family with one hand, while pulling closer to family with the other, clearly illustrates the adolescent's dilemma. This child, who depended on their parent's word as reality, will now have a reality of their own . . . and probably different than their parent's. Parents will be challenged with allowing their child to fail, as well as watching while they risk success.

As they move away from their parents, a teenager will seek support from others by embracing relationships with their peers. They will find excuses not to be with other adults, parents included. Teenagers ask parents to drop them off around the corner, not to talk to them while in public viewing range, and certainly never to show any affection, at any time, whatsoever. The peer group replaces the family unit for a time and becomes the prominent social influence in a teenager's life. For the most part, this is transitional. By early adulthood, most kids will find their way through their maze of friends and the black abyss of peer groups, and come back to their families. Just when parents thought their kids were gone, there they are wanting their room back. Of course, now the relationship has changed again, and former rules don't apply now that they're not teenagers anymore.

The same hormonal and developmental forces that are at work in other aspects of a teenager's life are active within their relationships as well. Best friends one day will be avoided the next. Favorite teachers and other significant adults will find their position fluctuating between hero status and an afterthought. Love is intense and often finished as quickly as it began. The current status of a teenager's relationship tends to be intense and for the moment. This perhaps explains why relationships can be so painful during this period of life. The intensity of adolescent emotions creates a wonderful, if not all consuming, black hole that can suck into it everything and everyone close by.

Relationships for teenagers at this age are based on being accepted by their peers, and teens are greatly influenced by the roller coaster of adolescent love. Major issues teenagers face within these relationships include struggles over authority and power, ego and acceptance, and sex. Though these may not be all-inclusive factors, to the adolescent they are the most powerful and prevalent. These relationships are based on conditions that are variable, risky, and very fluid, thus resulting in numerous problems. Teens base their acceptance on an ever-changing criteria of "what is cool." Unfortunately, this feedback is susceptible to daily change, which means that teens develop a very vulnerable external set of criteria which they also use to judge their internal self-concept. Thus, acceptance and identity can be a day to day adventure.

Probably the most remarkable relationship experience for teenagers involves romantic love. With hormonal explosions dominating this time of life, romance can be the most exquisite, and powerful, of all relationships. It can also be the most devastating, depressing, and ego-crushing experience of an adolescent's life. And when we add to this the fact that teens live primarily in the present, the highs are all that much sweeter, and the lows are all that much more debilitating.

Adults look at their teenager's relationship experiences and have difficulty understanding or appreciating the intensity of these ups and downs. Through their own life experience, adults know that they themselves will have other friends, loves, and experiences. This is, however, precisely where the adolescent can be at risk. Their sense of reality—the here and now—often excludes consideration of any other future possible relationships that may help soften the extremes of their current relationships.

As parents prepare their teenagers to move out into the world, parents need to become further aware of their children's needs, and also appreciate how the parent-teen relationship takes on various forms to meet these needs. Parent, friend, teacher, counselor, and mentor—these are all roles parents may assume from time to time in the lives of their adolescent.

Parent-Teen Dynamics

Parent-teen relationships come in a variety of arrangements. Depending on the family configuration, parents may find various alliances formed between teen and one or the other parent. In single parent families, this alliance may be clearer, but not necessarily less confrontational. Today, teens are out in the work force more than ever, and possibly interacting on levels in society not experienced by their parents when they were young. This may encourage a blurring of the parent-child roles and a questioning of rules and boundaries.

Parents of adolescents are caught in a dilemma. They have raised this child earnestly in an effort to create an individual who will become an effective and contributing member of society. But now it's time to allow that effectiveness to be tested. However, the risks of the adolescent world make this a scary proposition for parents. The parent-teen relationship, then, becomes one in which parents must blend their need to protect their child, while allowing this young adult to grow and test their strengths. This situation jeopardizes past relationship roles and brings boundaries into question and dispute. The results can include the distancing, non-communicative, and confrontational nature of parent-teen relationships. Communication has become a lost art at a time when parents and teens, perhaps more than ever, need to converse about life's most pressing issues.

Issues involving power and control are also part of this dynamic. Many parents might remember their authoritarian parents making it clear that "while you live under our roof . . . ." In other words, certain rules were not questioned within the family. Teenagers either chose to obey or chose not be under that particular roof. Parents today, however, sometimes face a different set of parenting rules. While they encourage their adolescent to take on more responsibility and control of their lives, they also struggle with giving up the control that was present in their earlier parent-child relationship. The dynamics of the parent-teen relationship center on reestablishing each other's roles, rules, and responsibilities. "Letting go" becomes the major challenge faced by parents, and knowing how much and when to let go is the art of adolescent parenting.

Peer Influence and Pressure

Many adolescents will insist that there is no such thing as peer pressure. They feel that **they** make their own decisions, and their friends are merely there to support this independent behavior. However, adults observing the fashion, language, mannerisms, and behavior of teens will note that teens do indeed seem to create a collective identity, which, to adults, obviously indicates peer group influence, or peer pressure. Adults themselves can see these influences in their own peer groups, and thus fully acknowledge the presence of peer pressure. Certainly the corporate and advertising worlds believe it exists. Images of what is cool and acceptable are splashed throughout adult life as men and women are bombarded with products that identify them to their selected peers.

As with any influence, peer pressure can be both helpful and a distraction. It serves to insulate and, at times, isolate adolescents, yet it also grants them acceptance and an identity at a time when these developmental tasks are of foremost importance. Peer groups serve as a refuge for the teenager from the family and from the adult world. Of course, parents and families experience this as a loss of a family member, and as an entry into the risky world of adolescence.

As with many aspects of adolescence, peers and peer groups can be the most anchoring influence or the most threatening influence in a teen's life. The power of the group can be seen upon the adolescent's entrance and exit from these groups. Getting into a group may not be easy, but to be accepted by the group is as necessary for the group as it is for the individual. Acquiescence and identity with the group serves to protect and extend the group's existence. Exits, on the other hand, can be perceived as a threat to the purpose and status of others in the group. Thus, adults will often see the group holding its members in at all costs.

Life in general is more complicated these days. Our society has a much richer variety of family configurations, and a wider definition of relationships is permitted in today's world. Families are no longer primarily two-parent configurations. Extended family does not exert the kind of influence it once did. People don't get married at the same point in their lives as they once did, and sexual identity is less narrowly defined. The media's influence on today's youth is illustrated in rather dramatic ways and can be formidable opponents to parents struggling to keep control. And as adolescents become more entrenched with their peers, they are further introduced to the variety of family arrangements, expectations, and communication patterns that exist in today's society. As a result, relationships for adolescents come in more shapes, sizes, and configurations than ever before. Weaving their way through the period of adolescence and these many varied relationships is no easy task for young adults. These influences and dynamics require more work on the part of adolescents as they form relationships, as well as on the part of those adults who wish to remain constant in their children's lives.

Adolescence is a time of contradictions, dilemmas, and conflicting forces. Relationships are no exception. Where parents once believed they had a cooperative child, now instead they may find they have a rebellious, inconsiderate teenager intent on making life miserable for everyone around them. Children who were once open and approachable, may now seem distant and remote. Instead of talking **to** their child, parents will be challenged to have a serious conversation **with** their child. Parents may feel as if their teen is slipping through their fingers like melting ice. In reality though, their relationship is changing. Transforming this connection into a healthy, functional relationship is a parent's greatest desire, and obviously in a teenager's best interest. This foundation will provide strength during crises, and encourage trust, love, and respect to prosper and develop.

In the pages that follow, we looked for resources that would offer parents a full perspective of changes that arise in the parent-teen relationship during adolescence. Many of these resources address the day to day conflicts that can occur between parents and teens, such as taking out the trash, cleaning up their room, meeting their curfew, etc. Other resources specifically address how parents and teens can handle more serious problems arising from peer relationships, such as alcohol or drug use, sex, violence and gang involvement, and other potentially life-threatening issues. Still other resources help parents in giving their child added responsibility so they learn to make their own decisions. The intent of many of these resources is to assist parents and teens in creating rules and boundaries, and establishing rights, privileges, and consequences that both can live with.

Other resources specifically focus on communication with advice on how to get a teenager to talk about their day, their views, their friends, anything. These resources offer tips on how to open a dialogue, words that are communication killers, suggested ways to say "no," advice on perfecting a parent's listening skills, and ways to handle disagreement. The intent of these resources is to help parents elicit something other than "uh-huh" or "fine" from their teenager.

To help you focus your search, we have divided these resources into the following categories:

In order to enhance the parent-teen relationship during adolescence, it will be helpful for parents to fully understand what their adolescent is thinking and feeling, and why they do what they do. We highly recommend that parents read the full-page reviews of resources we recommend in **Section II—"Understanding Adolescents."** Here, parents will find resources that describe characteristics of this age group so parents will know what they can logically expect in terms of their teen's behavior and emotions. By understanding their adolescent and appreciating the dramatic nature of their growth and development, communications and expectations between parent and teen may be better served.

In addition, for families that are dealing with specific crises, such as substance abuse, eating disorders, sexual behavior, and more, we also suggest parents read the full-page reviews of resources we recommend in **Section IV—"Critical Issues & Concerns."** Here, parents will find ways to maintain their inner family relationships while handling these intensely difficult situations.

Parent-Teen Dynamics

ART OF TALKING WITH YOUR TEENAGER (THE)

 Terrific Resource For:
Improving parent-teenager communications

 Recommended For:
Parent-Teen Relationships

Description:

This 211 page book outlines techniques for parents to use when relating to their teenagers. Centered on helping the parent figure out what kind of communicator they are, this book then examines the basics of communication—becoming a good listener, learning how to say no, keeping one's cool, how to handle disagreement, responding to major problems, and more. The author includes his tips on how to communicate effectively, coupled with ineffective door-openers, such as "Did you fail your test again today?" vs. "How was school today?" The author contends that if parents listen actively and curb their natural tendencies to dominate or accuse their teen, they will create an environment in which their teens will feel more comfortable as they relate their problems. Each chapter includes "Action Steps" which are exercises designed to help parents develop new communication skills, build their confidence, and help them practice the chapter's techniques while in action.

Evaluation:

Building on the foundations of good communication how-tos, the author provides numerous examples of good parent-teen conversations along with dead-end conversation "killers." Especially helpful is the chapter on "Five Keys to Communicating with Your Teenager." It details ways parents can show genuine interest in their teen, learn to control their emotions, develop a clear purpose when communicating with them, avoid conversation killers, and invest time with their teen. The "Action Steps" are also useful refreshers for rereading purposes. Also provided are tips and tricks for helping parents remember what they've learned. For example the acronym "C.A.L.M.L.Y." is offered to help parents remember to: Control their responses, Avoid vicious cycles, Listen to their teen's perspective, Motivate reconciliation, Learn verbal self-defense, and Yield when their teen is right. Offering ample hands-on advice, this book is recommended for parents interested in changing or enhancing the way they approach their teens.

Where To Find/Buy:

Bookstores and libraries

Overall Rating
★★★★
Written with compassion, clear and helpful with hints on how to communicate better

Design, Ease Of Use
★★★★
Examples, scripted dialogues; italics, bullets, numbered passages break up text info

1–4 Stars; N/R = Not Rated

Media:
Print

Price:
$9.95

Principal Subject:
Parent-Teen Relationships

ISBN:
1558504788

Edition:
1995

Publisher:
Adams Media

Author:
Paul W. Swets

**About The Author:
(From Cover Notes)**
Paul Swets is a husband, father, speaker and pastor. He earned a Doctor of Arts degree in English at the University of Michigan with research emphasis in the field of rhetoric. His first book, *The Art of Talking So That People Will Listen,* is in its fifteenth printing.

III. Parent-Teen Relationships

★★★★

Overall Rating
★★★★
Humorous at just the right times; a refreshingly insightful book about parents and teens

Design, Ease Of Use
★★★★
Witty writing makes for easy reading; organization of chapters is natural and logical

1–4 Stars; N/R = Not Rated

Media:
Print

Price:
$6.95

Principal Subject:
Parent-Teen Relationships

ISBN:
0812048768

Edition:
1992

Publisher:
Barron's Educational Series

Author:
Don H. Fontenelle, Ph.D.

About The Author:
(From Cover Notes)
Fontenelle is an experienced child and adolescent psychologist.

KEYS TO PARENTING YOUR TEENAGER

 Recommended For:
Parent-Teen Relationships

Description:
Consisting of 34 chapters, this 218 page resource covers topics ranging from changes during adolescence (parent and child) to different types of punishment. Other chapters focus on increasing parent-teen communication, learning to listen, and reestablishing trust once it has been violated. Fontenelle, an adolescent psychologist, outlines problems that arise from using punishment, as well as discussing the importance of consistency. Some chapters employ humor to explain a concept (for example, in listing parental changes during adolescence, he states that parents' "intelligence decreases, senility or amnesia develops," etc.); other discussions are more serious (alcohol, drugs, and suicide). A chapter addresses "What to Do If the Techniques in This Book Do Not Work." Two chapters conclude the book—"Memos From Your Teenager" and "Tips For Teenagers." In these chapters, Fontenelle puts into words the feelings experienced by both parents and teenagers that are sometimes left unsaid. Suggestions for further reading and an index are given.

Evaluation:
Although Fontenelle covers a great deal of information very quickly, he does a fantastic job of balancing advice with humor and seriousness. Most likely as a result of his own dealings with adolescents, he has a realistic understanding of young people's minds, and it seems as if he knows parents fairly well. His two concluding chapters are hilarious, and many parents and teens will find them entirely true. One excerpt from "Memos From Your Teenager" reads, "It seems as if your intelligence has decreased and, in fact, you're close to being stupid." Another reads, "It also appears that you have developed amnesia . . . you don't remember what it's like being my age." "Tips For Teenagers" then follows, advising a teen who has a problem talking with his parent to write the question down on paper and put it on the parent's pillow. Fontenelle says that "parents are pushovers for notes like this." The sections on punishment are realistic and informative—perfect for the parent who is at the end of his/her rope. ALL parents will benefit from reading this simple, yet unusually insightful, piece of work.

Where To Find/Buy:
Bookstores and libraries.

Parent-Teen Dynamics

PARENTS, TEENS AND BOUNDARIES
How To Draw The Line

 Recommended For:
Parent-Teen Relationships

Description:

Bluestein, a former counselor and teacher, tackles the broad issue of how to set boundaries, and manage and strengthen the parent-child bond. This book is divided into two parts; the first addresses the dynamics of parent-teen relationships, and the second offers 20 ways to build healthy family relationships. In Part One, several chapters encourage parents to recognize their motives, with a chapter cautioning parents against "all-or-nothing thinking." Bluestein also includes two chapters that explain what boundaries are, why they work, and how they benefit both "players" in the game. Part Two, with 21 chapters (about 5 pages each), asks parents to evaluate their communication responses within the family—"the big picture." This is divided into subtopics including love, trust, acceptance, negotiation, etc.; parents are invited to be aware of what they're doing right, and fine-tune other aspects in order to build a healthy relationship. Exercises are included so parents can reflect on the chapter's topic.

Evaluation:

Part Two's introduction, in discussing why parents shouldn't focus on fixing specific problems with their teenager's behavior, states that "focusing on these goals instead of the relationship can be rather shortsighted." This book offers a different approach to tackling the age-old issues involved with parenting teens. This 202 page resource asks parents to let go of what they think are the "real" problems (disrespect, late for curfew, academic failures). Instead, Bluestein argues that parents should focus on the relationship and strengthen the bond between parent and child. Setting boundaries, she believes, permits the parent to impose their own limits while preserving sanity, and in the long run, harmony. She does not, however, focus merely on restricting the teen. Rather, she encourages negotiation, trust-building, acceptance, and inevitably, acknowledging that the child is separate from the parent. This concise book is exceptional in its ability to see through to the hearts of issues and situations. A "must" for all parents.

Where To Find/Buy:

Bookstores, libraries, or order direct by calling 1-800-851-9100.

★★★★

Overall Rating
★★★★
A hope-filled, realistic book to help parents build a solid foundation with their child

Design, Ease Of Use
★★★★
Excellent organization; easy-to-use; language flows well and keeps reader interested

1–4 Stars; N/R = Not Rated

Media:
Print

Price:
$8.95

Principal Subject:
Parent-Teen Relationships

ISBN:
1558742794

Edition:
1993

Publisher:
Health Communications

Author:
Jane Bluestein, Ph.D.

About The Author:
(From Cover Notes)
Jane Bluestein, a well-known self-esteem expert specializing in building healthy adult-child relationships, is the author of 3 other books and 100 magazine articles. She lectures internationally and has appeared as a guest expert on the "Oprah Winfrey Show."

III. Parent-Teen Relationships

III. Parent-Teen Relationships

★★★★

Overall Rating
★★★★
Useful, explains specific actions to take for specific problems with step-by-step detail

Design, Ease Of Use
★★★★
Bold headings within chapters; numerous parent-teen dialogues; chapter activities

1–4 Stars; N/R = Not Rated

Media:
Print

Price:
$14.95

Principal Subject:
Parent-Teen Relationships

ISBN:
1559584416

Edition:
2nd (1994)

Publisher:
Prima Publishing

Author:
Jane Nelsen, Ed.D. and Lynn Lott, M.A., M.F.C.C.

About The Author:
(From Cover Notes)
Nelsen and Lott are both authors of parenting/family relationship books, including another book on discipline that they co-authored. Both have appeared on numerous TV shows, such as "Oprah," "The Today Show," and others. Nelsen is a mother of 7, and Lott a mother of 4.

Parent-Teen Dynamics

POSITIVE DISCIPLINE FOR TEENAGERS
Resolving Conflict With Your Teenage Son Or Daughter

 Recommended For:
Parent-Teen Relationships

Description:
This 431 page book includes three major sections. The first section, "The Individuation Process," introduces parents to teenagers, as well as to some of the main ideas in the book: mutual respect, long-range parenting, the value of mistakes, and communication. The second section, "Nonpunitive Parenting," consists of 9 chapters that address specific actions parents can take to "positively discipline" teenagers. Chapters include "The Teen Within You: Finding Your Unresolved Issues," "Control and Punishment: Fueling the Fires of Rebellion and Revenge," "Long-Range Parenting: Nurturing Individualism," "Following Through," "Teaching Life Skills," "Letting Go," "Working With Your Teen," "Communication That Really Works," and "Time That Counts." The last section focuses on drugs and dysfunctional behavior. The book also includes an appendix of activities which coordinate with the chapters.

Evaluation:
From the "Developing Capable People Series," this book helps parents empower teens with life skills. Based on the premise that parents should respect teens and teens should respect parents, the book not only invites parents to listen, support, love, and encourage their child, but also gives guidelines on using authority and saying "no" when needed. The last section on dysfunctional behavior is more of an overview, listing basic steps and actions only, so other resources will be needed for these parenting concerns. The book's strengths, however, include its 85 page appendix (a chapter-by-chapter workbook of activities) and Chapter 4 (the model for "learning from mistakes"). Chapters 13 and 14 contain useful, step-by-step actions for improved communication and cooperative problem-solving. Sample teen-parent dialogues and many lists of tips add to this book's usefulness. The style is easy to read, either cover-to-cover or by skimming. This book offers great hands-on tips for constructive parent-teen communications.

Where To Find/Buy:
Bookstores, libraries, or order direct by calling Empowering People at 1-800-456-7770 or by FAX at (801) 762-0022.

Parent-Teen Dynamics

TEENAGERS AND PARENTS
10 Steps For A Better Relationship

 Recommended For:
Parent-Teen Relationships

Description:

McIntire created the 10 steps of this 247 page text with these goals in mind: 1) that parents will raise a teen to be a competent adult; 2) that the family will be enjoyable to all of its members; and 3) that close friendship will remain once the ten steps have been implemented. The book is divided into 5 major categories within which are McIntire's 10 steps; an extensive table of contents is included. The first two steps ("Communicate in Positive Ways," "Watch Out for Blames and Games) are included under the category "Providing A Safe Place To Talk." Under "Encouraging Practice Of Skills They Need Now," McIntire includes the steps of "Coaching Teens about School and Social Skills," and "Make Room for Your Teen to Be Useful **and** to Be Weird." Other sections include "Coaching In Critical Areas," (alcohol, drugs, dating, sex, and cars), "Planning Reactions To 'Almost-Grown-Ups'," (punishment and alternatives), and "Caring for Yourself in the Parenting Job." Each chapter, or step, includes interactive exercises for parents, many examples, and sample dialogues. An index is included, as well as a page overview of the ten steps.

Evaluation:

This book is in its 3rd edition, and it is easy to see why. McIntire's 32 years in the field of family counseling and teacher consultation is evident here. Only someone with such hands-on knowledge could provide a similar type of knowledge to the public. The book provides a lot of solid, practical, well-organized advice for parents. It is also personal and easy to read, using tons of sample dialogues. Too many advice books give information and discuss research findings, but never really tell parents how to apply their newfound knowledge. This book gives sample conversations and has interactive exercises for parents, such as helping a teen find out their interests, abilities, and successes. Overall, it is extremely helpful and user-friendly. The table of contents is extremely thorough, so if a parent wished to find out about teens and drugs, they could find it immediately, or look in the index. This book is a must read for parents of teenagers, whether or not they are having communication difficulties. It may also be of use to teachers and students of family counseling and therapy.

Where To Find/Buy:

Bookstores, libraries, or order direct by calling 1-800-362-0985.

Overall Rating
★★★★
Excellent resource for parent-teen communication with plenty of hands-on advice

Design, Ease Of Use
★★★★
Engaging, personable; well-organized w/ detailed TOC, boxed highlights

1–4 Stars; N/R = Not Rated

Media:
Print

Price:
$11.95

Principal Subject:
Parent-Teen Relationships

ISBN:
0964055864

Edition:
3rd (1996)

Publisher:
Summit Crossroads Press

Author:
Roger W. McIntire

**About The Author:
(From Cover Notes)**
For 32 years, McIntire taught child psychology, and family counseling and therapy at the University of Maryland. He has been a consultant to teachers in preschools, grade schools, high schools, and colleges, and is the father of three children.

III. Parent-Teen Relationships

★★★★

Overall Rating
★★★★
The writing speaks directly to the reader; fast paced and yet uniquely informative

Design, Ease Of Use
★★★★
Easy to use; a quick look at the table of contents will lead the reader to issues of interest

1–4 Stars; N/R = Not Rated

Media:
Print

Price:
$19.95

Principal Subject:
Parent-Teen Relationships

ISBN:
1559723963

Edition:
2nd (1997)

Publisher:
Carol Publishing Group
(Birch Lane Press)

Author:
Lawrence Bauman, Ph.D. with Robert Riche

About The Author:
(From Cover Notes)
Lawrence Bauman, Ph.D. is a director of Inpatient Services at the South Beach Psychiatric Center in Staten Island, and has a private psychotherapy practice in New York City. He is married and the father of two teenagers.

Parent-Teen Dynamics

TEN MOST TROUBLESOME TEEN-AGE PROBLEMS AND HOW TO SOLVE THEM (THE)

 Recommended For:
Parent-Teen Relationships

Description:
This book is designed for the parent who anticipates or currently experiences problems with their teenager's attitude and/or behavior. There are, as suggested by the title, ten chapters, each of which deals with a specific parenting problem. The chapters are titled in the form of parental statements, the first of which is "My Kid Won't Take on Responsibility." Other chapter issues include anger, lying, laziness, academic performance, poor communication, lack of friends, drug use/bad friends, sex & AIDS, and the last chapter is entitled "My Kids Greatest Problem—Could It Be Me?" Each issue receives between 15–20 pages of attention, with the author describing the issue and why teenagers have problems with it. Then the author reports case studies from his own experience, presenting both the parent's and the child's view of the situation, offering ways to come to an agreement, and explaining how these case study issues were eventually solved. The author discusses rules and coping in his introduction, and there is an index.

Evaluation:
Bauman's knowledge about these teen issues seems particularly adept, and his own experiences substantially add to the book's credibility. Many of the case studies discussed will ring a few bells, with parents no doubt saying, "Hey! That's my kid!" Bauman believes that the key to helping teens over these issues is for parents to change their established parenting perspective, and to look for underlying causes for their teen's behavior instead. The solutions are very oriented towards the teenager; the author believes that parenting is a team sport, where the child is allowed to participate, too. For example, a parent who catches their child in a lie will inevitably feel hurt and will likely punish the child, but Bauman says that this will encourage future lying to avoid punishment. Better, he claims, to find out what is behind the lie; find out what the teenager is really hiding, and go from there using moderation. Parents having problems with any of these issues will be well-served by investing in this resource.

Where To Find/Buy:
Bookstores and libraries.

Parent-Teen Dynamics

GIVE THEM WINGS
Preparing For The Time Your Teen Leaves Home

Terrific Resource For:
Assisting parents in "letting go" of their children into adulthood

Recommended For:
Parent-Teen Relationships

Description:

In *Give Them Wings*, Kuykendall tells her own story of releasing her children at different stages of their lives. There are a wealth of topics in this 15 chapter, 231 page book, such as "bittersweet sixteen" (first driver's license, etc.), nurturing seeds (religion, character, financial responsibility), the senior year and choosing a college, saying good-bye, the first year of college & later years, first visits home, and moving back home after college. Bits and pieces of advice are scattered throughout this book. But the author's advice is clothed in her discussion of her own experiences and choices. She writes tips like "I won't nag," and "I won't manipulate by guilt." She advises parents to "see them as separate," "see them as unique." Although the book does have quite a few biblical references, and Kuykendall is obviously very involved in her religion, there are very few value judgments, and "rights" or "wrongs." She believes that parents and children make those decisions.

Evaluation:

This book offers a refreshing change from books which seem detached and fact-oriented to one which obviously has so much feeling. It's apparent that Kuykendall has been through a great deal with her children, and it's equally obvious how attached she is to them. This book would be valuable before, during, and after the separation, or "letting go," process. It's comforting to the reader, who will easily recognize the feelings that the author shares. Along the same lines, there are parts where the reader will laugh out loud, recognizing the subtle humor in the day-to-day lives of their children. Important to note is the fact that this book essentially covers all major parts of letting go, starting from the driver's license and progressing all the way through high school. There are no stones left unturned, and there is no shortage of advice. So, for the reader who wants to identify with someone, to feel good about a difficult time, or to receive a gentle push in the right direction, this is their book.

Where To Find/Buy:
Bookstores and libraries.

Overall Rating
★★★★
Inspiring, honest words of encouragement for parents of adolescents and young adults

Design, Ease Of Use
★★★
Easy to understand; author's advice is in boldface or italics

1–4 Stars; N/R = Not Rated

Media:
Print

Price:
$14.99

Principal Subject:
Parent-Teen Relationships

ISBN:
156179225X

Edition:
1994

Publisher:
Focus on the Family

Author:
Carol Kuykendall

About The Author:
(From Cover Notes)
Kuykendall is the "mother of three young people who are in the process of trying their wings for the first time." She is also Vice President of Educational Resources for Mothers of Preschoolers (MOPS) International.

III. Parent-Teen Relationships

★★★★

Overall Rating
★★★★
Great general resource that provides good information and advice, numerous scenarios

Design, Ease Of Use
★★★
Bullets, easily accessed info, best read as a whole; sample dialogues sometimes get lost

1–4 Stars; N/R = Not Rated

Media:
Print

Price:
$13.95

Principal Subject:
Parent-Teen Relationships

ISBN:
0452266165

Edition:
1991

Publisher:
Plume (Dutton Signet/Penguin Group/Penguin Books USA)

Author:
Mira Kirshenbaum and Charles Foster, Ph.D.

**About The Author:
(From Cover Notes)**
The authors are a husband and wife team of family therapists. They have taught and supervised other therapists, conducted research, and are the founding directors of the Brighton Family Therapy Associates. They have raised two children.

Parent-Teen Dynamics

PARENT/TEEN BREAKTHROUGH
The Relationship Approach

 Recommended For:
Parent-Teen Relationships

Description:

This book provides an alternate route to parents who have found the "tough love" approach doesn't work with their kids. It dismantles controlling or disciplinary approaches, pointing out that the teenager's one job in life is to get ready to leave home. Instead, the authors advocate that parents should develop good relationships with their kids, learn to talk with them, and find ways to address everyone's needs. Their "relationship approach" stresses ways to become the primary influence in a child's life, so they won't want to engage in harmful activities. Part One discusses why the control approach doesn't work, defines the relationship approach, and offers tips on how to get started. Part Two includes information on how to influence and protect a teenager, while still managing to get parental needs met. Part Three discusses the changes for both parents and teenagers during adolescence, and Part Four highlights problem areas, such as drugs, sex, the challenges of single parenting, and others.

Evaluation:

The "relationship approach" advocated in this book is clearly defined and modeled. This approach aims to break parents' assumptions that they need to limit their children and be their keepers. Instead, it stresses ways to listen to children's needs and help them come to terms with their maturity. It frees parents from the authoritarian, tough love stance, allowing parents to participate in their child's growth process. Throughout the book, the authors give numerous tips and pertinent advice on how to talk to adolescents, along with guidelines on how to compose one's self before speaking. The authors offer realistic solutions, providing detailed information on how to deal with specific problems. The section on problem-solving is especially helpful. It asks parents to apply their parenting skills—showing their love, working on communicating effectively, rewarding good behavior, etc. This is an excellent reference for parents who want to build solid, loving relationships with their children well beyond adolescence.

Where To Find/Buy:
Bookstores and libraries.

III. Parent-Teen Relationships

Parent-Teen Dynamics

SEIZE THE MOMENT, NOT YOUR TEEN
The Art Of Opportunity Parenting

 Terrific Resource For:
Christian parents wanting to strengthen their parent-child relationship

 Recommended For:
Parent-Teen Relationships

Description:
This 178 page book on Christian parenting has 9 chapters and 3 appendices. Discussions and advice on everyday living and issues are interwoven with the spiritual dimension of parents and teens. Much emphasis is also placed on the spiritual growth and discipline of parents as a way to become better parents. Many reflections from the parent's as well as the teen's viewpoints are given in this book. The author also shares his own personal experiences with parenting along with stories about other parents and teens. Each chapter ends with two sections called "What About You?" and "Extra Power for Parents from God's Word." "What About You?" raises questions related to the chapter that parents are to ask themselves for self-evaluation. "Extra Power" references Scripture and relates it to the contents of the chapter and to the reader's life. The appendices include "Values Reinforcers" (15 assets of healthy homes), "How to Be Ready to Seize the Moment" (10 skills to combat Satan), and a list of suggested readings.

Evaluation:
Seize The Moment is a must-read for Christian parents who believe that the key to better parenting is through spiritual growth. In fact, some parts of the book resemble a Bible study for parents. Sanders reaches into parents' heads with his logical and practical advice, as well as their hearts with his wisdom and insights. Parents will see that their own growth and walk with God are directly related to their relationship with their teen. Much warmth and compassion for teens is expressed by the author, as he reveals his own shortcomings as a parent and mistakes other parents have made. Many current teen-related issues are addressed in this book, but crisis situations often are not addressed in-depth. Two of the appendices, "Values Reinforcers" and "How to Be Ready to Seize the Moment," are short synopses of important highlights from the book and offer excellent reminders to parents in a quick-read form. Containing much valuable advice, this is a book parents will want to revisit over the years.

Where To Find/Buy:
Bookstores and libraries.

Overall Rating
★★★★
Warm, compassionate, Bible-based approach to general parenting concerns

Design, Ease Of Use
★★★
Consistent format; highlights in list form, bullets; helpful, concise appendices; no index

1–4 Stars; N/R = Not Rated

Media: Print

Price: $9.99

Principal Subject: Parent-Teen Relationships

ISBN: 0842369368

Edition: 1997

Publisher: Tyndale House Publishers

Author: Bill Sanders

About The Author: (From Cover Notes) Bill Sanders speaks in 150 public high schools each year, conducting seminars on critical teen issues. He has written many books on topics including teen-parent relationships, devotions for teens, and sex.

Overall Rating
★★★
Practical, warm and personal presentation of a Christian parenting approach

Design, Ease Of Use
★★★
Numbered & bulleted lists highlight main points; no index; generous notes section

1–4 Stars; N/R = Not Rated

Media:
Print

Price:
$18.99

Principal Subject:
Parent-Teen Relationships

ISBN:
1561796271

Edition:
1998

Publisher:
Tyndale House Publishers

Author:
Gary Smalley and Greg Smalley, Psy.D.

About The Author:
(From Cover Notes)
Gary Smalley, president of Today's Family in Branson, Missouri, is a speaker on family relationships, and the author of 14 books. Greg Smalley has a Psy.D. from Rosemead School of Psychology, and has written numerous articles on parenting and relationship issues.

Parent-Teen Dynamics

BOUND BY HONOR
Fostering A Great Relationship With Your Teen

Description:
This book, authored by a father-son team, has 13 chapters and 222 pages. It is a book on Christian parenting of teens and is Bible-based. The authors use many personal experiences from the teenage years of Greg Smalley and his siblings. They also draw from surveys of 5,000+ "former teens" and present case-study type scenarios. The book centers around the authors' beliefs that anger is the greatest wedge that drives parents and teens apart, and that "increasing honor and decreasing anger in the home are the two main principles in raising healthy teenagers." They define honor as placing "high value, worth, and importance on another person. . . ." Many principles and methods that were used by Gary Smalley and his wife in raising their children are presented. Numbered and bullet lists are given throughout the book to present information and outline main points. Topics covered include honoring children, anger, solving conflicts, strengthening parent-teen relationships, and maintaining or regaining teens' virginity.

Evaluation:
This unique author team has opened up their private lives and shared some of their intimate details in hopes that their readers might learn from them. The Smalleys use a light, warm, and often humorous approach to present subjects that can be sometimes serious in nature. They have learned to laugh at themselves and the fiascoes that they personally lived through while Greg Smalley was growing up. The many numbered and bulleted lists help present information in an easy-to-follow format; numerous lists are provided within chapters citing Biblical references about the topic discussed. There is a good, in-depth discussion of what honor means and how to honor one another (Chapter 2). Its strong point is in, as the subtitle says, teaching parents how to foster "a great relationship with your teen," although some of the suggestions may not be realistic for some families (such as creating a family contract). This book addresses many parent-teen issues, but does not delve into crisis situations.

Where To Find/Buy:
Bookstores, libraries, or order direct by calling 1-800-232-6459 (in Canada, call 1-800-661-9800).

Parent-Teen Dynamics

INFLUENTIAL PARENT (THE)
How To Be The Person Your Teen Really Needs

Description:

This 250 page book presents vignettes of parent-teen issues while highlighting common communication problems and ways to solve them. Chapter 1 focuses on how to set effective goals for parenting, while Chapters 2 and 3 discuss the "limited partnership" between parents and teenagers along with ways of getting the teen involved. Chapter 4 asks "Where Does Your Energy Go?" and offers tips for avoiding burnout. Chapters 5, 6, and 7 offer ways to positively influence a teen and increase one's effectiveness as a parent using "role" examples (teacher, mentor, friend, etc.) and "meaningful messages." Chapter 8 discusses four approaches parents can take to keep their teens "tuned in," whereas Chapter 9 highlights five types of resistance parents may encounter from teens. Chapter 10 explores ways in which parents can regain influence over their children's lives. Negotiating from one's "bottom line" and learning to bargain effectively with teenagers is the topic of Chapter 11. Chapter 12 focuses on knowing when to seek outside help. Chapter 13 outlines the author's eight steps to creative parenting and partnering.

Evaluation:

This "self-help" book's main strength lies in its realistic portrayal of the difficulties that can arise when parents and teenagers try to communicate and understand one another. The writing style is simple and easy to follow. There are no statistics and the teaching approach is light-handed. The author presupposes that the audience for his book is mainly interested in keeping the connections they have already established with their kids. He then does a fine job of continuing this connection by helping parents create a partnership with their teens based on mutual respect. The author acknowledges, however, that the relationship cannot be equal since most teens will be unaware of the amount of work that must necessarily come from the parent's side. Chapter 11's tips on negotiating with a teenager are particularly helpful with suggestions on healthy bargaining and fleshing out a bottom line when both parties are adamant about their needs. Using a humorous, compassionate, and spiritual approach, the book is a useful guide for changing how parents may approach raising and communicating with their teenager.

Where To Find/Buy:

Bookstores and libraries.

Overall Rating
★★★
Provides good advice on ways to create a healthy relationship with your teenager

Design, Ease Of Use
★★★
Easily read, not necessary to read sequentially; bullets, italicized and bold highlights

1–4 Stars; N/R = Not Rated

Media:
Print

Price:
$11.99

Principal Subject:
Parent-Teen Relationships

ISBN:
0877888876

Edition:
1997

Publisher:
Harold Shaw Publishers

Author:
David Damico

About The Author:
(From Cover Notes)
David Damico holds a masters degree in pastoral counseling. He provides workshops and seminars on parenting and personal growth. His books, such as *The Faces of Rage*, grow from his counseling experience.

III. Parent-Teen Relationships

Overall Rating
★★★
Well-written and very humorous; a must for any parent who needs help "letting go"

Design, Ease Of Use
★★★
To-the-point, matter-of-fact writing; must be read cover to cover but is easily read

1–4 Stars; N/R = Not Rated

Media:
Print

Price:
$11.99

Principal Subject:
Parent-Teen Relationships

ISBN:
0310200245

Edition:
1996

Publisher:
Zondervan Publishing House (HarperCollins Publishers)

Author:
Thom Black with Lynda Stephenson

About The Author:
(From Cover Notes)
Black is founder and director of the InGenius Center and vice president of Family Strategies, both at Family University in San Diego. He lives with his wife and three children in Illinois. He is the author of *Born to Fly!* and coauthor of *Discovering Your Child's Design.*

KICKING YOUR KID OUT OF THE NEST
Raising Teenagers For Life On Their Own

Description:
This book is organized into nine chapters, which deal primarily with, as the title suggests, letting go of the "child" and raising the teenager. The Introduction gives several examples of times when parents may ask "what happened to my **child**?" Chapter 1 addresses the necessity of "letting go" and offers insights as to what the goal of parenting ought to be. Chapters 2 and 3 dispel common myths of adolescence and give parents tips on how to positively direct the intrinsic energy of their child. Chapters 4, 5, and 6 offer parents advice on how to prepare themselves to deal with setbacks, how to accept the fact that their child may choose a different path, and ways to release control while maintaining authority. Chapter 7 suggests ways parents can find "the rightful place" in the lives of their teenagers; Chapters 8 and 9 conclude with thoughts on how to accept change and prepare teenagers for life in the 21st century. The author refers to experiences with his own children throughout.

Evaluation:
Black does a fabulous job of writing about serious issues while maintaining a very lighthearted tone. In the Introduction, he asks the reader to react to the truth of this statement: "Adolescence is a black hole waiting to suck in my child and there's nothing I can do to prevent it." Although the statement is funny, Black understands that many parents have heard so much about the possible pitfalls and difficulties during their child's teenage years that they may have resigned themselves to fate. Although it is best read cover to cover, the book is effectively organized starting off by stating that "the goal of parenting is to release well-balanced young adults into the world." Each of the remaining chapters then offers advice on the ordeals of parenting teens while keeping this goal in mind. What makes this book so readable is that it is written in a tone that any parent can understand. It also makes laughable some of the issues that parents struggle to deal with. All in all, parents will find Black offers excellent advice.

Where To Find/Buy:
Bookstores and libraries.

Parent-Teen Dynamics

LOVE ME ENOUGH TO SET SOME LIMITS
Building Your Child's Self-Esteem With Thoughtful Limit Setting

Description:

Using an interview format, the writers of *Parenting with Love and Logic* highlight their parenting technique. They believe that "love" allows children to grow through their mistakes while "logic" allows children to live with the consequences of their choices. This 65 minute audiotape explains how to set limits and offer children choices. Tips for dealing with specific situations are also given (homework, bedtime, clothes, music, friends, chores, using the car, curfews, sibling fights). The authors believe that setting firm limits builds children's self-concept and self-esteem and that children "desperately need limits." They differentiate between "fighting words" (telling them what not to do) and "thinking words" (giving them choices while implying the consequences will always be there). Fay states that if parents use thinking words, dignity, and respect, then their children will treat their parents the same way. A "direct correlation" between good school performance and setting limits on early behaviors is also suggested.

Evaluation:

Parents who don't have the time to read the authors' book will glean the important points through this audiotape. It is mostly directed at parents of teenagers with some advice for parents of younger children. It generally tends to be succinct, although the authors do ramble at times leaving the listener wondering where they are going. Several concrete examples of how to deal with certain situations are given, a quality lacking in one of their other tapes. Of particular use for many parents will be the numerous verbal examples given for what to say in given situations. Emphasis was on parents doing mental preparation by rehearsing what they will do and say to their child before a repeated behavior occurs. These exercises will help parents feel confident when entering into a confrontation with their teen. The author states that this will put the parent in control and avoid "brain drains" and arguments. Parents will find this tape a good reflection of the authors' key points and worth their time and money.

Where To Find/Buy:

Bookstores and libraries, or order direct by calling 1-800-338-4065.

Overall Rating
★★★
Offers parents verbal cues for staying in control of potential conflicts with their child

Design, Ease Of Use
★★★
Rambles at times, but fairly succinct in identifying main points; concrete examples given

---

1–4 Stars; N/R = Not Rated

Media:
Audiotape

Price:
$11.95

Principal Subject:
Parent-Teen Relationships

ISBN:
0944634354

Edition:
1996

Publisher:
The Love and Logic Press

Author:
Jim Fay with Foster W. Cline, M.D.

**About The Author:
(From Cover Notes)**
Fay, with over 30 years experience in education, is one of America's most sought-after consultants and presenters. He is the author of over 90 books, tapes, and articles on parenting and positive discipline.

III. Parent-Teen Relationships

Parent-Teen Dynamics

LOVING, LAUNCHING, AND LETTING GO
Preparing Your Nearly-Grown Children For Adulthood

Overall Rating
★★★
Inspiring Christian work for parents committed to staying involved in their child's life

Design, Ease Of Use
★★★
Succinct writing; summary paragraphs for each chapter offer parent-teen exercises

1–4 Stars; N/R = Not Rated

Media:
Print

Price:
$12.99

Principal Subject:
Parent-Teen Relationships

ISBN:
0805461868

Edition:
1995

Publisher:
Broadman & Holman Publishers

Author:
Virelle Kidder

About The Author:
(From Cover Notes)
Kidder is a contributing editor for *Today's Christian Woman* and the author of *Mothering Upstream*. She is the mother of four grown children.

Description:

Using a Christian perspective, Kidder's work attempts to answer and address the questions and concerns that parents have about "this last stage of parenting . . . to launch [their] children into adulthood in His keeping." She offers advice on various related issues including how to know when a young adult is ready to leave the home, ways to build closeness as a family, and how to help a teenager deal with typical everyday problems. The goal of her work, she says, is to help adults become "parents who warm God's heart and raise kids who are hungry for your values." The book is organized into three parts. Part One, "Loving," explains to parents how to love "effectively." "Launching," Part Two, advises parents how to prepare their child for adulthood; it offers ways to distract the child from everyday harms. Part Three discusses ways to get teenagers ready to "try their wings in adult life," along with advice for coping with the empty nest—"the Serendipity of Letting Go." Christian examples and inspiration are given throughout; each chapter concludes with ideas for parent-teen discussion.

Evaluation:

Perfect for the Christian parent who wants encouragement, advice, and directives on how to release their child into the world, this book effectively tackles one of the more difficult subjects of parenting. Kidder uses a tone that is lighthearted and fun, bringing into play her own experiences with her four children. The book does not address specific problems that arise for teenagers themselves; rather, it deals more with avoiding those difficult issues altogether. For example, in a chapter dealing with helping "your kids avoid entanglements," Kidder offers three tactics to employ. First, she says, parents should be deeply involved in their teenager's life. She then advises parents to keep the teen busy with "good stuff," like community service and youth groups. The last advice she offers is to "pray like mad." Because of the broad advice offered, this book's value may be limited only to those parents with a Christian background who are already deeply intertwined in the lives of their teens.

Where To Find/Buy:

Bookstores and libraries.

Parent-Teen Dynamics

PARENTING WITHOUT PRESSURE
A Whole Family Approach

Description:
Written for "anyone who wants to practice pro-active parenting skills," the author of this 159 page resource created this "win/win" approach in response to her daughter's turbulent teen years. She states that her approach offers "practical parenting techniques that focus on discipline, communication, self-esteem, and unconditional love;" she believes her techniques teach children accountability, responsibility, and behavioral consequences. The book is divided into two parts, the first of which outlines the features of her approach, such as establishing rules and boundaries, creating real consequences and incentives, and dealing with conflicts through arbitration/ communication. The second part contains "The Family Workbook," which consists of sample blank forms referred to in the book's first half ("rules we can live by," "fun times and evenings out," "daily stuff," etc.). Two appendixes contain a question-answer section about the workbook, and a problem-solution section for parent-child behavioral situations.

Evaluation:
The author, through her step-by-step program and supply of written forms, makes it possible for parents to back off from eruptive parent-child situations, keeping their cool and sanity. The teen, on the other hand, is allowed ownership in the decision-making process by helping create rules, solve problems, and determine consequences. The book doesn't center on parenting teens, but the author does present typical parent-teen problems, such as curfew, school progress, defiance, phone use, and more; sexuality is briefly discussed in Chapter 6 which focuses specifically on teenagers. The supplied forms are useful, and each chapter concludes with a "Homework for Parents" section which helps to focus parents on the chapter's advice, and offer additional ideas for positive family relations. Not for parents dealing with substance abuse, violence, or more serious issues, this book nonetheless offers parents a systematic approach for creating a family atmosphere of positive communication.

Where To Find/Buy:
Bookstores and libraries.

Overall Rating
★★★
Great step-by-step program, well thought-out and comprehensive

Design, Ease Of Use
★★★
Excellent use of forms, schedules, tracking slips; index would help, adequate TOC

1–4 Stars; N/R = Not Rated

Media:
Print

Price:
$14.00

Principal Subject:
Parent-Teen Relationships

ISBN:
0891097503

Edition:
1994

Publisher:
Pinon Press

Author:
Teresa A. Langston

About The Author: (From Cover Notes)
Langston developed the Parenting Without Pressure approach during her older daughter's turbulent teen years. She is a popular radio and TV guest, university lecturer, and seminar presenter. She also leads workshops for psychiatric hospitals, schools, churches, and more.

III. Parent-Teen Relationships

Overall Rating
★★★
Well balanced approach to parent-child interactions, religious, but not ecclesiastical

Design, Ease Of Use
★★★
Main points highlighted, bold; personal accounts indented, italicized; well-organized

1–4 Stars; N/R = Not Rated

Media:
Print

Price:
$9.95

Principal Subject:
Parent-Teen Relationships

ISBN:
0938179306

Edition:
1992

Publisher:
Mills & Sanderson, Publishers

Author:
Dr. Harold D. Jester

About The Author:
(From Cover Notes)
Jester is a licensed psychologist and Marriage and Family Therapist in Massachusetts. He is also a United Methodist minister who spent 20 years on active duty as an Air Force chaplain. He now serves as the director of a private counseling center in Springfield, MA.

Parent-Teen Dynamics

PULLING TOGETHER
Crisis Prevention For Teens And Their Parents

Description:
This 178 page resource is written for parents and adolescents by the director of the Massachusetts Society for the Prevention of Cruelty to Children. Jester discusses the many opportunities that parents and children have to actively contribute to the well-being of their family and their own personal lives. The book is divided into two main sections. Section One is addressed to adolescents and discusses how parental guilt and suffering complicates the parent-child relationship; ways in which parents use love, trust and guilt as weapons; the issues of rights, privileges, and duties in the child-parent relationship; a discussion of divorce; leaving home; thoughts on child abuse, and more. Part Two is addressed to parents and it revisits Part One, including questions to parents that the author deemed inappropriate for the first section. The book includes an index and appendices on supplementary resources, phone numbers for help lines, and a list of family discussion guidelines.

Evaluation:
This book offers practical advice to parents and adolescents wrestling with issues of communication and personal responsibility within the family unit. Jester asks parents to consider their children as moral beings, capable of making the decisions that will strongly impact their lives and well-being. By emphasizing the "self" in "self-help," Jester gives young people as much responsibility as their parents in making sure that the family unit works together with the welfare of all its members in mind. This book offers a refreshing change from others which ask the parent to look at their child as another species, incapable of taking responsibility for their actions or thoughts. There are many good chapters within this book, but Jester's chapter on "Rights, Duties, Privileges, Gratuities . . . " is particularly well done. He highlights ways in which parents can impose order and rules on their households without resorting to shouting matches or violent behavior. Throughout the book, he takes a religious viewpoint, but without becoming ecclesiastical. This is a great resource for parents and teens.

Where To Find/Buy:
Bookstores and libraries.

Parent-Teen Dynamics

AGE OF OPPORTUNITY
A Biblical Guide To Parenting Teens

Description:

As Tripp writes, "this is a book that believes that the truths of Scripture apply as powerfully to teens as they do to anybody else." Through most of his 253 page book, he uses biblical themes and Scriptural passages to illustrate his point that raising teenagers should be a fun, rewarding, and challenging experience. As he states, parents **and** teenagers who wish to please the Lord must "watch, pray, stand fast, and fight lest [they] fall into temptation." Tripp believes that struggles with culture's temptations are inescapable and always take place in a moral battlefield. He believes the struggle is about right & wrong, good & bad, human desire & God's will. The book focuses on parents and the belief that every situation is created by God as a challenge, or an opportunity. Only if parents listen carefully, and seize opportunities, will they be able to effectively guide their children, says Tripp. His view about the relationship of teens to parents? "This is spiritual warfare."

Evaluation:

This book requires readers with extremely religious minds, ones who firmly believe that everything is under God's control. The reader must also accept the belief that parents and family are the main channel through which God speaks, and that it is their duty to carry out His word and instill in the mind of their teen that following any other word is wrong. There is plenty of encouragement, mostly in the form of "if this happens, it's because God is creating an opportunity." Tripp also advocates parents completely immersing themselves in the lives of their child, making sure that they follow the set path of God. Family worship is stressed as a necessity, for without parental example, says Tripp, children have nothing. There is no moderation in this book, only demands that parents keep at it until their children acquiesce. As one of the most heavily biblically-oriented parenting books that exist, this book is recommended only to those who believe that following God's will is the one true way of helping their teenager.

Where To Find/Buy:

Bookstores and libraries.

III. Parent-Teen Relationships

Overall Rating
★★★
Christian book that believes parent-teen struggles are God's challenges/ opportunities

Design, Ease Of Use
★★
Chapters could be a bit more organized; unfortunate lack of index

1–4 Stars; N/R = Not Rated

Media:
Print

Price:
$14.99

Principal Subject:
Parent-Teen Relationships

ISBN:
0875526012

Edition:
1997

Publisher:
P&R Publishing

Author:
Paul David Tripp

About The Author:
(From Cover Notes)
Mr. Tripp is a counselor and academic dean at the Christian Counseling and Educational Foundation in Pennsylvania. He is also a lecturer in Practical Theology at Westminster Theological Seminary and a popular conference speaker.

★★★

Overall Rating
★★★
Offers good communication strategies with some specifics for parents of teens

Design, Ease Of Use
★★
Adequate table of contents & index; heavy text style, caps in chapter subheadings help

1–4 Stars; N/R = Not Rated

Media:
Print

Price:
$12.00

Principal Subject:
Parent-Teen Relationships

ISBN:
0380719541

Edition:
1994

Publisher:
Avon Books (Hearst Corporation)

Author:
Barbara Coloroso

**About The Author:
(From Cover Notes)**
Barbara Coloroso, a former schoolteacher, is an internationally known speaker in the areas of parenting, teaching, positive school climate, and nonviolent resolution.

Parent-Teen Dynamics

KIDS ARE WORTH IT!
Giving Your Child The Gift Of Inner Discipline

Description:
This book is based upon the author's parenting theory of teaching children to believe, think, and respect themselves, thus, becoming responsible, resourceful, resilient, and loving individuals who have the gift of inner discipline. She shows how to do this in 14 chapters. Chapter 2 highlights three kinds of families: "Brickwall," "Jellyfish," and "Backbone" and the characteristics of each; how they respond to various situations is explained throughout the rest of the book. Chapter topics include: keeping your cool, dealing with serious problems (getting your child out of jail, etc.), money, sexuality, and more. The author demonstrates that her "answer [to these situations] is more an approach to parenting than a collection of techniques." The author further states that having an attitude in which parents believe kids are worth it, treating them in a way parents would want to be treated, and behaving in a way that leaves dignities intact will provide an environment to help children develop self-discipline.

Evaluation:
The underlying theme in this book is "The Golden Rule." Drawing from her experience as a nun, and now as a parent of teenagers, the author outlines an approach that allows the child to be responsible for themselves instead of being reliant on external rewards, incentives, and punishments. The book's 253 pages offers insights on why discipline is not learned through threats and bribes, offering instead the impetus to teach children HOW to think. The book also provides some advice on how to buffer your child from the dangers of sexual promiscuity, drug abuse, and other self-destructive behavior; however, parents needing specific help will want to look elsewhere. Problem-solving patterns within the three family types (Brickwall, Jellyfish, Backbone) serve as excellent examples of how to establish good communication patterns between parents and teens. Although heavy with text at times, this book and its inspirational quotes will help parents find alternative ways to deal with "problems."

Where To Find/Buy:
Bookstores, libraries, or order direct by calling 1-800-238-0658.

Parent-Teen Dynamics

PARENTING TEENAGERS
Systematic Training For Effective Parenting Of Teens

Description:
This 154 page training manual for parents of teenagers seeks
to provide skills parents can practice so they can build better
relationships with their children. The authors recommend that
parents spend a week on each chapter, reading them in succession,
and studying the activities provided ("This Week," "Just For You,"
"For Your Family"). Each chapter provides an initial "Here's What
You Will Learn" section, bulleted sections of things to consider,
cartoons, concluding summary charts and "Points to Remember," and
hypothetical situations for parents to consider. The 7 chapters include
the following topics, in Part One—"Understanding yourself and Your
Teenager," "Changing Your Response to Your Teen," "Communicating
Respect and Encouragement, and in Part Two ("Developing the
Courage to Be Imperfect)—"Encouraging Cooperation and Solving
Problems," "Using Consequences to Build Responsibility," and
"Deciding What to Do" when disciplining your teenager (in two
chapters). The book includes an index.

Evaluation:
The layout for this book is a bit cluttered at times, making it hard to
read. But the information provided within is generally sound and will
be helpful to parents looking for better ways to communicate with
their teenager. The authors "STEPS" (or chapters) seem better used
as weekly parental workshops in learning how to cooperatively and
effectively talk with teens, and lovingly accept them for who they
are. The authors stress using "I-words" that encourage interaction,
and stress the importance of parental self-talk to determine goals.
The chapter on "Changing Your Response to Your Teen" is especially
helpful by providing parents with tools and behavioral changes
to help them become more effective parents. This guide gives
information on how to identify a teen's behavior goal, how to
encourage positive goals, how to examine parental and teen beliefs,
and how to practice reflective listening. This is a good general
resource for parents of teenagers, but treats many subjects lightly,
in short parenting sound "bites."

Where To Find/Buy:
Bookstores, libraries, or order direct by calling 1-800-328-2560.

Overall Rating
★★★
General information on how
to talk respectfully with
teens & set healthy limits

Design, Ease Of Use
★★
Somewhat cluttered;
good photos and cartoons;
bulleted info, helpful charts,
summaries

1–4 Stars; N/R = Not Rated

Media:
Print

Price:
$15.95

Principal Subject:
Parent-Teen Relationships

ISBN:
0812930142

Edition:
1998

Publisher:
American Guidance Service

Author:
Don Dinkmeyer, Sr., Ph.D.,
Gary D. McKay, Ph.D., Joyce
L. McKay, Ph.D., and Don
Dinkmeyer, Jr., Ph.D.

About The Author:
(From Cover Notes)
Don Dinkmeyer Sr. is a
clinical, and family and
marriage psychologist,
Gary McKay is a licensed
psychologist, Joyce McKay
is a Certified Professional
Counselor, and Don
Dinkmeyer Jr. is a licensed
marriage and family therapist.

III. Parent-Teen
Relationships

Parent-Teen Dynamics

RAISING THE ODDS FOR RESPONSIBLE BEHAVIOR

Overall Rating
★★★
Presents general, clear observations of parents' role in dealing with children's mistakes

Design, Ease Of Use
★★
Interview style informal, but tends to ramble; author lists step-by-step highlights

1–4 Stars; N/R = Not Rated

Media:
Audiotape

Price:
$11.95

Principal Subject:
Parent-Teen Relationships

ISBN:
0944634362

Edition:
1987

Publisher:
The Love and Logic Press

Author:
Jim Fay

About The Author:
(From Cover Notes)
Fay has 30+ years of experience as an educator and school principal, and is an educational consultant. He is the author of over 90 books, tapes, and articles on parenting and positive discipline.

Description:

Stating that "love allows children to grow through their mistakes," and "logic allows them to live with the consequences of their choices," Fay describes his Love and Logic® approach toward parenting in this 65 minute audiotape. The approach involves 5 steps: empathy for the child's mistakes, asking what the child is going to do about the problem, offering solutions of what others have done, looking at possible consequences for each solution together, and giving the child a chance to work it out. He outlines the whys and hows of his "Las Vegas plan" to raise the odds for responsible behavior with various narrative examples (toddler to adult) such as lying, alcohol abuse, bad grades, driving the family car, messy rooms, etc. Fay begins by offering his 4 step process for modeling responsibility—give a child responsibility they can handle, "hope and pray" they blow it so it will be a learning experience, allow them to deal with logical consequences, and then give the child the same task again.

Evaluation:

Emphasizing modeling, problem-solving, and ownership of the problem, coupled with a foundation of love, Fay believes that children "learn more from what they see than from what we tell them." Fay states that when others solve children's problems, they transfer ownership, and ultimately responsibility, from the child to themselves; instead mistakes should be viewed as opportunities for the child to learn responsibility. The "helicopter parent" who rescues their child in various circumstances (forgotten lunch, messy room, etc.) is described along with other pitfalls parents experience as they "own" their children's problems. Offering verbal examples to combat parental disappointment and anger, Fay makes a concerted argument for not stealing away those teachable moments, but instead insisting mistake should happen in the safety of the family. The interview style of the tape makes the author's points seem randomly placed, but his message is clear, concise, and general enough for most situations.

Where To Find/Buy:

Bookstores, libraries, or order direct by calling 1-800-338-4065.

Parent-Teen Dynamics

SEVEN-YEAR STRETCH (THE)
How Families Work Together To Grow Through Adolescence

Description:
Topics presented in this 8 chapter, 307 page book include such areas as: trust issues, parental control and letting go, teenagers' self-identity and social world, sexuality, risk-taking, attention deficit disorder, bulimia, homosexuality, substance abuse, jobs, and vandalism. A list of resources is given at the back of the book; no index is provided. Kastner, who is the psychologist of the author pair and whose clinical experiences and knowledge are represented in this book, illustrates a multitude of family scenarios gathered from her case studies, talks, and workshops. She analyzes each family's problem, discusses the resulting successful and/or unsuccessful outcomes of how the parent handled the situation, and provides alternate methods the parent could have used to better handle the situation. Kastner encourages "authoritative," not "authoritarian," parenting and devotes part of Chapter 2 to expound on what she calls "the holy triad of parenting" (thoughtful control, high warmth, open communication).

Evaluation:
Many of Kastner's illustrations are excellent, as are her analyses of the problems and her suggestions. Unusual to this book compared to others of its kind, are Kastner's discussion of the sample family dynamics. She begins each chapter with a "high-functioning, healthy" family struggling to cope with their teen's behavior or problem. As the chapter unfolds, she then dissects the issues involved, some of which are deep-seated. Many may find Kastner's guidance for parents a bit methodical at times, however. The book sorely needs an index. There is much covered and no easy way to find specific issues/ problems, as they are interspersed under chapter titles that often do not clearly define the chapter's content. The reader must either scan intensely through the book to find topics of interest or read the entire book. However, if parents have time to explore, the book provides a good overview on many different issues and problems, and will be useful for those who wish to obtain general parenting advice.

Where To Find/Buy:
Bookstores and libraries.

Overall Rating
★★★
Good, practical advice for parents; many vignettes of family problems

Design, Ease Of Use
★
Easy cover-to-cover reading, but lack of index makes quick referencing nearly impossible

1–4 Stars; N/R = Not Rated

Media:
Print

Price:
$23.00

Principal Subject:
Parent-Teen Relationships

ISBN:
0395735262

Edition:
1997

Publisher:
Houghton Mifflin

Author:
Laura S. Kastner, Ph.D., and Jennifer F. Wyatt, Ph.D.

About The Author: (From Cover Notes)
Kastner, a family therapist, is also a clinical associate professor of psychiatry and behavioral sciences at the University of Washington. Wyatt, a Seattle-based writer, has taught at both the college and high school levels.

III. Parent-Teen Relationships

Overall Rating
★★
Straightforward, effective family communication tips; workable solutions to problems

Design, Ease Of Use
★★★★
Detailed table of contents; logical order of chapters; two excellent appendices

1–4 Stars; N/R = Not Rated

Media:
Print

Price:
$14.95

Principal Subject:
Parent-Teen Relationships

ISBN:
0965065103

Edition:
1996

Publisher:
Real Life Press

Author:
Pat James Baxter, L.P.C., L.M.F.T. & Cynthia Dawson Naff, L.P.C.

About The Author:
(From Cover Notes)
Baxter is licensed in counseling, in marriage and family therapy, and has assisted families and teenagers for more than thirty years. Naff is an experienced teacher and therapist; she has successfully counseled many adolescents and their parents.

Parent-Teen Dynamics

AN OWNER'S GUIDE TO PARENTING TEENAGERS
A Step-by-Step, Solution-Focused Approach To Raising Adolescents Without Losing Your Mind

Description:
This 212 page book recommends solutions to existing problems between parents and teenagers. It is divided into three sections. The first answers basic questions about parenting; chapters, such as "What Happened?," "So Now What?," and "How to Speak the Same Language as Your Child," attempt to return the confused parent to equilibrium. Section II offers tips and techniques for maintaining control, such as developing family contracts, holding family meetings, and effective use of punishment; "Problems Deserving Special Attention" (lying, sex, alcohol, etc.) are included. Section III strives to help parents understand their child's desire for power and independence. Concepts such as passive resistance and attention-getting are discussed. A chapter is provided for the parent who is at "the end of their rope," with tips on toleration, changing the focus, and more. Two appendices are given—one includes sample forms to use for family agreements, and the second is a list of specific solutions to common problems.

Evaluation:
Self-help books targeted at parents can take on an air of lofty counselor to common parent. This book, however, is a refreshing contrast. The authors have adopted the get-down-and-dirty approach to parenting, and it's effectiveness is measured in the reader's laughs, combined with those internal thoughts of "why didn't I think of that?" An example: most parents, unsure of the consequences they provide in response to their teenager, stick to a tried-and-true "YOU'RE GROUNDED!" They've also seen, however, that this approach doesn't always work. The authors suggest a different approach—for example, if your child is irresponsible about taking out the trash, they suggest: "Put the trash on his bed . . . get his attention!" Although the solutions they offer are realistic, straightforward, and fair, heavy emphasis is placed on giving teens writing tasks about their behaviors which may or may not invite other power struggles. Best read by parents BEFORE they need to tackle problems, this guide will help families establish expectations, communication patterns, and effective discipline techniques.

Where To Find/Buy:
Bookstores, libraries, or order direct by calling (918) 587-1211.

Parent-Teen Dynamics

GOOD KIDS
How You And Your Kids Can Successfully Navigate The Teen Years

Description:

The information in *Good Kids* is based on research from 4,000 adolescents "who experience an optimal degree of wellness and health in the emotional, social, intellectual, and physical components of their lives." The authors embarked on their research in response to a parental cry for help; parents wanted to know how they could raise happy, secure, and healthy teenagers. Therefore, the book is designed to share with parents the "bright side" of adolescent lives. The text is 182 pages, and is organized into eight chapters. Chapter One introduces the "dark side" of teenagers—the horror stories the public hears from television and news. The rest of the chapters tell stories about both types; those teenagers who have been unsuccessful and those who are well-adjusted. Advice about topics covered include strong families, managing stress, optimism, spiritual wellness, developing bonds between people, and a chapter which tries to tie everything together. There is a topic index at the conclusion of the book.

Evaluation:

Good Kids is designed to help parents raise their child for success in the teenage years. The authors believe that the public has heard too much about all that is **wrong** with teenagers today, and therefore wrote a book to offer a ray of hope into the heart of a parent fearful of their child's impending teenage years. There is no question of this book's usefulness to the parent of a preteen. In fact, it is geared more toward parents of a child about to enter their teenage years, rather than toward parents with a child well into that period. The book should be read by those parents who wish to instill in their child a sense of security and spirituality, as well as the ability to bond with others. However, parents who are attempting to deal with problems that their child currently faces will be better served with a resource focused specifically on solving those problems once they have occurred. All in all, this book is valuable for raising a child to make beneficial choices in the pressure-filled world of adolescence.

Where To Find/Buy:

Bookstores and libraries.

Overall Rating
★★
A good resource for the parent of a preteen seeking to make teenage years easier

Design, Ease Of Use
★★★★
Consistent chapter layout—stories, summary advice for parent & teen, useful activities

1–4 Stars; N/R = Not Rated

Media:
Print

Price:
$17.95

Principal Subject:
Parent-Teen Relationships

ISBN:
0385484437

Edition:
1996

Publisher:
Doubleday (Bantam Doubleday Dell Publishing Group)

Author:
Nick Stinnett, Ph.D., and Michael O'Donnell, Ph.D.

About The Author:
(From Cover Notes)
Stinnett is a professor at the University of Alabama, and has been published in *USA Today, McCall's,* and *Parents* magazine. O'Donnell is Executive Director of the Center for Fathering. He lectures and does interviews around the world on youth and family issues.

III. Parent-Teen Relationships

Overall Rating
★★
Offers parents emotional support and solid advice on how to communicate with teens

Design, Ease Of Use
★★★★
Consistent format, each chapter contains objective & summary; bullets, bold headings

1–4 Stars; N/R = Not Rated

Media:
Print

Price:
$12.95

Principal Subject:
Parent-Teen Relationships

ISBN:
0943990955

Edition:
1994

Publisher:
Parenting Press

Author:
Louise Felton Tracy, M.S.

About The Author:
(From Cover Notes)
Tracy, a mother of six children, has 25 years of experience as a middle school counselor and social worker, and is also a private counselor. Tracy writes for various parenting magazines, and *Grounded for Life?!* received the *Parents' Choice* Approval Award in 1994.

Parent-Teen Dynamics

GROUNDED FOR LIFE?!
Stop Blowing Your Fuse And Start Communicating With Your Teenager

Description:
This 147 page book examines parenting practices of raising adolescents between the ages of 10 and 15 by providing a "child-rearing process that builds on communication, creative problem-solving, and individual strengths." Chapters 1 and 2 suggest that parents should assess their current parenting style to localize any family conflict, and then consider personal changes they can make to become more effective parents. The third chapter deals with parental division offering tips for how to communicate better with one's partner so that both parents will agree on how to deal with their adolescent. Chapter 4 concentrates on consequences and discipline, while Chapter 5 discusses ways to shift the focus of conflict highlighting "parent-owned problems." Approaches for changing parental attitudes are included in Chapter 6. Chapter 7 offers parents ideas for how to include their child in advance planning of family activities. Chapters 8 and 9 discuss how to approach problems at school and change problem behaviors. Chapter 10 deals with teen sexuality, and Chapter 11 emphasizes ways parents can persist as they parent their adolescent.

Evaluation:
Targeting 10 to 15 year olds as a good starting place for implementing change, the author states that "while middle school age children may challenge adult wishes and authority, they do not actively deny them." This book offers solid advice to parents interested in breaking free of an authoritative parenting style toward a more cooperative parenting stance. The advice, gleaned mostly from the author's personal experience with her own large family and 25 years as a middle school counselor, is sensible rather than scholarly. Much emphasis is placed on listening to children and changing parental behavior if needed when it interferes with communication. Each chapter is neatly begun with a "New Belief" and summarized with "Steps to Change" offering succinct and proactive advice. When parents feel as though they repeat the same speeches endlessly, are tired of the same recurring arguments and irreversible "hot spots," this valuable resource will soothe their frustrations and offer them a new direction.

Where To Find/Buy:
Bookstores, libraries, or order direct by calling 1-800-992-6657.

Parent-Teen Dynamics

TURBULENT TEENS OF PANICKING PARENTS

Description:

This book is meant to be a practical, supportive guide to parenting a teenager. Written by a high school guidance counselor with almost 20 years of experience with teens, its intent is to provide hope and guidance for a variety of important issues. Each chapter includes an overview of the given topic, and concludes with questions and exercises ("Coming To Grips") to help parents practice the chapter's information. Topics covered include: talking to teens, getting them to pay attention, minding parent's words, and more. One chapter includes a large interactive section that allows parents to explore their individual parenting style. Major issues, such as school, sex, date rape, drugs, and alcohol, are discussed in separate chapters. Each of the 13 chapters is divided into many subsections and includes several examples of dialogues between counselor/parent and teen. Additionally, an introduction and bibliography are included in this 190 page text.

Evaluation:

Gordon's experience as a counselor is illustrated in this resource, and she speaks in a personal, often humorous voice. She covers many arenas of potential parent-teen conflict, and offers parents advice about how to talk to their teens about drugs, alcohol, and sex. However, parents must be careful to discern Gordon's opinions from their own when choosing courses of action. For example, she strongly states that teens should abstain from sex until marriage, yet she offers very little help on how to teach teens abstinence. There is a slight religious overtone to parts of the book, which will be comforting to some. For those who have different beliefs, the tone is easy to overlook or bypass. What stands out in this book is the liberal use of case study examples from Gordon, and the exercises for parents at the end of each chapter which act as checkpoints to review the essential points of each chapter. Parents should come away from this book with an understanding of effective ways to talk to their teenagers. Use it with other objective guides.

Where To Find/Buy:

Bookstores and libraries.

Overall Rating

★★

Great guide for teen-parent communication, sprinkled with author's opinions

Design, Ease Of Use

★★★

Humorous, yet practical; parent exercises and sample dialogues provided

1–4 Stars; N/R = Not Rated

Media:
Print

Price:
$10.99

Principal Subject:
Parent-Teen Relationships

ISBN:
0800756207

Edition:
1997

Publisher:
Fleming H. Revell (Baker Book House Company)

Author:
Jeenie Gordon

About The Author: (From Cover Notes)
Gordon is a conference speaker, the author of three books, and a single parent. She has been a high school guidance counselor for nineteen years, and has appeared frequently on *Focus on the Family*, and other radio broadcasts.

III. Parent-Teen Relationships

Overall Rating
★★
Offers Christian perspectives in describing conversation-stoppers used by parents

Design, Ease Of Use
★★
Easy-to read; moderately ambiguous chapter titles; no index

1–4 Stars; N/R = Not Rated

Media:
Print

Price:
$8.99

Principal Subject:
Parent-Teen Relationships

ISBN:
1556614047

Edition:
1994

Publisher:
Bethany House Publishers

Author:
William L. Coleman

**About The Author:
(From Cover Notes)**
Coleman has written 30+ Bethany House books on various topics. He combines his experience as a pastor, researcher, writer, and speaker, and is noted for his communication in the area of family relationships and practical spirituality.

Parent-Teen Dynamics

EIGHT THINGS NOT TO SAY TO YOUR TEEN
Ways To Talk With Teens That Really Work

Description:

This 157 page "what NOT to do" parenting book aims to help parents keep the lines of communication open by describing things parents sometimes say that hurt communication. Offering a Christian perspective, it is designed to prevent adults from being counterproductive in dealing with their teenager. The book is divided into three parts. Part One is called "How Do You Do It," and attempts to calm the frustrated parent. The author talks directly to the parent, uses examples from his own life, and quotes Scripture to support his points and reassure the parent. The second part of the book dives into "The Big Eight." Such things as "When I was your age . . ." and "You'll look back someday . . ." are a few of the conversation-stoppers that are discussed and discouraged (usually a 6–8 page discussion for each). The last part explains how to avoid sending "mixed messages" which interfere with effective communication. The book concludes by reassuring parents that they aren't alone.

Evaluation:

Some books mention things to avoid when dealing with teenagers, but this book really lists them, offering a new angle. Also, rather than simply explaining what NOT to do, and leaving the parent wondering "Well, now what?," Coleman offers a great deal of suggestions on how to communicate with the teen. Especially noteworthy is a section called "Top Ten Places to Talk With Teens." This provides interesting perspectives on where teens will be most receptive to conversation—while a parent is playing sports with them, or in the car, sitting on the floor in the living room, in a restaurant, and other places. The author also lists a few places where kids tend to clam up, locations where parents traditionally run things—the den, at a "family conference," at breakfast (they need space in the morning), and more. The book is written with quite a few Scriptural references; however, parents without a Biblical background will also benefit from this book, an excellent helper for those who need to communicate effectively.

Where To Find/Buy:
Bookstores and libraries.

Parent-Teen Dynamics

EMOTIONALLY HEALTHY TEENAGERS
Guide Your Teens To Successful Independent Adulthood

Description:

Kesler's goal in this 165 page book is to assist parents in letting go of their child, without the pain and hassle that typically comes when teens begin to get the familiar restlessness. In order to facilitate this goal and communication his points, he developed ten major principles, which he believes can help parents "lighten up" and let go. There are ten chapters (plus an introduction and epilogue), and each principle is embodied in a statement. Examples of these are: "Love your spouse more than your kids," "Expect obedience; don't beg for it," and "Teach your teen the concept of cause and effect" (about youth and consequences). Other sections focus on helping a child find a niche, working with (vs. against) one's kids, listening rather than lecturing, and looking at the funny side of problems. His most serious chapter, "Do As I Do," teaches parents to live, love, and obey Christ, thus passing their value on to their teen. There is a rather humorous chapter on rebellion, and the book concludes with the value of giving teens "bites of freedom."

Evaluation:

This book looks at raising and letting go of teenagers from a rather matter-of-fact, no nonsense point of view. An excellent book, Christian parents needing some guidance and advice will be reassured by Kesler's humor and encouragement. Some chapters are extremely well-done, most notable of which is Chapter 7 which asks parents to relax and laugh sometimes. Kesler also discusses the occasions when teenagers will mess up. For example, he offers a situation in which a boy comes home drunk, the family learns from it, and the boy vows to never drink again; he also writes about a scenario in which two parents catch their daughter in bed with her boyfriend. These are very real teenage issues, but it does seem that Kesler departs a bit too quickly, sometimes, from the issue being discussed. However, *Emotionally Healthy Teenagers* does have excellent advice about consequences, albeit a bit simple at times, and will be great for the Christian parent who needs a bit of Christian backing and guidance.

Where To Find/Buy:

Bookstores and libraries.

Overall Rating
★★
Good advice for Christian parents; some universal applications & ideas

Design, Ease Of Use
★★
Inadequate index; writing is easy-to-understand; bold-faced excerpts are a nice touch

---

1–4 Stars; N/R = Not Rated

Media:
Print

Price:
$10.99

Principal Subject:
Parent-Teen Relationships

ISBN:
0849940699

Edition:
1998

Publisher:
Word Publishing

Author:
Jay Kesler

**About The Author:
(From Cover Notes)**
Kesler is the president of Taylor University and the host of the daily radio broadcast, "Family Forum." His books are foundational works for parents and counselors nationwide. Kesler is the former president of Youth for Christ, and has three grown children.

Overall Rating
★★
Heartwarming, simple, yet insightful portrayal of "what they did right"

Design, Ease Of Use
★★
Rambles a bit due to numerous personal narratives; no index, but can be read quickly

1–4 Stars; N/R = Not Rated

Media:
Print

Price:
$8.99

Principal Subject:
Parent-Teen Relationships

ISBN:
1556612494

Edition:
1992

Publisher:
Bethany House Publishers

Author:
William L. Coleman

**About The Author:
(From Cover Notes)**
Coleman is the author of 30+ Bethany House books on a variety of topics. Combining his experience as a pastor, researcher, writer, and speaker, he is noted for his effective communication in the area of family relationships and practical spirituality.

Parent-Teen Dynamics

TEN THINGS YOUR TEEN WILL THANK YOU FOR . . . SOMEDAY

Description:

Coleman, the author of *Eight Things Not To Say To Your Teen* (among others), got the idea for this book when, at a seminar, he asked "a group . . . to write down what they thought their parents [had done] right." He was intrigued by the answers, and investigated further. The book is his finished product; the goal is to help parents know when to fight their battles, and when to let go. There are ten choices that parents make, Coleman believes, that wind up working greatly in favor for the child. These choices or major topics are laid out in the forms of "Thanks"—for example "Thanks for letting me dream," "Thanks for Forgetting What We Said," etc. In-between each of the ten chapters is a short section (sometimes related, sometimes not) that lists Coleman's specific advice—a type of "here's what I think" section. Here, the author stresses what's important about parenting to him—things such as a father's love, watching out for children's feelings, protection, avoiding "unfinished conversations," and more.

Evaluation:

To some degree, this book offers a hindsight view into parenting. The first impression upon reading the introductory passages is that this book might be one-sided, because, since the ideas come only from parents themselves, they might not have a clear view of their teenagers' perspectives. As the reader dives into the book, though, it becomes apparent that this is not the case. Coleman writes from a Christian perspective, which he uses to support many of his points. He states the importance of letting children live their dreams, for example, and supports this with a biblical passage that "a crushed spirit dries up the bones." Coleman is humorous in the right spots, and his advice is concise and on-target. Parents will benefit from this book, not simply because of Coleman's "ten things," but because of his inserted recommendations and cautions—simple insights with grand implications. The book is heartwarming, and most parents will gain some new ideas, as well as realizing what they may take for granted.

Where To Find/Buy:

Bookstores and libraries.

Parent-Teen Dynamics

WHAT MAKES YOUR TEEN TICK?

Description:

Coleman has written over thirty books for Bethany House Publishers, and blends his experience as a pastor with his knowledge of family dynamics. Consisting of 20 chapters, this 155 page book presents parents with an overview of the teenage years. It gives parents clues on how to deal with their teens, and information to help them understand what teens are going through. Sample topics include teens' physical development, four questions that teens seek answers to, how to develop teen esteem and understand their frustration, teen tension, and brooding. Some chapters provide practical advice, or interactive questions and tips. One chapter provides conversation starters, while others list what teens still need from parents, effective bribes, how to argue with a teenager, and questions that test how well a parent knows their teen. A note from the author, an introduction, and a conclusion are included. Most of the chapters have several subdivisions not listed in the table of contents.

Evaluation:

The teenage years, as experts will agree, are a tough transition period for both teens and parents. This book focuses on the turmoil teens go through, and ways in which parents can understand and help their teens without being overly intrusive or authoritarian. It provides guidelines for parents who aim to develop a friendly, knowledgeable voice with their children. Coleman provides a practical, spiritual voice for parents, and lets them know that no one does a perfect job raising children. The best parents, according to Coleman, are the ones that admit they need guidance and support raising their kids. This book provides many pointers and tips from how to open up conversations with one's teen to how to argue with them. The writing is clear and honest, and the format is easy to read and follow. At times Coleman's religious outlook shines through, but he does not push his views upon the reader. An index or a list of parent resources would compliment the book. Parents, pastors, and school counselors could find this resource useful.

Where To Find/Buy:

Bookstores and libraries.

Overall Rating
★★
Practical, spiritual advice for parents on understanding and communicating with teens

Design, Ease Of Use
★★
Clear tone, short chapters with several subdivisions; needs index and support resources

1–4 Stars; N/R = Not Rated

Media:
Print

Price:
$7.99

Principal Subject:
Parent-Teen Relationships

ISBN:
1556613229

Edition:
1993

Publisher:
Bethany House Publishers

Author:
William L. Coleman

About The Author:
(From Cover Notes)
William Coleman is known for his experience in the area of family relationships and practical spirituality. He has experience as a pastor, researcher, writer, and speaker, and he has been married over 30 years.

III. Parent-Teen Relationships

★★

Overall Rating
★★
Good general insights and inspirational messages on Christian parenting

Design, Ease Of Use
★
No table of contents or index, however, it is concise and is easy reading

1–4 Stars; N/R = Not Rated

Media:
Print

Price:
$8.99

Principal Subject:
Parent-Teen Relationships

ISBN:
0784704090

Edition:
1995

Publisher:
Empowered Youth Products (The Standard Publishing Company)

Author:
Dr. David Olshine and Dr. Ron Habermas

**About The Author:
(From Cover Notes)**
Olshine, chairman of the Youth Ministry Department at Columbia International University in Columbia, SC, has been actively involved in youth ministry for 17+ years. Habermas is McGee Professor of Biblical Studies at John Brown University in Siloam Springs, Arkansas.

Parent-Teen Dynamics

DOWN BUT NOT OUT PARENTING
50 Ways To Win With Your Teen

Description:
Down But Not Out Parenting contains 50 short essays in its 96 pages. Each essay typically covers 1–2 pages. The authors "are committed to scriptural guidelines of parenting," as evidenced through the author's contextual messages and scriptural references in many of the essays. The essays speak to parents about their teens on many different topics, including giving your child space and respecting their need for space, being a good listener vs. doing all the talking and being a "know-it-all," helping your child grow spiritually, building traditions, learning what teens want in parents, and more. This book seeks to encourage parents in their parenting, offering insights and ideas, and striving to help parents be more sensitive to their teens, all in the name of improving parent-teen relationships. Statistics about teenagers and many stories are given in the authors' "50 ways to win with your teen."

Evaluation:
The authors write, "Parenting is tough. But the sacrifice brings incredible joy." This attitude is evident in the authors' "50 ways." The authors write with a positive tone toward teens, not denying, however, that there can be extreme difficulties. But they encourage parents to give teens the benefit of the doubt and hold them loosely so they can have a chance to grow. This book's short essay format makes for light and easy reading. Many concerns related to the teenage years are addressed in a friendly and humorous way. It is a good Christian parenting resource for practical ideas, supportive insights, and general information about the teenage years. This book does not address crises situations at any depth and serves mainly to provide parents with a better understanding of their teen and to perk up the parent-teen relationship.

Where To Find/Buy:
Bookstores and libraries.

Parent-Teen Dynamics

REACHING THE HEART OF YOUR TEEN
Basics Of Communication Between Parent And Teen

Description:
Gary and Anne Marie Ezzo believe that it is possible to pass through the teenage years without rebellion and strife. They attempt to teach parents, through a Bible-based method, how to develop healthy, supportive relationships with their teens. The 208 page book is divided into four parts—"What You Need To Know About Teen Rebellion," "Reaching The Heart Of Your Teen," "Opening the Lines Of Communication," and "Maintaining Hearts." Part One discusses rebellion, myths of adolescence, and the power of the parent-teen relationship. The sections following discuss how to use authority, build credibility with teens, develop family structures, and communicate. Each chapter contains questions for review, which act as checkpoints for parents. Also, many chapters contain guidelines for parents in enclosed sections—for instance one chapter contains information on evaluating a youth ministry. There is a good deal of biblical reference in this book, including several biblical passages and references.

Evaluation:
The Ezzos present a Bible-based guideline for those parents who have difficulty communicating with their teens. They chose to share their positive parenting experiences with others as a means to teach and enlighten, and provide hope or guidance. Although the Ezzos put a lot of heart and faith into the book, it tends to fall short on practical help or advice. Additionally, the writing in the book is quite wordy and rambling. The Ezzos tend to go on and on about a subject, and never get to the heart of the matter. Some of the special sections (within chapters) that are boxed off, such as "Common Traits Of Strong Families," are helpful, but solid, practical advice is meager here. The Ezzos' premise is that spiritual guidance and faith in God will help those families in need. Those parents searching for a Bible-based alternative to the secular parenting books that flood bookstore shelves will find this book reassuring; it places ultimate responsibility in the hands of God and families' faith in Him. However, those not familiar with the Bible are apt to get lost in the book's wordiness.

Where To Find/Buy:
Bookstores and libraries.

Overall Rating
★★
Biblically-based alternative to parenting teenagers

Design, Ease Of Use
★
Cites scripture throughout; parental review questions; wordy, rambling; meager index

1–4 Stars; N/R = Not Rated

Media:
Print

Price:
$9.99

Principal Subject:
Parent-Teen Relationships

ISBN:
1576730220

Edition:
1997

Publisher:
Multnomah Books
(Questar Publishers)

Author:
Gary & Anne Marie Ezzo

**About The Author:
(From Cover Notes)**
Gary Ezzo is the author of several Bible-based parenting books. He is also the executive director of Growing Families International. Anne Marie Ezzo is a childbirth instructor and RN with a background in pediatric nursing.

III. Parent-Teen Relationships

Overall Rating
★★
Concepts and methods illustrated through numerous situational anecdotes

Design, Ease Of Use
★
Must be read cover to cover; chapter summaries useful but bulleted tips would also help

1–4 Stars; N/R = Not Rated

Media:
Print

Price:
$15.00

Principal Subject:
Parent-Teen Relationships

ISBN:
1559582200

Edition:
1993

Publisher:
Prima Publishing

Author:
Robert J. Mac Kenzie, Ed.D.

About The Author:
(From Cover Notes)
Mac Kenzie, Ed.D., an educational psychologist and family therapist has more than 13 years experience working with family behavioral problems. He provides family counseling and leads parent/teacher training workshops nationwide.

Parent-Teen Dynamics

SETTING LIMITS
How To Raise Responsible, Independent Children By Providing Reasonable Boundaries

Description:
Mac Kenzie's discipline approach is aimed at helping parents "teach their children how to make acceptable choices and to truly understand the consequences of unacceptable behavior." Aimed primarily at schoolage children, these methods are also illustrated from age 2 through the teenage years. This 334 page guide contains twelve chapters. The first three chapters of the book are focused on "the family dance" and what doesn't work when establishing and learning rules. Chapters 4–8 illustrate ways that encourage cooperation, accountability, successful problem solving skills, and consequences. Chapter 9 shows parents how these methods can be applied to teenagers, with Chapters 10 and 11 offering suggestions on how these methods can be used to conquer conflicts involving chores and homework. Chapter 12 offers advice on how to implement this approach and how to deal with problems inherent in making this change. Advice on how to start a parent help group, a list of additional resources, and an index complete the book.

Evaluation:
Although this book is intended as a discipline guide for parents, teachers, and caregivers, it can also be helpful for anyone interested in improving the way they communicate with children. Emphasis in this method is placed on teaching rules and expectations for acceptable behavior without sending mixed or conflicting messages. Using many staged examples and diagrams to illustrate a point, the author has managed to meld the techniques together in a complementary progressive approach; useful for many will be the way he contrasts various parental responses to a given situation (permissive, democratic, punitive). All chapters conclude with a summary and a list of "Parent Study Group Questions" that provide parents and caregivers with useful skill-training exercises. However, parents will need to read the book cover-to-cover and stay focused to fully benefit from this technique. If they can clearly see the author's points and direction through the multitude of parent-child stories, it may be worth their time.

Where To Find/Buy:
Bookstores and libraries, or order direct by calling (916) 632-4400.

Parent-Teen Dynamics

WONDERFUL WAYS TO LOVE A TEEN
. . . Even When It Seems Impossible

Description:

Family therapist Judy Ford has written this guide as a follow-up to her best-selling *Wonderful Ways to Love a Child*. This compact (6" x 6"), 176 page book gives 69 two-page essays on "the art of relating" to teenagers. Designed for busy parents, its short-essay format is divided into three sections: Serenity, Spirit, and Security. "Serenity" contains essays, such as "Laugh About Inconsistencies," "Choose Power Struggles Wisely," and "Treasure Being Together as a Family." "Spirit" provides insight on letting your teen grow inwardly to become the individuals they were meant to be. "Security" gives advice on teaching teens self-assurance by believing in them, giving them room to grow, as well as being there for them. A list of phone numbers of resource organizations, helplines, and hotlines is provided at the end of the book.

Evaluation:

This book offers a practical, easy-to-read format that can be read quickly by busy parents or by parents who seek advice on issues they may be facing at the moment. This book offers encouragement and helpful advice, but in small bites, sometimes too small to do the topic justice. Ford generally takes a light, upbeat approach to dealing with teens. For example, in discussing parent-teen communication, Ford suggests parents be still and smile, that "if life with your teenager sometimes doesn't make sense, you'll be ahead when you smile." She acknowledges problems with raising teenagers, but she doesn't include details of the extreme struggles some parents may face. As she presents parent-teen issues and conflicts, one can see that Ford values teenagers as people who have the potential to blossom into wonderful adults. Each essay can be read in a matter of minutes. Reading this book is like sitting at the kitchen table talking to a friend, but parents wishing more serious discussion of the topics need to look elsewhere.

Where To Find/Buy:

Bookstores, libraries, or order direct by calling 1-800-685-9595.

Overall Rating

★

Presents issues parents face throughout their teens' stages, in a condensed fashion

Design, Ease Of Use

★★★

Short-essay format w/clear, concise writing; many parent-teen scenarios; lack of index

1–4 Stars; N/R = Not Rated

Media:
Print

Price:
$10.95

Principal Subject:
Parent-Teen Relationships

ISBN:
1573240230

Edition:
1996

Publisher:
Conari Press

Author:
Judy Ford, M.S.W.

**About The Author:
(From Cover Notes)**
Ford, M.S.W., has worked with teens and families for almost 30 years—from gang turf in Los Angeles to crisis intervention in hospital emergency rooms. The best-selling author of *Wonderful Ways to Love a Child*, Ford lives with her teenage daughter in Kirkland, WA.

Overall Rating
★
Lighthearted look at teenager-parent relations

Design, Ease Of Use
★★
Collection of brief essays/personal stories; humorous with some black-line drawings

1–4 Stars; N/R = Not Rated

Media:
Print

Price:
$10.00

Principal Subject:
Parent-Teen Relationships

ISBN:
0965704807

Edition:
1997

Publisher:
Triple F Press

Author:
Linda Fink

**About The Author:
(From Cover Notes)**
Fink was the author for twelve years of a newspaper column called "Homespun Humor" published in *The Sun*, a weekly Oregon newspaper. *How To Live With Teenagers* is her second book. She has two sons.

Parent-Teen Dynamics

HOW TO LIVE WITH TEENAGERS
I Give Up. How?

Description:

How To Live With Teenagers is a collection of short essays first published in *The Sun*, a weekly Oregon newspaper. The essays are humorous takes on life with teenagers. Fink divided the book into three main parts, consisting of "How Parents Mess Up Teenagers," "How Teenagers Mess Up Parents," and "How Messed Up Are We?" The parts, respectively, contain eleven, seventeen, and twenty essays. A few thoughts from the author are provided at the beginning of each part. Sample titles from the first part are: Misconceptions, Smoke Signals, and I'd Rather Do It Myself. Titles from Part Two include: Kid Costs, Chaperone, Spring Break, and College Crime. The final section includes such essay titles as: Growing Up, Yuppie, Christmas Tree Fight, Broken Heart, and The Opposite Sex. Essays are typically less than five pages long, and some contain illustrations. The book is 149 pages long and contains 48 essays in all.

Evaluation:

As the back cover declares, "If you can't think of anything funny about teenagers, read this book." Fink's philosophy on raising teenagers is to laugh. The book is full of unusual takes on typical topics in the lives of teenagers. For instance, Fink describes one of the ways parents mess teens up—by trying to force them to read. One of her sons loved to read, and she believes he did so because she was always trying to pull him away from books. An example of how teenagers mess parents up is given in an essay about Fink's sons pretending they were orphans. Then Fink uses the fact that she didn't miss her youngest son (and he didn't miss her) when he went away to college as proof that they were both messed up to begin. The essays lighten topics that normally give parents headaches. Fink makes life more bearable through humor, often a seldom used tool in teen psychology. While this book won't teach parents any practical skills for raising teenagers, it will teach them to lighten up and enjoy the comedy as it unfolds.

Where To Find/Buy:
Bookstores and libraries.

Parent-Teen Dynamics

RAISING A THOUGHTFUL TEENAGER
A Book Of Answers And Values For Parents

Description:
Rabbi Kamin, in his introduction, writes what he believes are the most important aspects of parent-teen dynamics: looking, listening, and loving. Following this statement, the rest of the book is a collection of chapters which deal with a wide variety of issues. Such issues include those topics that are commonly faced by parents and teens, such as sex, drinking, death, religion, and more. Each of the 22 chapters presents a question as posed by a child; for example, the chapter dealing with sex & intimacy is titled "How Old Should I Be to Have Sex?" The typical length for each chapter is about 11 pages. The chapters are arranged in a fairly similar fashion—the author offers some background and scriptural reference (if applicable), then talks about some experiences with which he has dealt. Then, bits and pieces of advice are offered. Rather than specific words, Kamin usually offers ideas for parents to contemplate. He does mention certain things NOT to say, and usually offers the parent some words of encouragement.

Evaluation:
The author looks at a teenager's world from a perspective that differs from what is traditionally used. Kamin has a gift—he has the ability to soothe the reader with words. On occasion, his language actually lulls the reader as does a lullaby. There is no question that this is enjoyable reading. However, the parent who needs concrete answers (and they DO exist) may not be satisfied with this book. In addition, this book makes two questionable assumptions: 1) that teenagers really do ask their parents these questions, and 2) that teenagers ask these questions at all. There are a few chapters which specifically do not belong—"When Will The World End?" and "Is It Okay For Me To Say What I Think?" are two such issues which seem a bit abstract. Although this is enjoyable reading, and some parents may find ideas on how to talk to their kids, it is more likely that parents will finish the book and say, "Yeah, that sounds nice. So what do I really do?" This resource is more like a feel-good novel, than a practical guide.

Where To Find/Buy:
Bookstores and libraries.

Overall Rating
★
A lot of words without much advice; Kamin makes some questionable assumptions

Design, Ease Of Use
★
Hard to find the advice he offers; table of contents is very general; no index

1–4 Stars; N/R = Not Rated

Media:
Print

Price:
$10.95

Principal Subject:
Parent-Teen Relationships

ISBN:
0452274206

Edition:
1997

Publisher:
Plume (Dutton Signet/Penguin Books USA)

Author:
Ben Kamin

**About The Author:
(From Cover Notes)**
Ben Kamin is a senior rabbi at the Temple-Tifereth Israel, a 145-year-old Reform congregation of 1,600 families in Cleveland, Ohio. He writes regularly for the *Cleveland Plain Dealer* and appears frequently on radio and television.

III. Parent-Teen Relationships

Parent-Teen Dynamics

RAISING TODAY'S TEENS

Overall Rating

★

Ambitiously offers online parental counseling, but no forums exist for off-hours help

Design, Ease Of Use

★

Site map needed; unorganized lists of Qs; purple graphic throughout is rather cloying

1–4 Stars; N/R = Not Rated

Media:
Internet

Principal Subject:
Parent-Teen Relationships

Internet URL:
http://www.talkzone.org/

Description:

Billed as a "national helpline for parents raising teens," this site's "trained parent counselors . . . provide problem-solving techniques and communication solutions to parents, to help strengthen parenting skills." There are 11 options on their homepage, 7 of which include: a profile and contact info on the site's creators, participation in a survey, "amusements" (a parent-teen cartoon when we visited), links to other sites, and more. The other 4 options center on offering advice and information to parents of teens. At "Online Counseling," parents may enter chat rooms (private or shared) for "free, private, and confidential" counseling (Monday–Friday, 10 am–5 pm Mountain Standard Time) or parents may speak directly to a counselor (1-800-475-TALK). Past Q and As are available through the "Bulletin Board," and visitors may request copies of the site's *Raising Teens* magazine through "Publications." "Ask Beth" includes articles from the Boston Globe's columns (since 1964) which answer various teens' questions.

Evaluation:

Aiming to relieve the stresses involved with parenting teenagers, this site's online counseling service may fulfill the immediate needs of some parents, that is, unless those frustrations fall outside of the time slots when the counselors are present. In lieu of that possibility, one would then hope that parents could access discussion groups in which parents have hashed out and shared ideas for dealing with parent-teenage problems and crises. However, no forums are evident. Perhaps this is an oversight that will be corrected in the site's future planning. Parents **can** scan the "Bulletin Board" archive in search of answers to their questions, but the list lacks any grouping by topic; parents will need to scroll through the whole list. This site's goal is applaudable—offering parents person-to-person contact so they can find alternative solutions to family problems. However ambitious this site is though, it falls short of its mark. Look to other more interactive and comprehensive sites supporting parental conversations and feedback.

Where To Find/Buy:

On the Internet at the URL: http://www.talkzone.org/.

PEER PRESSURE REVERSAL
An Adult Guide To Developing A Responsible Child

Terrific Resource For:

Hands-on techniques to deal with peer pressures

Recommended For:

Parent-Teen Relationships

Description:

Scott, who has been counseling and lecturing since 1970, has developed a method for avoiding peer pressure called "Peer Pressure Reversal." This 235 page book presents her program in a step-by-step, skills-oriented, practical guidebook. It is written for adults and consists of six chapters, beginning with an introduction about negative peer pressure. The second chapter, the heart of the author's program, depicts the three main steps of Peer Pressure Reversal (PPR)—checking out the scene, making a good decision, and acting to avoid trouble. Actual methods of how to teach PPR are presented in Chapters 3 and 4, offering separate guidelines for parents and teachers. Each section within these chapters is broken down and numbered according to its place in the program, with sample titles such as schedule, introduce, discuss, practice, and feedback. The final chapters are devoted to reinforcing PPR and summarizing the skills learned. Scott uses steps, simple diagrams, and examples to teach her program. She includes additional resources for parents dealing with peer-pressure problems.

Evaluation:

Parents, teachers, or other caregivers who witness their children falling prey to the whims of their friends should get a lot of tips from this book. It provides a solid, practical plan for talking to kids about peer pressure and how they can avoid it. The writing is simplistic at times, but the simplicity aids the easy-to-follow format. For each step in the PPR plan, Scott not only offers suggestions for discussions, but also provides examples of the plan in use. She offers responses children can use when faced with an uncomfortable situation. Scott understands most children's needs to remain cool in the eyes of their peers, and several of her suggestions are humorous and lighthearted. This book teaches parents and teachers how to help their kids keep their opinions, yet still keep their friends. The only possible problem with Scott's plan may be her assumption that children will listen to their parents or teachers. Perhaps the best teachers for children are other children who have learned the skill of PPR, not adults. Overall, Scott offers a unique solution for overcoming peer pressure that teachers and parents should at least consider.

Where To Find/Buy:

Bookstores, libraries, or order direct by calling 1-800-822-2801.

Overall Rating
★★★★
Hands-on, practical guide to dealing with peer pressure

Design, Ease Of Use
★★★★
Step-by-step format makes author's points clear, logical; plentiful examples

1–4 Stars; N/R = Not Rated

Media:
Print

Price:
$14.95

Principal Subject:
Parent-Teen Relationships

ISBN:
0874254086

Edition:
2nd (1997)

Publisher:
HRD Press

Author:
Sharon Scott

About The Author:
(From Cover Notes)
Scott is a licensed professional counselor and marriage and family therapist, an award winning author, lecturer, and consultant who specializes in counseling services and training programs. Her programs focus on intervention and prevention strategies for all ages.

Overall Rating
★★★
Excellent insight; helpful for the parent who also wants to be a friend to their teen

Design, Ease Of Use
★★★
Teen, parent quotes enlightening; chapter themes don't always follow chapter titles

1–4 Stars; N/R = Not Rated

Media:
Print

Price:
$12.95

Principal Subject:
Parent-Teen Relationships

ISBN:
1577490037

Edition:
1995

Publisher:
Fairview Press

Author:
Valerie Wiener

About The Author:
(From Cover Notes)
Wiener, a professional communicator for 30 years, has been actively involved in youth communications projects since the early 1970s. She has received national recognition for her programs with teenagers, and is also the author of *Power Communications*.

Peer Influence, Pressure

GANG FREE
Influencing Friendship Choices In Today's World

Description:
Wiener believes that there are very few resources which deal with the friendships forged by teenagers. Her book, then, attempts to fill in this gap, and is based on "46 books and hundreds of articles," as well as "original research with 216 teenagers." This 207 page, two-part book highlights two specific topics, the first of which is called "How America's Teenagers Make Friends." It is filled with original quotes from the kids involved with Wiener's research, as well as Wiener's commentary. Chapters focus upon self-concept, peer impact, and group identification. The second part—"Getting Parents Involved"—is designed to help involve parents in the life of their child. It highlights the changing roles of families over time, communication techniques, and ways to teach by example. There are thirteen chapters in all, a foreword, a preface by Wiener, and a table of contents. The end of the book contains an afterword, a bibliography, and an index of key concepts.

Evaluation:
The subtitle of this book, "Influencing Friendship Choices In Today's World," is one of those phrases that parents probably do not want their child to see. Few teenagers appreciate parental influence over their choices of friendships. Therefore, it may seem at first glance that this book is a subtle manipulation tool to assist parents in changing or "helping" their child pick "good" friends. A closer look, however, does not support this immediate opinion. The book's second section really centers around effective, moderate, and open communication with teens. It teaches ways in which a parent can positively interact with their child. Part One, contrary to initial expectations, discusses the difficulties teenagers face in today's world, focusing on how they make choices; it also talks about how important peer evaluation can be. All in all, this book is an excellent tool for helping parents gain insight to their teen's peer relations. Be aware though—the title is misleading; parents should keep it out of sight of their teen!

Where To Find/Buy:
Bookstores and libraries.

Peer Influence, Pressure

COPING WITH PEER PRESSURE

Description:

Directed toward adolescents and focusing on peer pressure, this 215 page resource aims to provide "simple, organized information to guide (them) through this crucial time." The author discusses the nature of peer pressure, viewing the peer group as a transition between the dependent life of the family and the independence of maturity. This book explains the nature of peer influence, the reasons why adolescents give in to peer pressure, and how to identify the patterns of negative peer pressure, such as drugs, alcohol, sex, gangs, cults, etc. The author does not offer a textbook solution for how to get through adolescence, but instead believes that "Everyone has unique skills, personalities, and family histories. Finding, understanding, and living successfully with these differences is what adolescence is all about." Other chapter topics include the effects of peer pressure on special populations (gifted children, learning disabled, etc.), the effects of loss on adolescents, the positive benefits gleaned from one's peer group, and more.

Evaluation:

The best thing about this book is its compassionate, yet direct tone. The chapter on sexuality is particularly effective. Its use of personal narratives shows how complicated the issue of sexuality really is and how adolescents' choices can affect their future. Another well-done aspect of this book is its discussion of the positive effects of peer pressure. Peers hold the unique position of being an adolescent's bridge from dependence to independence. They help through losses, breakups, and life's major and minor disappointments. "Friendship is a vote of confidence that helps teens to learn the attitudes and skills that lead to independence and responsibility." The author neatly concludes by detailing ways adolescents can move beyond peer pressure by knowing themselves, forming and testing their own opinions, developing skills, learning how to make decisions, and not fearing mistakes. Although written for adolescents, this guide affords parents an insider look at the personal challenges their teen faces with their peers.

Where To Find/Buy:

Bookstores and libraries.

Overall Rating
★★★
Good examination of pressures placed on teens; also points out positive aspect of peers

Design, Ease Of Use
★★
Essay format makes cover-to-cover reading necessary; bold subheadings help

1–4 Stars; N/R = Not Rated

Media:
Print

Price:
$6.95

Principal Subject:
Parent-Teen Relationships

ISBN:
1568381832

Edition:
5th (1997)

Publisher:
Hazelden (Rosen Publishing Group)

Author:
Leslie S. Kaplan

About The Author:
(From Cover Notes)
Kaplan, Ed.D, is an educational administrator with the York County Public Schools in Virginia, a Licensed Professional Counselor, and a National Board Certified Counselor. She has written articles dealing with adolescents and counseling appear in various journals.

III. Parent-Teen Relationships

Overall Rating
★
Well intentioned but offers little concrete advice or how-tos

Design, Ease Of Use
★★★
Pamphlet format is easy to read; bold subheadings

1–4 Stars; N/R = Not Rated

Media:
Print

Price:
$1.95

Principal Subject:
Parent-Teen Relationships

ISBN:
1562461516

Edition:
1998

Publisher:
Johnson Institute

Author:
Johnson Institute

Peer Influence, Pressure

WHAT TO DO WHEN YOU'RE WORRIED ABOUT YOUR KID'S CHOICE OF FRIENDS
For Parents, Teachers, And Other Caregivers: The Parenting For Prevention Series

Description:

The developers of this 12 page pamphlet aim to help parents "teach kids how to choose good friends and companions and how to avoid those who may spell 'trouble'." As part of the Parenting for Prevention Information Series, it details the various steps that parents can take if they are concerned with their children's choice in friends. Advice offered suggests that parents should: get to know their children's friends; learn to recognize "trouble behavior," such as acting out, foul language, etc.; learn to foster their child's interests and hobbies; try and draw other children to their home where parents can supervise activities; be fair but firm; recommend and participate in alternative activities; suggest alternative friends; and teach their child the value of friendship. The pamphlet provides general information on how to accomplish each of these suggestions.

Evaluation:

This flimsy pamphlet provides little in the way of new or directly helpful information for parents concerned about their children's choice in friends. Twelve pages in length, it gives only snippets of highlights in its coverage, brief examples of ways to communicate, and rudimentary examples of things not to do or say. For example, the section on giving "yourself the 'home court' advantage," or ways to encourage your child's friends to visit your home, suggests all the benefits of this suggestion, but offers no real advice on **how** to get kids to hang out in your home. This resource is far too general to be of any real use or persuasion. This subject matter is better covered in even the most general textbook resources where the subject receives the attention it justly deserves.

Where To Find/Buy:

Bookstores, libraries, or order direct by calling 1-800-231-5165.

CRITICAL ISSUES
& CONCERNS

INTRODUCTION

No doubt parents are familiar with the commercial declaring "this isn't your father's oldsmobile" referring to how products have changed from the past to the present. Well, more has changed than just cars. In many ways, it's not even the same world as it was even one generation ago. Our children have to deal with a world that not only feels more risky and dangerous, but **is** riskier and **is** more dangerous. Our homes are bombarded with an incredible amount of information and current events thanks to the immediate nature of modern day communications. However, this may also taint our perceptions of safety. Professionals have found that people who have never been directly touched by violence and crime may display the same symptoms as those who have been victimized. This influx of communication, or "information overload," can create anxieties and fears within parents that may then be transmitted to their children.

Being a teenager in today's world is a different experience than it was for past generations. Issues such as substance use and abuse, teen pregnancy and unplanned parenthood, adolescent depression and suicide, violence, and even death have become common terms in describing adolescence. These factors are more than enough to make the prospect of parenting an adolescent a scary proposition.

Do parents have any control over influences that might affect their family? Psychologists continue to debate whether or not adolescent behaviors are a result of learning or a result of genetics. Behaviorists believe that a person begins learning how to cope in the world from the minute they draw their first breath outside of the womb. Other theorists believe that behavior is a result of brain chemistry and function. Still others believe that much of our behavior is genetically predisposed. A comprehensive viewpoint then might include acknowledgment of what we do and what we don't have control over.

Some conditions are clearly genetically based. For example, some teens will be genetically predisposed to feelings of depression and may perhaps seriously contemplate suicide. Still others may be predisposed to substance abuse and the various conditions and diseases which can ensue. Parents don't have control over the genetic make-up of their children. They can, however, be aware of their family's genetic history and educate their child about any predisposed risks.

Parents do have influence over how their child chooses to cope with adversities during their transition through adolescence. This parental impact will continue to show its significance throughout other stages of their child's life. Parents are important role models to teens, although this may seem difficult to appreciate in the heat of parent-teenage struggles and arguments. The old adage of "do as I say, not as I do" is constantly challenged by teens who are quick to use parental behavior to justify their own. If parents tell teens not to drink and drive, parents had better be prepared not to drink and drive themselves. Teens are exposed to more choices, greater freedom, and blossoming new physical abilities, and consequently their adolescence may be littered with struggles along the way. This is a period of real risk for adolescents and obviously a time of great concern for parents.

Perhaps the most often discussed and most clearly visible problem that parents worry about is their child's possible use or abuse of various substances, whether alcohol, nicotine, or drugs. Yet, unknowingly, parents may have already taught their child to use these substances to mitigate the pains of life, to lower social inhibitions, and, yes, to be accepted by mainstream society. Alcohol is the drug of choice for most adolescents and adults in our society, and it is the single most toxic; the American Academy of Pediatrics recently cited findings that said the majority of teenagers begin drinking at the age of 14. Teenagers' use and abuse of alcohol often results in extremely destructive behaviors to the teen, to property, and to others. Adolescents may be genetically predisposed to substance abuse or they may have learned to use drugs or alcohol to blunt life's impacts. Whichever the case, when adolescents use or abuse substances, they may also inadvertently create a strong foundation for other serious issues. Drugs and alcohol are major players and open the gateway to potential problems, such as sexual behavior, AIDS, teen pregnancy, crime, depression, and risky behaviors which might lead to injury or death.

Media and other communication modes have constructed an image of a teenager in our society that is difficult for teens to actually replicate in real life. Girls are given an unrealistic and unhealthy image to live up to and seek. As a result, female adolescent smoking is increasing, and eating disorders such as bulimia and anorexia are prevalent in some teen populations. Society continues to encourage boys to express aggression, and consequently they learn to identify with heroes who suppress women, and those who glorify violence.

Adults decry reports of delinquent behavior by adolescents, they fear gang activity, and are shocked by the growing number of juveniles being placed in prisons. And the last few decades highlight an epidemic of teen suicidal behavior linked to depression, stress, and perhaps an inability for teens to make effective connections in this rapidly paced world.

This may all sound so hopeless, but remember that life is a balancing act. There are difficult and frightening aspects to adolescence, just as with any other time of life, but there are also wonderful and exciting aspects as well. Parents shouldn't lose sight of the fact that most teens transcend adolescence with success. However, that doesn't mean that parents should sit back and be complacent about this probability. Being a parent of an adolescent is hard work, and the harder a parent works, the greater the likelihood that their child will make it to adulthood as an integrated, effective person. Critical issues, concerns, and problems are out there lurking, and it's likely that every family will have to deal with them in some form or another.

Even though adolescence can bring about a separation of teens from their families, families continue to be the greatest constant influence in children's lives. So what can parents do to strengthen their adolescent and soften the impact of adolescent traumas? Our society has seen drastic changes in the family's structure and the way it functions compared to the last generation. Where once the extended family was intimately involved in parenting matters, now families are more nuclear. And many of these families have changed from a heterosexual two-parent household to that of a home consisting of a single parent, same sex parents, or a variety of other household hierarchies.

The high incidence of divorce in our society has added terms and concepts such as "blended families" and "co-parenting." Consequently, the body of research dealing with the impact of divorce and custodial arrangements has grown immensely. However, the interpretation of that impact seems as varied as the kinds of households that have evolved over the last generation. One thing that is certain is that the ways in which parents and families deal with divorce becomes crucial to how well this event is integrated into children's lives. Certainly some of the critical issues and concerns identified as part of adolescence can spring from how families struggle or manage to thrive during the process of divorce. As a result of a divorce and its reconfiguration of their family, children will perhaps be even more concerned with issues involving predictability, safety, and acceptance within the makeup of their "new" family. The family, then, has the most potential for helping adolescents either transcend or run aground during this very risky, if not terribly thrilling, time.

As parents observe their adolescent's behavior, both the endearing and the disturbing, they are reminded of their child's earnestness to seek acceptance, as supported by recent research. For example, kids join gangs in their quest for relationships that are familial, and teenagers' sexual behavior often becomes a powerful expression of their need for love. Other frequently observed self-destructive behaviors, such as acting-out, eating disorders, drinking and drug use, and delinquency and destruction, seem to be based on, or at least motivated by, the need for teens to be accepted.

Parents must understand the risks involved with adolescence, as well as reminding themselves of the wonderful and exciting aspects of being a teen. Parents must also acknowledge and appreciate the important role they play in the success of their adolescent's journey. More that just knowing that these risks exist, parents need to know how their family and child may be vulnerable. Parents need to fully understand how the choices they make also impact their adolescent. They need to keep a watchful eye as their child struggles to be accepted by others, especially their peers. Some parenting experts say that if your child makes it through adolescence alive, then you've succeeded as a parent. Given this discussion about sex, drugs, and rock-and-roll (or perhaps more appropriately grunge, rave, or techno), parents may think this isn't too far from the truth.

The discussions below will introduce you to some of the issues you and your teenager will encounter during adolescence. Following this section, you'll find our recommendations for resources that can help parents deal with each of these issues.

Substance Abuse

Substance use and abuse are perhaps the most visible issues that concern parents during adolescence. The use of substances, including alcohol, drugs, and nicotine, is at the crux of a great deal of adolescent social behavior and disastrous decisions. Like their parents before them, most adolescents today choose alcohol as their drug of choice. Unlike their parents, however, adolescents' use of drugs typically begins at an earlier age nowadays. Research shows, however, that the younger a person is when they start experimenting with substances, the more likelihood that they will become dependent. Thus there is a greater probability today that if a teenager uses substances, they may wind up becoming a victim of abuse and dependency.

The stronger nature of controlled substances today also is a major contributing factor. Yes, it's true, this is not your parents' marijuana. The marijuana of today is stronger and more potentially lethal, and the presence of rock cocaine and its inexpensive price tag spells important differences and massive trouble for today's adolescent drug users. Yet by far the drug of choice for adolescents is still alcohol, considered to be the most toxic and damaging drug available to our youth. Because it is the most easily accessed, because it has the air of social acceptability, and because adults grant teenagers tacit permission to use it, it has become an eroding force in adolescents' lives.

Whether controlled substances are used for peer group acceptance or as a form of self-medication, the use of drugs, alcohol, and nicotine is the single most widespread destructive behavior affecting adolescents in our society. As a society, we tend to employ many changing strategies to try and deal with this issue. From parent-child contracts to taking a no-tolerance stance, the message all professionals agree on is that parents and teens should delay this behavior for as long as possible. Research indicates that the longer a teen postpones their first use, the less probability they will develop dependent behavior. The exception to this, of course, are those adolescents who may be genetically predisposed to addiction. Parents need to consider all these factors, and help prevent substance abuse in the first place, thus saving themselves and their teen the anguish and heartbreak of dealing with intervention, treatment, recovery, and aftercare programs.

Sexuality and Pregnancy

Sexuality is probably the greatest example of the best and worst of adolescence. The wonderful world of sexual attractions and romantic relationships begins to unfold for young people during this time. The physical and emotional growth adolescents undergo represent perhaps the most extreme areas of adolescent change. This sexual maturation process is filled with mystery and fascination for both boys and girls. However, this same process for many parents is filled with anxiety and dread. Not only are adolescents reaching sexual maturity at an earlier age, but we also live in an age when the consequential sexual behavior can be fatal. "Having that talk" may seem like one of the most uncomfortable discussions for parents of adolescents, yet in today's world the stakes of not doing so are greater than ever.

When parents were youths, perhaps their primary concerns with early sexual behavior consisted of becoming pregnant or contracting VD. But now, the fears of pregnancy and the transmission of sexually transmitted diseases have been joined by the panic of becoming infected with the virus that causes AIDS. This fact alone mandates a more aggressive stance by parents to communicate information about sexuality and sexual behavior. As with many issues of adolescence, the challenge for adults lies in finding ways to share this information with adolescents without talking down to them or discouraging a healthy development of their sexuality.

Parents often become confused and concerned about how much of their own past sexual behaviors should be divulged to their children. This is especially true for parents who transcended their adolescence during a time of sexual revolution and free choice. Parents may need help clarifying their own values regarding sexuality, or, as experts state, the message parents send becomes wishy-washy and open for direct challenge by their teens. In addition, parents need to be aware of the dramatic changes that have occurred concerning birth control methods, pregnancy options, and other sexuality choices since parents were teens. Parents may need updated information that they can pass on to their child. And when discussing sexuality, many professionals advise parents to not just focus on the physical aspect—"the birds and the bees"—but also help teens understand that there are emotional elements at risk as well. Too many times, adolescents who choose to engage in early sexual behavior do not realize the repercussions or feelings that arise when a relationship ends, especially one in which sex was involved.

Besides the transmission of sexually transmitted diseases, and the possible damage to an adolescent's healthy emotional development, there is the chance of pregnancy. Since a teen typically evokes an attitude of "living for the moment," unplanned pregnancies may be more a concern for parents than for their child. Yet, with the concerted efforts of many social, religious, and media groups this generation may be the best informed ever about the consequences of sexual behavior.

Of the many issues faced by parents, an adolescent having a child is perhaps one of the most disruptive behaviors that can occur during adolescence. This outcome is a slingshot for teens right into adulthood. The responsibility of child-rearing comes at a time when teens themselves are reaching for independence from their childhood, and forming their own identity. Yet, teens must accelerate or abandon these tasks in exchange for the adult-like responsibilities of raising and supporting a child. Parents of the teen often wind up dealing with their own sense of loss as well, letting go of the wishes and hopes they had for their child's future. They may also lose a great deal of their own freedom and independence while helping their teen raise and support their grandchild.

The different ways pregnancy impacts adolescent boys and girls is complex, and tied to social values and gender roles. Being immediately immersed into "the real world," results in ending, or at least postponing, the hopes and dreams of many young people. Statistics, show that teenage marriages, especially those originating because of pregnancy, begin at a great disadvantage. Additionally, the ability of teenage couples to raise and support a child often relies on the couple's parents, putting a great strain on most families. As confusing as life can be as an adolescent, and as difficult as it is for anyone to raise children nowadays, the prospect of being a teenage parent ushers in a harsh dose of reality and life.

Eating Disorders

An eating disorder is a disease that is predominantly found in adolescents, and its basis can be found in their misconceptions about self-image and control. This disease centers on a child's unhealthy relationship with food, and if not treated it can lead to serious medical problems or complications. Bulimia Nervosa, Anorexia Nervosa, and Compulsive Overeating are examples of some of the most commonly recognized eating disorders. Latest statistics show that eating disorders are on the rise in the U.S., and some experts say that anorexia, in particular, has the highest death rate of any psychiatric illness.

Bulimia often begins in early to mid-adolescence, and usually occurs in girls. The process of bingeing and purging food is a very dangerous and damaging behavior. Typically the bulimic child eats excessively and rapidly using food to satisfy their emotional need for fulfillment, and then feels guilty thereby ridding their body of the excess food through the use of laxatives, diuretics, vomiting, or excessive exercise. Anorexia is more often found in later adolescence and early adulthood. It includes a fear of being fat, obsessive-compulsive behaviors focused on food, and weight loss through restricted intake of food and/or starvation. This is compounded by the child's distorted body image in which the anorexic sees her body only in terms of its negative characteristics, and thus continues the starvation process regardless of how thin they have actually become. Although it is typically found in women, recent studies show evidence that this disorder is becoming an affliction also affecting young men. Compulsive Overeating is similar to bulimia in that the individual binges, however, the compulsive overeater does not engage in the purging process. As with bulimia, the overeater usually tries to fulfill their emotional needs with food. They then become addicted to food much as an alcoholic becomes addicted to alcohol.

What are some factors that may cause eating disorders? One influence is the way society and the media pervasively and constantly bombard us with unattainable images of what is considered physically desirable. Another factor has to do with the way certain families are structured and how family members may struggle for control. Divorce, depression, sexual abuse, and other factors can also substantially contribute to this disorder. For developing adolescent girls, the arrival of normal fatty areas on their body may signal internal distress, whereas for pubescent boys, misconceptions of masculinity and athletic appearance distort their perceptions which can result in overexercise, dieting, and other resolutions.

We do find that both boys and girls who are affected by eating disorders typically exhibit traits such as perfectionism, obsessive beliefs and compulsive behavior surrounding food, rigid values of success, and distorted views of their self-image. These behaviors and diseases are not to be taken lightly. Though treatable, they present a powerful and potent enemy.

Delinquent Behavior and Gangs

Young people today, as a result of their continual search for identity and peer group acceptance, face serious choices as they grow into adulthood. One of the most serious threats centers on an adolescent's desire to belong and be part of a group, which may be fulfilled through participation in a gang or through delinquent behavior with their peers. There has been an alarming increase in the number of juveniles arrested for murder, as high as 119% nationwide according to some studies. Gang representation is no longer solely felt in urban cities, but has spread into smaller communities and rural areas. We hear news reports plastered all over about drive-by shootings, retaliatory killings, drug-centered crimes, robberies, and other violent behavior . . . much of which is attributed to gang involvement. And all of which can spell serious trouble when we consider the vulnerable state of our adolescents.

Experts have found that the "gang," whether it be a child's peer group or a particular gang (Skinheads, Crips, Bloods, Asian, Hispanic, girl gangs to name a few), replaces an adolescent's need to belong to a family. Here adolescents find what's missing in their lives—a set of governing rules and consequences, the feeling of belonging and being accepted, and support and guidance from other members. Obviously, some teens will be more vulnerable than others to making the catastrophic decision to become a gang member, others may simply become involved with a questionable crowd. Whatever the decision an adolescent makes, the repercussions can be disastrous, destructive, and at worst case, deadly.

Parents need to recognize whether their adolescent's conduct is a normal developmental pattern or a signal for future antisocial behavior. Families should realize the importance of communicating with their child while finding ways to resolve family disputes. Parents need to be wary for warning signs that indicate possible gang involvement, whether it be the clothing, jewelry, or colors their teen chooses to wear, the language they use with their peers, or the air freshener swinging freely in their car. Parents and teens need to recognize signs of gang involvement in their community in order to disallow gang penetration within their child's school. But foremost, families need to help their child find ways to belong outside the family that don't involve choices of life and death.

Depression, and Suicide

Whether it is related directly to adolescence or caused by other factors, adolescent depression is an on-going concern in our society. The many challenges adolescents face in terms of their ego growth, their identity, and the enormous physiological changes they undergo may make teens more vulnerable to depression than other age groups. Also, depression can originate from other factors such as biochemical makeup or genetic base. In these cases, the dynamics of adolescence may dramatically trigger or influence depression.

Depression that occurs during adolescence may present symptoms that are different from those exhibited at other ages. We commonly think of a depressed individual as having characteristics which include withdrawal, relationship dysfunction, sleep disturbance, decrease in daily functioning, energy loss, etc. Adolescent depression can be expressed in these ways, but may also be characterized by acting-out behavior, spontaneous and self-destructive behavior, risk-taking behavior, increased drug use and abuse, violent behavior, and contemplation of suicide.

Adolescent suicide has been a particular concern during the past decade. The phenomenal numbers of attempted and completed suicides among adolescents and teens illustrate how depression has reached epidemic proportions. Experts theorize about the roots and causes of this devastating behavior, but the trend continues to increase. Our society has become much better about talking openly about suicide and death by suicide, which has helped in creating preventative strategies and public awareness. The now-known possible connection between depression (and inherent suicidal response) and substance abuse has opened parents' eyes to an additional danger that arises when their teen uses alcohol or drugs. The bottom line is that adolescent depression and suicidal behavior originate from cognitive, genetic, biochemical, and interpersonal influences. As we continue to increase and improve our preventative strategies, and as we expand our intervention strategies, the message to our teens must be made clear—life contains problems, but there are many choices for how to solve these problems. Although a teen may "live for the moment," suicide, however, is never the right choice.

Divorce

The biggest influence in a teen's life is their family. It stands to reason, then, that if the influence of the family is critical to healthy development and functioning, then dysfunction in the family will certainly have an impact on a teenager. When adolescent behavior becomes dysfunctional, one of the first places to examine is the family and its dynamics. Over the years, studies have told us different things. On one hand, we have been told that it's better to keep the household intact, even if there are confrontation and interpersonal problems. On the other hand, we have also been told that a dysfunctional family could have adverse effects on its children. Obviously, with the divorce rate as high as it is in this country, we seem to have made our choice as a society. Divorce has ushered in new concepts and nomenclature into family life. Terms such as "blended families," "co-parenting," and "shared custody," have become commonly used along with the concept of the "single parent family."

There is no doubt that a divorce in the family can be disruptive to the entire family system. Many divorce situations include interpersonal problems between the two dominant family figures. This presents obstacles to clear communication among family members, along with difficulty in helping children cope in healthy ways. These situations, however, whether effectively resolved or angrily confronted, present a series of losses to children. These losses can include the loss of the child's family of origin, separation from one or the other parent, separation from siblings, and if moving is involved, the loss of friends and familiar environments. It's important to understand that the cognitive understanding and behavioral expression of these losses will be different for each child. Many times adults incorrectly assume that a teenager is better equipped than a young child to handle the changes arising from a divorce. But, the various coping strategies, support systems, developmental abilities, and life experiences of the child will greatly influence how the child deals with the divorce.

Certainly, many children who grow up in households where a divorce has taken place develop into healthy functioning adults. As with other aspects of adolescence, the impact of divorce greatly depends on many variables, primarily, of course, the parents themselves. A divorce impacts the family as a whole, thus the strategies used for dealing with divorce should involve the entire family, and not just include the divorcing parents. Divorce is a fact of life in our society, and as such, needs to be given the necessary attention to help adolescents traverse the uneven terrain they often find themselves encountering when parents get divorced.

Death

Although adults see adolescence in terms of new beginnings, adolescence is also about endings—the ending of childhood, of dependence on parents and family, and the loss of innocence. The adolescent's growing ability to handle more complex cognitive thinking also allows them to acknowledge and begin dealing with abstract concepts such as permanence, loss, and death. And for the first time, many teens must begin to acknowledge the mortality of parents, friends, and themselves.

The cognitive realization that some things are irreversible is a part of adulthood visited upon teens at different times. Some adolescents, growing up in environments where death and loss are a part of everyday experiences, develop these understandings early in life. These young people have a perception that life is short, and death is imminent, and this is part of their everyday reality. For other adolescents, this may be a time when they experience the abstract concept of death and their own mortality for the first time.

Complicating this is the reluctance of our society to acknowledge death, loss, and the mourning process as normal outcomes of life. Generally speaking, we don't handle issues involving death very well in this society. Some societies and cultures have constructed rituals for grief and mourning that better attend to the necessary processes of dealing with death. As parents, the younger we begin to help our children understand and deal with issues of death and loss, the more prepared they will be to integrate these realities into their lives as adolescents.

General Overview of Critical Issues

In this section, we have included some additional resources that address the serious concerns that parents and adolescents may face during adolescence. These resources may not include all of the topics discussed above, and they may not necessarily go into the specifics of subjects like substance abuse treatment or recognition of gang involvement. But they can, however, offer parents an overview of various issues that may arise and general suggestions for how parents can help their family and teenager survive these critical problems. Use these resources to gain an understanding of the various forces that may influence your child's adolescence. An all-inclusive guide can not only help answer your general questions but help you appreciate the magnitude of this time period. All-inclusive guides, by their very nature, don't offer in-depth information in any one area. Whenever you find you need help in a specific area, check other recommendations we have made for the topics we've identified.

We all need help in sifting through the mountain of information and advice that is available about how to raise children nowadays in our society. To help you understand and deal with the major critical issues you may face during your child's adolescence, we have divided our resources into several categories to help focus your search for answers. Resources that we highly recommend are included at the beginning of each topic's subsection and other resources we have reviewed follow those.

Remember the challenges are great, the rewards are infinite, and the goal of parenting an adolescent is to help them become an integrated member and effective person in our society. Keep abreast of the pitfalls that may lie in your child's path, know when to intercede and when to back off, and appreciate the complexities of the choices that are flaunted in your teen's face. By doing so, you will help your teenager successfully navigate their journey toward adulthood, and help preserve your confidence and trust that the path won't be too full of thorns and perils.

★★★★

Overall Rating
★★★★
Outstanding presentation of the how-tos of communication, from confronting to listening

Design, Ease Of Use
★★★★
Fast-paced, highly appealing; varied, offering both parent-teen scenarios & discussion

1–4 Stars; N/R = Not Rated

Media:
Videotape

Price:
$34.98

Principal Subject:
Critical Issues & Concerns

Publisher:
Legacy Home Video

Author:
Legacy Home Video

DRUG FREE KIDS
A Parents' Guide

 Terrific Resource For:
Parent-teen role-played scenarios concerning substance abuse issues (videotape)

 Recommended For:
Critical Issues & Concerns

Description:
This one hour videotape explores parents' concerns about adolescent substance abuse. Included within the tape's dramatic reenactments and role-playing vignettes are actors such as Jane Alexander, Ned Beatty, Melissa Gilbert, Bonnie Franklin, and others. The tape begins by listing warning signs that signal a child may be using drugs or alcohol. The message throughout is that parents have a right to "come down hard" if they suspect their child is abusing substances; the creators make the distinction between being your child's friend and being a responsible friend to your child. Various communication techniques are illustrated, along with ways to confront 3 different scenarios (when parents don't think their child is using drugs, but want to find out; when parents see warning signs, but aren't sure; when parents know, but don't know how serious it is). Parent-teen issues (parties, sex, peer pressure, curfew, school performance, etc.) are also role-played; the negative and positive elements of communication are discussed. The tape concludes by suggesting ways other groups can help—doctors, school, government, and more.

Evaluation:
Parents won't find a better videotape available that offers insight into constructive ways parents can communicate their values about substance abuse to their teen. Despite its price, many parents will receive maximum benefit from the visual-auditory components of this presentation. The numerous role-played scenarios illustrate the "dos" and "don'ts" of how to communicate as a team. Especially useful are those scenes that depict ways parents can: confront a teen, get to the underlying problem a teen faces in terms of peer pressure, discuss the effects of drugs or alcohol on sexual behavior and a teen's responsibility, and deal with parental anger and disappointment in a teen's behavior. Also illustrated are ways to redirect youth and help them learn better ways of coping with stress; this is coupled with the reminder that parents too need to look at what coping skills they are modeling. Centered on communication patterns as the key toward resolving parent-teen issues, this tape is a "must-have" for any parenting library.

Where To Find/Buy:
Bookstores, libraries, videotape dealers, or order direct by calling Total Marketing Services at 1-800-262-3822.

IV. Critical Issues & Concerns

Substance Abuse

DRUG PROOF YOUR KIDS
The Complete Guide To Education, Prevention, Intervention

Terrific Resource For:
Christian parents wanting to prevent or treat substance abuse in their teen

Recommended For:
Critical Issues & Concerns

Description:
Using a biblical approach, this 222 page book aims to educate parents on the dangers of drugs, so they can then inform their children. The 13 chapters include facts about drug abuse and alcoholism, reasons why kids take drugs or alcohol, prevention tools (parents, God, unconditional love, behavior and discipline, control, contracts, friends, etc.), intervention, choosing treatment, relapses, and more. In order to validate their points, the authors combine facts and personal narratives of parents who have dealt with these issues. They believe there are techniques parents can use to keep their kids drug-free. They discuss the mixed messages parents send with their own drug and alcohol use, and ask for changes within the family unit. A discussion leader's guide after the appendix provides guidelines for parent discussion and strategy groups. Also given is a chapter-by chapter personal study guide (about 40 pages) which invites parents to observe their lives and their children's lives in order to effectively "drug-proof" their kids.

Evaluation:
This book draws on the authors' combined experience in youth ministry. Comprehensive and complete, it provides a Christian approach to instilling drug-free values in children. Using compassion and honesty, the authors provide personal narratives, facts, and statistics to illustrate their advice. Its tone is rather confessional, and it does a fine job of personalizing the struggles many parents undergo as they deal with sources that glamorize drugs and alcohol. The chapter on "Roadblocks and Building Blocks" is helpful. It highlights specific ways parents can help their children build self-esteem in a society obsessed with materialism and "feeling good." Also well-done are the chapters on "Treatment" and "Handling Relapse." Information is provided on "wrong reasons for choosing a treatment program" and "relapse indicators" which are areas often ignored in other resources. This resource will be helpful to Christian parents concerned with finding ways to teach their children about the hazards of drug use.

Where To Find/Buy:
Bookstores, libraries, or order direct by calling 1-800-4-GOSPEL.

★★★★

Overall Rating
★★★★
Comprehensive resource for Christian parents interested in "drug-proofing" their kids

Design, Ease Of Use
★★★★
Excellent layout; can be read all the way through or accessed randomly

1–4 Stars; N/R = Not Rated

Media:
Print

Price:
$10.99

Principal Subject:
Critical Issues & Concerns

ISBN:
0830717714

Edition:
2nd (1995)

Publisher:
Regal Books (Gospel Light)

Author:
Stephen Arterburn and Jim Burns

About The Author:
(From Cover Notes)
Arterburn is the author of 17 books, and cofounder and chairman of Minirth-Meier New Life radio broadcasts. Burns is also an author, and president of the National Institute of Youth Ministry in San Clemente, CA. He also lectures about youth ministry and parenting.

IV. Critical Issues & Concerns

★★★★

Overall Rating
★★★★
Excellent resource, balanced between clinical and personal needs of families and teens

Design, Ease Of Use
★★★★
Well-referenced, easy to access for information

1–4 Stars; N/R = Not Rated

Media:
Print

Price:
$10.95

Principal Subject:
Critical Issues & Concerns

ISBN:
1562460153

Edition:
1991

Publisher:
Johnson Institute

Author:
Peter R. Cohen, M.D.

About The Author:
(From Cover Notes)
Cohen is a child and adolescent psychiatrist, medical director for Child and Adolescent Mental Health Services of Montgomery County, Maryland, and medical director for Chemical Dependence Programs at the Psychiatric Institute of Montgomery County.

Substance Abuse

HELPING YOUR CHEMICALLY DEPENDENT TEENAGER RECOVER
A Guide For Parents And Other Concerned Adults

 Recommended For:
Critical Issues & Concerns

Description:
This 139 page book provides information to parents of chemically dependent teenagers. The author believes that recovery is important for the entire family of an addicted teenager. He details the problems faced by a family during crisis intervention, treatment, and recovery, describing tasks to lead a teenager and their family throughout their transition. Cohen outlines 4 stages of recovery along with their associated tasks: "Crisis Control" (crisis identification, problem assessment, intervention, contracts), "Stability and Structure" (detoxifying and withdrawal, awareness of powerlessness and unmanageability, creating a recovery plan), "Consistency and Balance" (teenager and parental tasks), and "Attachment." Also discussed are various treatment programs (short-term, intermediate, long-term), as well as ways to help teens if they relapse. Each chapter includes information on behaviors to expect, answers to parental questions, and tasks to get through the stage. The book also includes a list of readings, an index, the 12 steps of Alcoholics Anonymous, and the 12 steps of Al-Anon.

Evaluation:
Cohen describes recovery as a lifelong process or the family, with no guarantees except a lot of hope that the family can recover together. He treats teenage chemical dependence as being distinct from the adult experience of addiction. Cohen sees helping a teenager recover from chemical dependency as a loving act, carried out by parents willing to give their child the necessary time and attention. The advice in this book is realistic and sound, giving parents the support they'll need to confront their crisis honestly and with compassion. The chapter on how parents can help themselves is especially insightful, offering parents ways to deal with the crisis without shutting off important areas of their personal lives. Cohen advocates acknowledging personal powerlessness, admitting personal shortcomings, healing, developing a relationship with a "higher power," and helping others as a means of finding personal recovery. This book is recommended for any parent dealing with chemical dependency in their family.

Where To Find/Buy:
Bookstores and libraries.

Substance Abuse

PARENTING FOR PREVENTION: HOW TO RAISE A CHILD TO SAY NO TO DRUGS AND ALCOHOL

For Parents, Teachers, And Other Concerned Adults

 Recommended For:
Critical Issues & Concerns

Description:

This 242 page book is based on the premise that teaching kids life skills/social skills will prevent alcohol use and other drug problems. The author makes it clear that this is not a book for parents whose kids are "already seriously into chemicals." Instead, it is intended for parents who want a long-range prevention program, and are willing to spend time developing "well-balanced kids in a healthy family setting." As such, 130 pages of the book are spent defining parents' and teenagers' roles along with needed skills. The book's first part cites numerous facts about drugs and drug use, and dispels "mistaken beliefs;" this is followed by "A Job Description for Parents" (prepare kids for the real world and meet their deepest human needs), and "A Job Description for Kids" (learn to accept responsibility). Part 2 describes ways to help kids develop life skills (communicating, making decisions, refusing, etc.) through modeling, reinforcement, and consistency. Part 3 is addressed to parents with alcohol/drug problems.

Evaluation:

Wilmes' no-nonsense approach and positive guidance will most likely help any parent raise a child to be a capable, well-balanced person. Hopefully, his promise that parents will "gain new insights into a whole host of everyday parenting problems as well as practical skills for handling them" will bear witness for those who follow his recommendations. The book is easy-to-read and easy-to-use, with each chapter beginning with a teen/parent scenario. The chapters on life skills are excellent and quite specific, always ending with lists of "Things to Do" and "Things to Avoid." While Chapters One and Two do specifically discuss alcohol, this book isn't a resource for parents already dealing with teenage alcohol/drug use; it is also not for parents looking for a "quick-fix" to a problem; rather it is for parents seeking a whole approach to parenting. The resource list and detailed index also make this a good reference tool. As a preventive resource, this one can't be beat due to its positive tone, realistic advice, and constructive follow-through.

Where To Find/Buy:

Bookstores, libraries, or order direct by calling Johnson Institute at 1-800-231-5165, or contacting them at 7205 Ohms Lane, Minneapolis, MN 55439

Overall Rating
★★★★
Its "Things to Do" and "Things to Avoid" help parents take proactive steps

Design, Ease Of Use
★★★★
Easy to use; short chapters with many headings, visuals, and lists; excellent index

1–4 Stars; N/R = Not Rated

Media:
Print

Price:
$13.95

Principal Subject:
Critical Issues & Concerns

ISBN:
0935908463

Edition:
2nd (1995)

Publisher:
Johnson Institute

Author:
David J. Wilmes

About The Author:
(From Cover Notes)
Wilmes is a father of two sons and professional counselor

IV. Critical Issues & Concerns

Overall Rating
★★★★
Useful advice and helpful solutions; honest approach to the difficulties of peer pressure

Design, Ease Of Use
★★★★
Well organized, good use of subheadings, italics, ample index

1–4 Stars; N/R = Not Rated

Media:
Print

Price:
$14.95

Principal Subject:
Critical Issues & Concerns

ISBN:
1557043183

Edition:
2nd (1998)

Publisher:
Newmarket Press

Author:
Robert Schwebel, Ph.D.

**About The Author:
(From Cover Notes)**
Schwebel, with a doctorate in clinical psychology, has worked for 25+ years in preventing and treating tobacco, alcohol, and other drug problems. He has worked in private practice and in the public sector, developing drug treatment programs for various agencies.

Substance Abuse

SAYING NO IS NOT ENOUGH
Helping Your Kids Make Wise Decisions About Alcohol, Tobacco, And Other Drugs—A Guide For Parents Of Children Ages 3 Through 19

 Recommended For:
Critical Issues & Concerns

Description:
This 288 page guide details ways to raise drug-free kids. It includes advice, stories, and sample dialogues. The author believes that parents should: start when children are young; create a climate for communication; show by example how children can meet their own needs without drugs; help kids learn to resist peer pressure; establish give-and-take discussions with teens; stay alert for potential drug problems; and know how to respond to problems. New changes in the second edition include: recommendations to parents on discussing their own use of substances; what to do about non-voluntary drug testing; a chapter on tobacco; more information on marijuana; how to deal with dishonesty in children, especially adolescents; and interventions for kids already abusing substances. Part Two, of three parts, is specifically written for parents of teens and focuses on how to open dialogues with teens, listen to each other, and make valid agreements. The book includes an introduction by Dr. Spock and an index.

Evaluation:
This book deals honestly with the importance of peer pressure in the lives of children. Rather than taking a harsh stance, it advocates dealing compassionately with the pressures kids face, and understanding that saying "no" is the hardest thing to do when kids are in peer group situations. The book provides information on drug use, abuse, and dependence. The author asks parents to examine their own beliefs so that they can understand the messages they send their kids. He discusses ways to strengthen children's thinking processes from a young age so they can make responsible decisions later on. This guide also gives parents a helpful overview of major drugs along with warning signs of dependence. The analyses of the sample dialogues are helpful and captures many parent-teen scenarios. Providing many insights on how to empower the family, Schwebel understands the trials facing parents and teens, and has provided a great resource for them, offering a step-by-step program for success in fighting the drug battle.

Where To Find/Buy:
Bookstores, libraries, or order direct by calling 1-800-669-3903, or (212) 832-3575, or by contacting Newmarket Press at 18 East 48th Street, New York, NY 10017.

Substance Abuse

SAY NO! TO DRUGS
A Parent's Guide To Teaching Your Kids How To Grow Up Without Drugs And Alcohol

 Recommended For:
Critical Issues & Concerns

Description:

Part of the Good Foundation series, this 45 minute videotape recommends that "talking to your kids honestly and often about the realities of drug or alcohol use can help shape proper attitudes at an early age." To that end, the tape combines professional advice from various substance abuse prevention organizations (National Federation of Parents for Drug-Free Youth, PRIDE, etc.) and staged vignettes of a family dealing with concerns and questions from their teenagers. Based on understanding adolescents' underlying motives and consequent behavior (to fit in, appear grown up, etc.), the tape then offers parents how-tos for dealing with various situations, primarily focused on teaching children how to handle peer pressure. Sample dos and don'ts are included for parent-teen conversations and reasons not to take drugs or drink. Also provided are a list of substance abuse warning signs, ten ways to teach children how to say "no," contact information for support organizations, and a suggested reading list.

Evaluation:

The production quality of this video is rather amateurish, and the family scenes are rehearsed and staged. But parents will find its message succinct and direct. The tape's bottom line is that parent-teen communication is the key to preventing problems. It illustrates numerous ways parents can convince their child about the dangers of substances without sounding preachy, and within normal daily family chatter. It supports the fact that parents must educate themselves, take a firm stand about drugs and alcohol, and enforce their rights (search of children's rooms), but also gently asks parents to allow children to make informed decisions, and take responsibility for their actions. Beneficial to many parents will be the tape's "Ten Ways to Say 'No'." Here, parents are given a quick rundown of alternatives children can use to get out of sticky situations with their peers, such as, sounding like a "broken record," changing the subject, using reverse peer pressure, and more. Useful for engaging parents in productive conversations with their teen about peer influence and substances, this tape, although stale, offers some good advice.

Where To Find/Buy:

Bookstores, libraries, video dealers, or order direct by calling Library Video Company at 1-800-843-3620 or (610) 645-4000.

Overall Rating
★★★★
Prevention tips based on parent ed, parent-teen communications, firm expectations

Design, Ease Of Use
★★★
Flows well, many problem-solving examples through (rather stale) family vignettes

1–4 Stars; N/R = Not Rated

Media:
Videotape

Price:
$19.95

Principal Subject:
Critical Issues & Concerns

ISBN:
1557590176

Edition:
1986

Publisher:
Video West

Author:
Video West

IV. Critical Issues & Concerns

Overall Rating
★★★★
Realistic approach to and advocacy for assessment, treatment, and aftercare transitions

Design, Ease Of Use
★★
Easily read; indented headings get lost, need bolder highlights; good chap. summaries

1–4 Stars; N/R = Not Rated

Media:
Print

Price:
$12.95

Principal Subject:
Critical Issues & Concerns

ISBN:
1880197022

Edition:
1992

Publisher:
Gylantic Publishing Company

Author:
Shelly Marshall

About The Author:
(From Cover Notes)
A graduate of Metropolitan State College in Denver with a B.S. in Human Services with a speciality in Drugs and Alcohol, Marshall is the best selling author of *Day By Day and Young, Sober and Free*. She also has a Th.B. degree in counseling.

Substance Abuse

TEENAGE ADDICTS CAN RECOVER
Treating The Addict, Not The Addiction

Description:

Teenage Addicts Can Recover analyzes the current state of understanding and treatment of the addicted adolescent. The author directs her concerns to both parents and recovery personnel in the field of teenage addiction. Speaking as a recovering drug and alcohol addict and the mother of a recovering drug and alcohol addict, Marshall uses concise language to subscribe parents to a model of recovery that she believes offers teens a successful recovery. Section One covers the assessment phase of addiction. Four chapters in this section identify the troubled teen, explain the parents' role in treatment and recovery, answer questions about teenage drug addiction, and discuss professionals' prejudices about teenage addicts. Section Two discusses qualities of treatment programs that work. The three chapters in this section outline the problems of assessment and treatment, expectations and goals of treatment, and specific procedures for dealing with young people. Section Three analyzes the transition after recovery-"aftercare."

Evaluation:

Easily read, this book examines treatment programs for teenage addicts. The author, with her considerable experience in treating and studying teenage addicts, examines such issues as "Is alcoholism really a psychological problem, a family problem or a disease?" With honesty and support, Marshall presents the challenges parents face while seeking the best recovery help possible for their addicted adolescent. She offers the same clear-eyed advice to professionals dealing with addicted teenagers, advising them to examine everything from their practices in hiring staff to the personal relationship existing between patient and therapist. The only real drawback of this book might be the author's overt touting of the AA 12 step program; some people might be put off with its religious tone, although her reasoning is too compelling to be overruled. As a parent supporting other parents seeking help their children deserve, her concern shines through, making this a good resource for parents and administrators.

Where To Find/Buy:

Bookstores, libraries, or order direct by calling (303) 797-6093.

Substance Abuse

NATIONAL CLEARINGHOUSE FOR ALCOHOL AND DRUG INFORMATION

Description:

Presented by the Substance Abuse and Mental Health Services Administration (SAMHSA), this site offers features for both professionals and parents. Areas for parents include: "Publications/ Catalog," "Alcohol & Drug Facts," and "Searchable Databases;" the homepage also accesses "Research & Statistics" on substance abuse. "Publications" can be sorted by audience (college students, community coalitions, family & friends, youth & teens, etc.) or subject (specific drug names, general substance abuse fact sheets, etc.); "Quick Docs" and an online guide—"Straight Facts About Drugs and Alcohol" are also available within "Publications" with various charts, bulleted tips, and resources along with information on specific drugs (from alcohol and cocaine to nicotine and opiates/ narcotics), how to determine if someone has a problem, how to get help, and more. "Alcohol & Drug Facts" are available both through the homepage and through "Publications." The site hosts 11 different search engines, one of which offers 6 criteria (private/public-owned, services, type of care, type of payment, etc.) for locating treatment and prevention programs.

Evaluation:

One aspect of this site that makes it novel is its search capabilities. Being able to conduct searches based on subject or audience will help parents narrow the site's field of reference for their specific needs. In particular, SAMHSA's search facility for finding prevention and treatment programs fills the void left by other resources that emphasize how to detect substance abuse, but then offer no assistance on where to get help. The search amounts to only names and contact information, but this is a start for many needy families. The main problem we found with the site was its organization. The headings on its homepage seem obvious, until you retrace your steps to find the information again. Information is buried deep and one can become lost trying to relocate given articles or tips. The facts and publications are useful, and the search engine will meet many parents' personal criteria making this site a definite stop. But parents should keep an eye on where they find the information they need, so their return trip will be smoother.

Where To Find/Buy:

On the Internet at the URL: http://www.health.org/.

Overall Rating
★★★★
Offers facts on substance abuse, search engine for finding prevention/treatment programs

Design, Ease Of Use
★
"Titles" on homepage offer unclear path when retracing contents; search facilities good

1–4 Stars; N/R = Not Rated

Media:
Internet

Principal Subject:
Critical Issues & Concerns

Internet URL:
http://www.health.org/

IV. Critical Issues & Concerns

★ ★ ★

Overall Rating
★ ★ ★
Focuses mainly on diagnosis, intervention/confrontation, not treatment or recovery

Design, Ease Of Use
★ ★ ★ ★
Bulleted highlights, bold headings, sample contracts, checklists, questionnaires, etc.

1–4 Stars; N/R = Not Rated

Media:
Print

Price:
$12.95

Principal Subject:
Critical Issues & Concerns

ISBN:
0935908420

Edition:
2nd (1996)

Publisher:
Johnson Institute

Author:
Dick Schaefer

About The Author:
(From Cover Notes)
Dick Schaefer is Director of the Touch Love Center in Fargo, North Dakota. He is a licensed Addiction Counselor and holds a Master's Degree. He has worked with chemically dependent teenagers for nearly 30 years.

Substance Abuse

CHOICES & CONSEQUENCES
What To Do When A Teenager Uses Alcohol/Drugs

Description:
Schaefer has worked with chemically dependent teenagers for over 30 years. He reasons that "it takes a system to crack a system" and presents a course of action for parents to take in dealing with their chemically dependent teenagers. He explains why kids use alcohol and drugs, the addiction process, and the stages of the disease of addiction. In addition, he discusses what the tasks and self-esteem needs are for adolescents: the need to determine their own vocation, to establish their own values, to explore their own sexuality, and to establish their authority; these unfulfilled needs for addicted youths are then linked to their treatment process so that they can take responsibility for and pride in their own recovery. Other topics discussed in this book include: how to intervene in an addicted person's life, the professional's role in confrontation, and ways of reintegrating the adolescent into sobriety. Schaefer includes salient facts and studies to back up his beliefs in the course of treatment he prescribes.

Evaluation:
Schaefer repeatedly states that the most important thing that young people need to be aware of is that they are responsible for their choices and their own recovery. From ascertaining that the teenager is dependent on drugs to helping them reenter the world sober and in control of their lives, Schaefer provides a step-by-step approach which many will find invaluable. Parents will find numerous tips for helping their child without taking on the added responsibility of their child's recovery. The chapter on confrontation is effective giving advice on setting reasonable limits and ways of taking back the home environment. Schaefer also discusses the four Cs of confrontation: choices, consequences, contracts, and control. Contracts offer a good vehicle for teenagers to take responsibility for themselves, giving them some control over their environment, while helping them learn to make good choices. This book is a great resource for parents needing practical step-by-step help that works for the good of the whole family.

Where To Find/Buy:
Bookstores, libraries, or order direct by calling 1-800-231-5165 or (612) 831-1630, or by contacting Johnson Institute, 7205 Ohms Lane, Minneapolis, MN 55439-2159.

IV. Critical Issues & Concerns

Substance Abuse

DRUGS AND KIDS
How Parents Can Keep Them Apart

Description:

Relying on his experience as a chemical dependency counselor, the author highlights ways of keeping kids off drugs in this 258 page book. He details what parents can do if they find out their children are on drugs, along with tips on alternative ways of making them feel positive about themselves. Somdahl emphasizes the idea of the family as a team, with the parent being the "key player" in the life of the adolescent; he then highlights attributes of a winning team and those of a losing team. The 7 chapters in the book deal with the parents' roles as key players, early intervention and denial, enabling factors, the evaluation process of substance abuse, addiction treatment and the benefits of the recovery process, family communication, and key points in parenting to help parents deal more effectively with their children. The book also contains a list of recommended reading, a list of other resources, and an index.

Evaluation:

Somdahl's commitment to keeping kids off drugs is obvious throughout the book as he provides solid information on how parents can keep kids away from the lure of drugs. He stresses the importance of families working together as teams, taking responsibility for their roles as well as helping each other succeed in life. He then describes the necessary qualities involved with being a key player: experience and education, the ability to play under any circumstances, commitment, unity, faith, and hope. Somdahl recommends that parents be active in their children's lives. Doing so, he believes, invites kids to feel part of the family group, joined together in a sense of team spirit, thus helping them not engage in poor peer groups involved with substances. Chapter Five is particularly helpful. It presents tips for good communication (listen, observe, and respond), ways to implement family agreements to keep kids off drugs, and 12 steps to discussing drugs. Parents are given warning signs to be aware of in this book, as well as many helpful communication tips.

Where To Find/Buy:

Bookstores, libraries, or order direct by calling 1-800-644-DIMI (3464).

Overall Rating
★★★
Good general information with examples of what kids need from their parents

Design, Ease Of Use
★★★★
Large print; bulleted information and bold subheadings; can be read randomly

1–4 Stars; N/R = Not Rated

Media:
Print

Price:
$14.95

Principal Subject:
Critical Issues & Concerns

ISBN:
0931625300

Edition:
1996

Publisher:
Dimi Press

Author:
Gary L. Somdahl

About The Author:
(From Cover Notes)
Somdahl is a licensed Youth Chemical Dependency Counselor with the Carondelet Behavioral Health Center of Pasco, Washington, a father, and a trainer of parents on the subject of keeping kids off drugs. He lives in Richland, Washington.

IV. Critical Issues & Concerns

Overall Rating
★★★
This straightforward, informative guide enables parents to deal with teenagers' issues

Design, Ease Of Use
★★★
Sometimes a bit wordy; excellent use of space and logical progression

1–4 Stars; N/R = Not Rated

Media:
Print

Price:
$9.95

Principal Subject:
Critical Issues & Concerns

ISBN:
0830625372

Edition:
1993

Publisher:
Human Services Institute/Tab Books (McGraw-Hill)

Author:
Belinda Terro Mooney, A.C.S.W., C.A.C.

About The Author:
(From Cover Notes)
Mooney is developer and former director of the Adolescent Dual Diagnosis Unit at Laurel Heights Hospital in Atlanta. She is currently a private consultant who conducts training workshops nationwide.

Substance Abuse

LEAVE ME ALONE!
Helping Your Troubled Teenager

Description:

This is a resource for parents of kids who have serious problems with chemical dependency and an associated psychiatric disorder. Applying the term "dual diagnosis," the author explains in her 176 page, 9 chapter book exactly what this concept means and how it's diagnosed. Chapter One explains dual diagnosis, while the second offers some real-life examples and how these children's problems evolved. The third chapter describes parents' viewpoints, and the fourth defines "normal adolescence." Chapters Five and Six delve deeply into the issues of chemical dependency, and psychiatric and emotional problems. Chapters Seven, Eight, and Nine advise parents about getting help for their child, describe the typical family problem of codependency, and ways to let go after the problems are (or aren't) solved. Each chapter concludes with a summary and list of exercises "to help you understand." Appendices include questions parents can answer to help them realize the situations facing their child.

Evaluation:

For parents who are prepared to address the fact that their child may have a serious dependency and psychiatric problem, this book will be a big help in understanding causes and treatments. Void of humor, this book offers straightforward facts and advice. The author takes a no-tolerance position on alcohol use by teenagers, and offers strict guidelines to keep families emotionally and spiritually healthy. The information is very comprehensive, especially in the psychiatric disorders chapter, addressing many areas from anxiety to bulimia. Although the book is generally clear and readable, the author's use of academic language sometimes may leave the lay person confused. The major drawback to any book of this sort is that adults may inappropriately diagnose their child as having or not having a chemical problem or psychiatric disorder. As always, what some consider normal teen behavior might be considered a form of substance abuse by others. Overall, this is an excellent resource, novel in its comprehensive approach at looking at alternative roots of chemical dependency problems.

Where To Find/Buy:

Bookstores and libraries.

Substance Abuse

TEEN ADDICTION
Formerly titled Happy Daze

Description:

The author, a faculty member of the Suzanne Somers Institute for the Effects of Addictions on Families (in Palm Springs, CA) draws on her experience as a "recognized authority" on adolescent addictions to provide information for parents, teachers, and counselors of chemically dependent teens. This 178 page reference uses case studies, facts, and research results to give information on the nature and treatment of addiction. Topics discussed include: the beginnings and progression of dependency, development (normal adolescent vs. the dependent adolescent), children of alcoholics, ways that adolescents are enabled, adolescents in recovery, the family in recovery, and ways community and families are working toward establishing "healthy perspectives." Case studies highlight the author's points and the author's endeavor to shorten the road to recovery for dependent teens and their families. The book includes a bibliography, and a chapter which discusses suggested resources and support organizations.

Evaluation:

Though the volume of case studies are overwhelming at times, this book manages to provide ample advice on how to identify and help a chemically addicted teenager. It provides a general overview of the problem of teen addiction and treatment with an empathetic and down-to-earth voice. The chapter on "The Progression of Dependency" is helpful with its explanation of the addict's rationale along with how the disease of dependency progresses. The chapter on "The Dependent Adolescent" is also insightful offering parents narrative benchmarks to determine whether or not their teen's behavior and perspectives are "normal" teenage fare, or something to be concerned about. The print is tiny, but the author has done a fine job capturing the book's contents with bold, succinct captions; the case studies are italicized to differentiate them from the author's points. However, there are other, more in-depth resources available on the subject of teen addiction, and this book would make a great companion to those.

Where To Find/Buy:

Bookstores and libraries.

Overall Rating
★★★
Useful information which is overwhelmed by case studies at times

Design, Ease Of Use
★★★
Best when read all the way through; case studies italicized; index is necessary

1–4 Stars; N/R = Not Rated

Media:
Print

Price:
$4.99

Principal Subject:
Critical Issues & Concerns

ISBN:
0345362829

Edition:
1994

Publisher:
Ballantine Books (Random House)

Author:
Marti Heuer

**About The Author:
(From Cover Notes)**
Heuer has designed and implemented adolescent and family mental health and addiction treatment programs throughout the Midwest and California. She also lectures and provides training seminars on adolescent addictions and family issues pertaining to addictions.

IV. Critical Issues & Concerns

Overall Rating
★★
Great coverage of substance abuse prevention measures, recognition signs, and more

Design, Ease Of Use
★★★★
Well-organized, w/ bullets, tables of info; excellent graphics of drugs/paraphernalia

1–4 Stars; N/R = Not Rated

Media:
Internet

Principal Subject:
Critical Issues & Concerns

Publisher:
U.S. Department of Education

Internet URL:
http://www.health.org/pubs/
parguide/index.htm

Substance Abuse

GROWING UP DRUG FREE (INTERNET)
A Parent's Guide To Prevention

Description:

Divided into eight "chapters," this website offers online the U.S. Department of Education's free publication by the same name. Chapter titles include: "What Parents Can Do" (general parental guidelines to communicate rules and expectations regarding alcohol and drugs); "Applying the Principles" (from preschoolers to high school students; suggested activities for each age group are included); "What to do if Your Child is Using Drugs" (symptoms, pictures of paraphernalia, etc.); "Getting Involved" (ideas for forming school, community, and parent support groups); "Making It Work" (an example of how parents and community volunteers made a difference); "Specific Drugs and their Effects" (alcohol, tobacco, cannabis, inhalants, cocaine, stimulants, depressants, hallucinogens, narcotics, designer drugs; tables outline drug type, slang street terms, appearance, how used); "Resources" (5 page list of various agencies/ organizations, book lists, videos for more help); and "References" (chapter-by-chapter bibliography).

Evaluation:

Parents, either those worried about how to avoid the dangers of substance abuse, or those wondering if their teen is already involved, can get a wealth of information here. Especially useful sections are "Applying the Principles," "What to do if Your Child is Using Drugs," and "Specific Drugs and their Effects." Most sites barely touch on offering ways to prevent substance abuse. The DOE's guide, however, offers specific and comprehensive strategies for teaching young children from age 3 and up refusal, decision-making, and interpersonal skills. The emphasis throughout and the suggested activities offered build on children's self-confidence. Coupling this with teaching children about the ills of alcohol and other drugs makes for a dynamite package. Pictures and detailed descriptions are provided of drugs and drug equipment along with a substantial list of symptoms. Areas not covered include intervention, treatment, and recovery. This guide does a fine job of offering education, support, and guidance.

Where To Find/Buy:

On the Internet at the URL: http://www.health.org/pubs/parguide/ index.htm. The publication can also be received by calling 1-800-624-0100 (in the Washington, DC area, call 732-3627).

Substance Abuse

HOW TO TELL IF YOUR KIDS ARE USING DRUGS

Description:

Asking parents to confront the statistics, Dimoff and Carper point out that most adolescents in our society are experimenting with drugs and alcohol. With that as a premise, they provide information on the following: the four stages of drug abuse and the most common types of drugs used at each stage; a listing of the major drug categories (signs of use, typical forms, street names); discussion of the reasons why kids use drugs; red flags signaling drug use; specific advice on how to confront a child who's using drugs, and how to create and promote a drug-free home environment. The sections on "red flags" include discussions on changes in personality, changes in appearance, changes in activities and habits, drug paraphernalia, and legal problems. This 152 page book also includes a chapter on denial and enabling, and the ways in which parents condone their children's drug use by not forcing them to confront the problem. It also covers user denial, providing information on how to deal with both forms effectively.

Evaluation:

Their book starts with the chilling premise of, "Have your children tried drugs? In all likelihood, yes." The authors then set out to help parents prevent their children from becoming part of the drug abuse statistics. Believing it's never too early to talk to kids about drugs, they provide age specific topics for discussion. The chapters on "red flags" are very well-done. They discuss the warning signs and implications of drug use. These sections offer more in-depth descriptions than most other resources on this subject. The chapter on how to help is also useful. It aids parents in determining whether or not their child is experimenting with illegal substances, and provides information on how to intervene (create a united front, talk with others, decide on a goal, identify likely defenses, talk to your child only when he or she is not high, etc.). Aimed at recognizing the signs of drug use and intervening with drug abuse, this resource provides concrete advice. But parents will need other resources to sort out treatment programs and aftercare.

Where To Find/Buy:

Bookstores and libraries.

Overall Rating
★★
Good guide for recognizing the signs of drug use; little info on treatment & recovery

Design, Ease Of Use
★★★★
To the point and precise; easily referenced with bold subheadings, lists of highlights

---

1–4 Stars; N/R = Not Rated

Media:
Print

Price:
$9.95

Principal Subject:
Critical Issues & Concerns

ISBN:
0816029164

Edition:
1992

Publisher:
Facts on File

Author:
Timothy Dimoff and Steve Carper

**About The Author:
(From Cover Notes)**
Dimoff is a former narcotics detective and the president of Substance Abuse Counseling Services in Tallmadge, Ohio. Carper is an experienced freelance writer.

IV. Critical Issues & Concerns

Overall Rating
★★
Unrealistic advice ignores adolescent struggles, and gives this book little credence

Design, Ease Of Use
★★★★
Easy to read format with detailed TOC, ample index, list of support orgs and resources

1–4 Stars; N/R = Not Rated

Media:
Print

Price:
$13.95

Principal Subject:
Critical Issues & Concerns

ISBN:
1571456252

Edition:
1998

Publisher:
Laurel Glen Publishing

Author:
Glen Levant

About The Author:
(From Cover Notes)
Glen Levant is the president and founding director of D.A.R.E. America Worldwide.

Substance Abuse

KEEPING KIDS DRUG FREE
D.A.R.E. Official Parent's Guide

Description:
Stating that "preteens generally get their first exposure to drugs from other kids, peers and playmates," this book attempts to inform parents about things they can do to "drug proof" their children. Part One focuses on how kids get into trouble with drugs, including discussions of how parents can build children's self-esteem, the media's portrayal of drugs, violence in the home and community. Part Two provides drug information: spotting the signs and symptoms of drug use, discussion of alcohol and tobacco—the "gateway drugs," marijuana, inhalants, steroids, illegal stimulants (cocaine, crack, meth), and "designer drugs" (heroin, hallucinogens). Part Three discusses problem-solving techniques and strategies for raising drug-free kids. The book includes an index and appendices which consist of a glossary of drug terms and a resource guide for parents. Chapter notes are also provided. Within the text are blocked vignettes containing teens' and preteens "stories" and their decisions about substance use.

Evaluation:
This book attempts to pack too much information on various subjects (drug and alcohol use and abuse, gangs, parenting techniques, etc.) into its 276 pages, and loses coherence as a result. It also gives unrealistic advice, such as its list of "Ways To Say No," which fails to take into account the nature of peer pressure. It asks kids to step outside their safety zone at a time when they identify more with their peers than with their family, and at a time when "Just Say No" has become a cliche for many young people. The book's facts and figures are accurate, and it certainly gives parents information on how to drug proof their kids. But the advice is often one-dimensional, showing little compassion for the adolescent. The "tough love" policy works up to a point, but adolescents are individuals, and one approach will not work for every child. Other books on this subject provide more realistic and compassionate approaches to teaching adolescents about the perils of drug use and abuse. We suggest these resources over this one.

Where To Find/Buy:
Bookstores, libraries, or order direct by calling 1-800-284-3580.

Substance Abuse

OUR CHILDREN ARE ALCOHOLICS
Coping With Children Who Have Addictions

Description:

Sally and David B. wrote this book to help families deal honestly with the problem of alcoholism, or as they further explain, "addictive disease." More specifically, it is written for parents of alcoholic children. They advocate 12-step programs such as Al-Anon, which is mainly composed of partners, spouses and grown children of alcoholics. These programs, say the authors, discuss ways parents can combat the feelings of fear, shame, anger and grief by learning to "detach with love" from their child. Part One of this 174 page book chronicles the authors' personal struggle with their four children's alcoholism. It includes the children's perspectives, as well as those of the authors. Part Two discusses addictive disease and its effect on families. Part Three presents stories by parents and their addicted children. The children range in age from teenagers to middle-aged adults. Part Four concludes with a bibliography, a list of community resources, suggested audiovisuals, catalogs, and a glossary.

Evaluation:

This is an excellent resource for parents already involved in or interested in beginning 12-step programs to help deal with alcoholism in their family. The authors relate their personal and moving account as they painfully discover that all four of their children had become addicted to alcohol and/or drugs. This helps provide powerful testimony to the authors' belief that 12-step programs work. Throughout the book, they stress the importance of parents "detaching with love," the process by which parents learn to live their lives with joy in the face of their children's suffering. For example, Sally B. struggled with her own drinking problem for decades before getting help, and had to work hard to let go of the guilt and fear in her life. The section on addictive disease is especially helpful with its information on the genetic and socio-cultural factors of addictive disease. The authors' story adds power and humanity to the facts, and the advice they give will help parents who are suffering under similar circumstances.

Where To Find/Buy:

Bookstores, libraries, or order direct by calling 1-800-557-9867.

Overall Rating
★★
Highly personal account of a family's struggle with alcoholism

Design, Ease Of Use
★★★★
Easy to read; accessible, bold subheadings

1–4 Stars; N/R = Not Rated

Media:
Print

Price:
$13.95

Principal Subject:
Critical Issues & Concerns

ISBN:
1888461020

Edition:
1997

Publisher:
IsleWest Publishing (Carlisle Communications)

Author:
Sally and David B. (anonymous)

About The Author:
(From Cover Notes)
Sally and David B. wrote this book to "provide relief and reassurance for beleaguered parent of alcoholics and addicts." They wish to remain anonymous in accordance of Al-Anon tradition.

IV. Critical Issues & Concerns

Overall Rating
★★
Provides overview of the problem of addiction with no in-depth treatment

Design, Ease Of Use
★★
Good bold headings, inset blocks of highlighted info; brief index, general TOC

1–4 Stars; N/R = Not Rated

Media:
Print

Price:
$19.95

Principal Subject:
Critical Issues & Concerns

ISBN:
0894909150

Edition:
1997

Publisher:
Enslow Publishers

Author:
Miriam Smith McLaughlin & Sandra Peyser Hazouri

About The Author:
(From Cover Notes)
Miriam Smith McLaughlin and Sandra Peyser Hazouri are the co-authors of several educational books They are nationally recognized trainers in the areas of families, substance abuse, grief and loss, and service learning.

Substance Abuse

ADDICTION: THE HIGH THAT BRINGS YOU DOWN

Description:
Assuming the reader has little knowledge of the subject matter, this 104 page resource outlines the basics of addiction. The book's six chapters: highlight the differences between healthy families and addicts' families, discuss how families work as systems, provide information on the "disease of addiction," and discuss roles family members take on when one of them is an addict. There are also chapters which discuss what to do when the teenager is the addict and how to treat the family affected by addiction. The authors also provide insight into children's roles within the family hierarchy, stating that the most common roles for children are those of scapegoat, "hero child," "lost child," "mascot child," and that of "chief enabler." A chapter on "Help for Addicts' Families" provides general information on resources available in schools, in the community, in the form of support groups, and within the medical community in the form of intervention. A list of recommended further reading is included.

Evaluation:
This book never strays from the general. Its co-authors are "nationally recognized" trainers in the areas of families and substance abuse, and the book has the feel of a seminar for teenagers. Parents will find that, at best, it is a beginning guide on how to determine whether your family might be experiencing a problem with drug abuse. The section on family dynamics is well done. It defines the family as a system, and when one family member is unable to do their part, the other members must adjust in order to keep the family going. In a family with an addict, change is not allowed since any shift in the family structure destroys the tenuous balance. Children, then, assume certain coping mechanisms to survive in this otherwise impossible situation. *Addiction* provides clear, easy-to-understand perspectives on what it means to be a member of a family where someone is an addict. It will be a bit too simplistic for most people, but is useful when used in conjunction with other more detailed references.

Where To Find/Buy:
Bookstores and libraries.

Substance Abuse

DESPERATE PRETENDERS

Description:

In her book, Cantrell reveals deep, dark secrets of her family's life with a teenage drug and alcohol abuser. The story is written in first person as she opens pages of her diary. Cantrell, herself, grew up in a dysfunctional home with an abusive, alcoholic father as well as an alcoholic grandfather. She married a verbally abusive alcoholic and two of her sons became alcohol and drug abusers. Her story in *Desperate Pretenders* is about her second son, Danny. Cantrell describes her son's first experiences with drugs, cigarettes, and alcohol in the 7th and 8th grades, through the full grips of his 3-year addiction (including expulsion from one school after another, being unable to keep jobs, chronic lying, running away, arrest for DUI and subsequent jail time, parental verbal abuse, and unsuccessful participation in numerous treatment programs). Cantrell shows that she played the role of enabler and rescuer, giving Danny numerous chances, wanting to believe his lies that he will change, while struggling to keep the family together. Their seemingly hopeless situation is resolved as Danny succeeds through a program called "Straight."

Evaluation:

This book offers understanding to parents who are struggling with a child addicted to drugs and alcohol. Frustrated parents in these circumstances will no doubt see themselves in this book, as addiction strikes each victim (the abuser and his or her family) with similar effects. Although it may be of little consolation to the parent entrenched in the addiction cycle to know that someone else's child has gone through the destructive effects of drugs and alcohol, the book does offer hope. It is recommended reading for hurting parents, as they likely can see parts of their lives reflected in Cantrell's and be able to draw from her experiences. The descriptions of the family's countless failed attempts to rehabilitate Danny climaxes with their ultimate success, not without setbacks, through the program "Straight," with Danny later even helping a newcomer to the program. Although it must be read cover-to-cover, this 111 page book may give the reader renewed hope.

Where To Find/Buy:

Bookstores and libraries.

Overall Rating
★★
A very honest, revealing story about the cycle and destructiveness of alcohol/drug abuse

Design, Ease Of Use
★★
Written like a novel, the story flows well, but must be read cover-to-cover

1–4 Stars; N/R = Not Rated

Media:
Print

Principal Subject:
Critical Issues & Concerns

ISBN:
1878951041

Edition:
1990

Publisher:
Autumn House Publishing Company

Author:
Elaine Cantrell

About The Author: (From Cover Notes)
Cantrell is the mother of four children, two of whom were drug and alcohol abusers. Her book chronicles her family's struggles with her son Danny.

IV. Critical Issues & Concerns

Overall Rating
★★
Good general information, but very generic; good list of resources

Design, Ease Of Use
★★
Sidebar titles; eye-catching w/colorful photos/illustrations; no TOC or index

1–4 Stars; N/R = Not Rated

Media:
Print

Price:
FREE

Principal Subject:
Critical Issues & Concerns

Publisher:
U.S. Department of Education

Author:
U.S. Department of Education

Substance Abuse

GROWING UP DRUG FREE (PRINT)
A Parent's Guide To Prevention

Description:
This book is a general reference which details steps parents can take to educate their kids about the harmful effects of drugs. The following topics are discussed within the guide's 52 pages: what parents can do to educate and communicate with their children about drugs and their harmful effects, ways to apply the principles, what to do if a child is using drugs, how to get involved in school and community programs, a list of specific drugs and their effects, along with a list of resources and references. "Applying the Principles" includes a K–12 guide to educating kids about the effects of drugs and alcohol, along with a list of things children should understand by the end of grades 3, 6, 9 and 12, along with a list of suggested activities for each age group. There are no table of contents or index.

Evaluation:
The DOE's guide offers specific and comprehensive strategies for teaching young children from age 3 and up refusal, decision-making, and interpersonal skills. The emphasis throughout and the suggested activities offered build on children's self-confidence. Coupling this with teaching children about the ills of alcohol and other drugs makes for a dynamite package. Pictures and detailed descriptions are provided of drugs and drug equipment along with a substantial list of symptoms. The checklist of things a child should know at different stages of their development is particularly helpful, as are the communication tips in each section. Especially useful sections are "Applying the Principles," "What to do if Your Child is Using Drugs," and "Specific Drugs and their Effects." Areas not covered include intervention strategies, treatment options, and recovery. Offering education, support, and guidance, this guide is a good general resource, it's free, but should be used with more detailed resources on the same subject.

Where To Find/Buy:
Bookstores, libraries, or order direct by calling 1-800-624-0100, or by contacting Growing Up Drug Free, Pueblo, CO 81009, or National Clearinghouse for Alcohol and Drug Information, P. O. Box 2345, Rockville MD 20852.

Substance Abuse

NATIONAL INSTITUTE ON DRUG ABUSE (NIDA)

Description:

Stating that the National Institute on Drug Abuse "supports over 85% of the world's research on the health aspects of drug abuse and addiction," their website features the agency's "capsules," "Infofax," "publications," and "research reports." The site contains options for professionals with two sections addressing parents' needs—"Publications" and "Information on Drugs of Abuse." "Publications" offers NIDA's online guide "Preventing Drug Use Among Children and Adolescents" which lists various prevention principles ("Prevention programs should target all forms of drug abuse"), risk factors associated with abuse, community tips for preventing drug abuse, descriptions of "research-based drug abuse prevention programs" (10), and more. Also available is NIDA's brochure "Facts About Marijuana" using a Q and A format. "Information on Drugs of Abuse" links the visitor to NIDA's information bank with one page fact sheets available on various substances along with a chart listing common drugs, street names, medical uses, etc.

Evaluation:

What NIDA's website lacks in visual interest, they make up for in their outlay of facts. Worried parents will find ample information here to help take notice of warning signs involved with substance abuse. The brochure addressing marijuana use and symptoms, and the drug-specific "Capsules" and "Infofax" offer basic information. Unusual features include the half page descriptions on the site's chosen drug abuse prevention programs, and the chart listing common drugs. Rather disappointing, however, was NIDA's online guide of "Preventing Drug Use." It's not clear whether this guide is intended for parents, educators, or community leaders, but its overall messages are broad and inconclusive. For example, when discussing risk factors, NIDA states that children move from using legal substances to illegal drugs, "but it cannot be said that smoking and drinking at young ages are the cause of later drug use." Use this website for quick facts about particular drugs, but use other sources for specific prevention and treatment advice.

Where To Find/Buy:

On the Internet at the URL: http://www.nida.nih.gov/.

Overall Rating
★★
Offers basic facts on specific drugs through one page fact sheets, online publications

Design, Ease Of Use
★★
Visually uninteresting; navigation somewhat awkward, visitors likely to get lost

1–4 Stars; N/R = Not Rated

Media:
Internet

Principal Subject:
Critical Issues & Concerns

Publisher:
National Institute On Drug Abuse

Internet URL:
http://www.nida.nih.gov/

IV. Critical Issues & Concerns

Overall Rating

★★

Logical, sensible discussion of blood alcohol levels, abstinence, but little direct advice

Design, Ease Of Use

★★

Straightforward TOC, lack of index or support organizations, can be accessed randomly

1–4 Stars; N/R = Not Rated

Media:
Print

Price:
$16.95

Principal Subject:
Critical Issues & Concerns

ISBN:
0914783572

Edition:
1992

Publisher:
The Charles Press, Publishers

Author:
Roger E. Vogler, Ph.D. and Wayne R. Bartz, Ph.D.

About The Author:
(From Cover Notes)
Vogler is Professor of Psychology at Pomona College, and a clinical psychologist at the Center For Behavior Change in Pomona, California. Bartz is Professor of Psychology at American River College in Sacramento, California

Substance Abuse

TEENAGERS & ALCOHOL
When Saying No Isn't Enough

Description:

Teenagers and Alcohol discusses parental concerns about teenage drinking. The authors draw on their experience as psychologists to help parents become actively involved in keeping their kids away from alcohol abuse. Their proposed program has 9 steps, each of which is explained within this 147 page book's 3 parts, 9 chapters. Part One includes the first 3 steps—understand the problem, get the facts about alcohol, and learn how to maximize parental influence. The program's next 4 steps are described in Part Two, and include information on how to influence decisions about drinking, how to foster non-drinking behavior, how to teach "sensible drinking" (if non-drinking fails), and how to handle teenage alcohol abuse. Part Three concludes with the final 2 steps—ways to help preteens understand issues surrounding drinking and alcohol abuse, and how to change society's perspectives of alcohol consumption.

Evaluation:

Seeking to find a viable alternative to the failing "Just Say No" campaign, the authors provide parents with "the tools necessary to take an active role in guiding their children toward making responsible choices about alcohol." The authors' 9-step program is balanced and sensible, but a bit too logical and dry. What's missing in this guide? Direct advice on how to help teens deal with peer pressure, warning signs of alcohol use, and input on treatment and recovery options. They do acknowledge that it might be impossible to keep a teenager from abstaining from alcohol. They then educate a teen on the effects of alcohol usage, along with ways for the teen to determine the stages of drunkenness, and knowing when it reaches dangerous levels. Of course, realistically if a teen becomes drunk, this information will most likely not be remembered nor be helpful. This resource provides numerous facts about blood alcohol levels, but is best saved for classroom use and discussion, and not relied on as a primary resource at home.

Where To Find/Buy:

Bookstores and libraries.

Substance Abuse

WHEN THE DRUG WAR HITS HOME
Healing The Family Torn Apart By Teenage Drug Use

Description:

This book addresses what to do when you have discovered your child has a drug problem. Stamper draws on her experience as a clinician and supervisor of "one of the nation's most highly regarded adolescent chemical dependency programs" in this 139 page book. She provides a combination of her own insights, statistics, and real examples of teens who have struggled with drug abuse and the families who were torn apart by the fallout of addiction. Chapter One discusses the reasons why kids use drugs. Chapters Two and Three respectively discuss the stage of denial and how to access treatment facilities. Chapter Four deals with the healing process. Chapters Five and Six focus on life after treatment and how to deal with relapses and cross-addictions. The book concludes by discussing prevention myths and facts. The author seeks to empower parents in their battle against addiction, by giving them the tools to make changes in their own lives that will in turn "make it uncomfortable for your kid if he or she does not change."

Evaluation:

This book doesn't provide any startling new revelations or formulas for parents seeking help in dealing with their addicted teenagers. Drawing from her experiences as an open treatment manager, Stamper provides basic information and advice for parents who are wondering what they can expect from the treatment process. Her most important parenting rule is simple, "do what you need to do so you can feel good about yourself and your life." She provides composite stories of the kids and families she has encountered in her work, giving a realistic look at what it means to struggle as a family with the problem of substance abuse. Stamper doesn't lay blame or define an enemy. She approaches the problem on a personal level, as an advocate for kids. This book is a good basic reference for parents wondering what they can expect from the treatment process for their teenage drug abuser. It should be used in combination with other materials though.

Where To Find/Buy:

Bookstores, libraries, or order direct by calling 1-800-544-8207.

Overall Rating
★★
General resource for parents seeking help for their drug-addicted adolescents

Design, Ease Of Use
★
Easy to read, simplistic format; no hierarchy in headings makes it confusing at times

---

1–4 Stars; N/R = Not Rated

Media:
Print

Price:
$11.95

Principal Subject:
Critical Issues & Concerns

ISBN:
1577490517

Edition:
2nd (1997)

Publisher:
Fairview Press

Author:
Laura Stamper

About The Author:
(From Cover Notes)
Stamper is a clinician and supervisor in "one of the nation's most highly regarded adolescent chemical dependency programs."

IV. Critical Issues & Concerns

Overall Rating

★

Brief lists of substance abuse symptoms but nothing else to support parents' needs

Design, Ease Of Use

★★★

Easily navigated, no graphics; extensive list of linked resources and supportive articles

1–4 Stars; N/R = Not Rated

Media:
Internet

Principal Subject:
Critical Issues & Concerns

Internet URL:
http://www.acde.org/

Substance Abuse

AMERICAN COUNCIL FOR DRUG EDUCATION

Description:

Affiliated with Phoenix House ("the nation's leading non-profit drug abuse service organization), this website's creators offer 6 options at their homepage, including membership (individual or corporate) and a "Learning Trip" of how chemicals react in the body; Macromedia Flash plug-in is required for this area. "Grown-Ups" offers parents facts about marijuana use along with a generalized list of physical and behavioral/psychological symptoms of drug use; capsulated symptoms for specific drugs (marijuana, alcohol, depressants, stimulants, tobacco/nicotine, heroin, inhalants, hallucinogens) are also given. The site's online "Library" hosts links to other resources and websites, along with a supporting list of news articles (Newsweek, Wall Street Journal, etc.) and professional journals. "Drugs Don't Work" outlines the ACDE's workplace program for organizations who desire a drug-free workplace policy. Various ACDE publications can be purchased through snail mail (42¢ to $15.00) and are listed as well.

Evaluation:

Understandably, as this site states, "information is a powerful tool in the effort to fight drug abuse." Unfortunately, this site misses their own mark. Parents **will** get a brief list here of symptoms inherent with substance abuse, but nothing more. More helpful would have been descriptions of drug slang, paraphernalia, and possible treatments and resources, not to mention some suggestions on how to prevent substance abuse in the first place. More emphasis is spent on scare tactics ("children and youth who use alcohol, tobacco and/or marijuana are more likely to go on to experiment with more potent and more seriously harmful drugs) than on direct constructive input ("it is important that parents . . . emphasize non-use messages"). Learning how to teach your child to avoid involvement with drugs, knowing what to look for if you suspect they are involved, and knowing when and where to look for help for substance abuse problems are crucial and powerful tools. Look elsewhere though because this site's toolbox is empty.

Where To Find/Buy:

On the Internet at the URL: http://www.acde.org/.

Substance Abuse

COMING TOGETHER ON PREVENTION

Description:

Stating that "only when society . . . changes its norm, will the prevention message become part of our daily lives, and children be given the chance they deserve to realize their potential," this 26 minute videotape focuses on ways to prevent substance abuse. Highlighting three prevention models tested by the National Institute on Drug Abuse, this tape focuses on the need for early intervention with children. The first model is a school-based program called Reconnecting At-Risk Youth (Seattle, WA). The program suggests that, since students are often introduced to drugs and alcohol by their peers, high-risk students should be involved in a one quarter course on "personal growth." The second program is family-based (Denver, CO) and focuses on changing the family dynamics for those families in which a parent abuses drugs or alcohol. The final program—Project STAR (Students Taught Awareness and Resistance) in the Kansas City area—focuses on a community-based collaboration to teach resistance skills to kids.

Evaluation:

Worried parents seeking comrades in the fight against substance abuse will find some elements of this tape useful. This video offers parents an overall perspective of how schools, families, and communities can pull together to give children a direct anti-drug message. Although NIDA doesn't go into specifics about the success rate of the 3 model programs shown in this tape, those research results hopefully can be found elsewhere. Some parental questions will be answered by viewing this tape, but many more questions will be left unanswered. For example, many parents want advice or direction about how they themselves can prevent children from abusing drugs. But they won't find those answers here. Although the message of early intervention is clear, what isn't clear in this tape is what parents as a family unit can do to influence their kids' decisions. This tape is best used to help parents, professionals, educators, and community leaders form an alliance so they can collaboratively make a difference with children at risk.

Where To Find/Buy:

Bookstores, libraries, videotape dealers, or order direct by calling 1-800-729-6686 or (301) 468-2600.

Overall Rating
★
Shows how collaborative efforts can impact substance abuse, but nothing just for parents

Design, Ease Of Use
★★★
Succinct, informative; some research data not supplied (success rates of program)

1–4 Stars; N/R = Not Rated

Media:
Videotape

Price:
$12.50

Principal Subject:
Critical Issues & Concerns

Edition:
1994

Publisher:
National Clearinghouse for Alcohol and Drug Information (NCADI)

Author:
National Institute on Drug Abuse Videotape Series

Overall Rating

★

Disappointing lack of real information from a well-respected program and curriculum

Design, Ease Of Use

★★★

Straight-forward but otherwise dull site; excerpts available from D.A.R.E. publication

1–4 Stars; N/R = Not Rated

Media:
Internet

Principal Subject:
Critical Issues & Concerns

Internet URL:
http://www.dare-america.com/

Substance Abuse

D.A.R.E.

Description:

Developed originally by the L.A. Police Department and the L.A. Unified School District to "provide children with the information and skills they need to live drug-and-violence-free lives," the homepage of their website offers separate features for kids, educators, officers, and parents. Within "Parents," visitors can get a "quick look" and an overview of the D.A.R.E. (Drug Abuse Resistance Education) program including one paragraph explanations of their mission, curriculum, lessons, funding, and more. An article on "The Scourge of Drugs" lists facts about the drug epidemic in America along with the effects, costs, and benefits of the D.A.R.E. program. Parent testimonials are also included within this feature. The "D.A.R.E. Archive" contains past articles (2 when we visited). Excerpts from D.A.R.E.'s publication *Keeping Kids Drug Free—D.A.R.E. Official Parent's Guide* will appear monthly; a 2 page excerpt from Chapter Two of Part One was highlighted during our visit along with a 1-800 number to order a copy.

Evaluation:

D.A.R.E. has long been considered a guiding force in many school districts' drug education and prevention programs. We found their website, however, lacked the substance of their respected curriculum. All that can be found at this site are the basic cold facts of D.A.R.E.'s war on drugs. Parents won't get any information about substance abuse prevention, symptoms, or treatments. It's a shame D.A.R.E.'s book couldn't be published en masse at their website to support their mission of providing "information and skills." Instead the push seems to be on purchasing it (but not online). Also, the site states that "most people choose not to see [drug abuse] . . . to fight it, we must face it head on." But instead of facing it head on here, parents are informed of the ills of substance abuse and how money spent on D.A.R.E. compares to the costs of incarceration. Parents hoping to get real guidance in either preventing substance abuse in their children or in treating a suspected problem will most definitely need to explore other avenues.

Where To Find/Buy:

On the Internet at the URL: http://www.dare-america.com/. Their publication may be ordered by calling 1-800-284-3580.

Substance Abuse

HOW TO TELL WHEN KIDS ARE IN TROUBLE WITH ALCOHOL/DRUGS

Description:

Part of a series of 15 pamphlets published by the Johnson Institute, this 41 page guide defines chemical dependency and then provides an overview of its four phases. Phase One includes the teen who uses alcohol/drugs and learns about the "Pleasurable Mood Swing." The discussion in Phase Two centers on the teen who regularly uses alcohol/drugs and now **seeks** pleasurable mood swings. Phase Three occurs when the teen abuses alcohol/drugs and is now "Harmfully Involved." Phase Four includes the teen who is addicted to alcohol/drugs and is now chemically dependent. For each phase, information is provided on the characteristics of use ("starts to make self-imposed rules to govern using"), the chemicals of choice (over-the-counter, marijuana, cocaine, alcohol, etc.), and the possible consequences (social—legal, school, home, friends; personal—physical, mental, emotional, spiritual). Questionnaires are given at the end of the book to help parents determine their child's involvement with substances.

Evaluation:

The foundation of this pamphlet is that "teens who use alcohol or other drugs do not become chemically dependent overnight. Rather they usually progress through four different phases of use, each phase taking the teen deeper and deeper into trouble." This guide for parents, teachers, and other caregivers provides a bare-bones approach to helping parents determine whether or not their child has a problem with alcohol or drug use. Part of the Parenting for Prevention series, this pamphlet might offer counselors or other professionals an opening dialogue for discussions centered on ways to alert parents to the warning signs of substance abuse. However, this guide will not address most parents' needs. For example, other guides offer photos of drugs and related paraphernalia as realistic evidence of warning signs; it is absent here. For better coverage, parents will need other sources that can provide the nitty-gritty details of substance abuse along with guidance on how to deal with their child's addiction to drugs or alcohol.

Where To Find/Buy:

Bookstores, libraries, or order direct by calling 1-800-231-5165.

Overall Rating
★
Basic overview of 4 phases of chemical dependency; best used only as a starting point

Design, Ease Of Use
★★★
Concise w/ large print, bold margin headings; pics of drugs/paraphernalia would help

1–4 Stars; N/R = Not Rated

Media:
Print

Price:
$4.95

Principal Subject:
Critical Issues & Concerns

ISBN:
1562461427

Edition:
1998

Publisher:
Johnson Institute—QVS

Author:
Johnson Institute

About The Author:
(From Cover Notes)
For more than thirty years, the Johnson Institute has worked to restore shattered careers, heal relationships with coworkers and friends, save lives, and bring families back together.

Internet URL:
www.johnsoninstitute.com

IV. Critical Issues & Concerns

Overall Rating
★
Outlines the pitfalls of marijuana use, but no constructive input or recognition of signs

Design, Ease Of Use
★★★
Teen testimonials and factual discussion work well; other segments random and jumbled

1–4 Stars; N/R = Not Rated

Media:
Videotape

Price:
$12.50

Principal Subject:
Critical Issues & Concerns

Edition:
1995

Publisher:
National Clearinghouse for Alcohol and Drug Information (NCADI)

Author:
National Institute on Drug Abuse Videotape Series

Substance Abuse

MARIJUANA: WHAT CAN A PARENT DO?

Description:

During the course of its 14 minutes, this videotape by the National Institute on Drug Abuse explains why parents need to educate their adolescents about the inherent dangers of marijuana use. By combining teen testimonials and parent interviews, emphasis is placed on how parents need to be aware of everything that goes in their children's lives. The biological facts of marijuana use are given, from its ability to damage memory and impair judgement to behavioral conditions arising from using higher levels of marijuana, such as truancy, delinquency, and arrest. The correlation between marijuana use and negligent driving, sexual behavior, and AIDS is explored. Also discussed is the disparity for some parents (who experimented themselves with marijuana during their adolescence) and the parenting role they now play. This videotape reinforces the need to "make time to spend time" with one's child, getting to know their friends and friends' families, and to continually monitor and supervise a child's activities.

Evaluation:

Nothing of much consequence can usually be accomplished in a 14 minute time span, and this is evidenced here. Upon viewing this tape, parents will get the feeling that their children should not experiment with drugs. This, of course, is not an earth-shattering revelation. What's lacking in this tape are the how-tos and what-ifs—how to talk to your child about peer pressure and its influence on your child's decision-making abilities, how to recognize signs and paraphernalia associated with possible marijuana usage, how to encourage your child not to experiment in the first place, and what to do if your child has indulged or has a serious problem. The tape opens with a mother's dialogue emphasizing that the only way to prevent your child from getting involved with drugs is to "be open with them, to talk to them, warn them, but keep talking about where they are." Unfortunately, the tape offers no conversation openers, but instead leaves the viewer with many unanswered questions and a veritable feeling of worry and threat.

Where To Find/Buy:

Bookstores, libraries, videotape dealers, or order direct by calling 1-800-729-6686 or (301) 468-2600.

Substance Abuse

NATIONAL FAMILIES IN ACTION

Description:

Hosted by the National Families in Action, a national prevention effort to cut regular drug use among adolescents and adults, this site features 5 options on their homepage. Two sections highlight publications and products that can be purchased through the site's "Catalog," along with a 15 page listing of referral organizations for additional help. "Ask the Experts" is an electronic version of the NFIA executive director's syndicated column about drug abuse from the 1980s; this feature includes frequently asked questions, but no longer responds to submitted questions. A fourth feature at their homepage, has links to various other "Cultural/Ethnic Partners" (white, African American, Hispanic/Latino, Asian American, Pacific Islander, Native American) in an effort to build a family movement to protect children from drug use and drug dealing. "Drug Info" offers one page of information on substances (alcohol, tobacco, heroin, LSD, cocaine, marijuana, PCP, etc.), their effects, street names, and legal status.

Evaluation:

Short and sweet, but not complete, are words that best describe this site. Parents searching for capsules of information that explain the effects of various substances will certainly find it here, but they will get no direction on how to deal with substance abuse. Some tips are contained within the FAQ segment, but only in short bits, and parents will have to wade through the 10 pages of questions and answers in hope of finding the pertinent advice they need. In light of the organization's efforts to build a "family movement," one would also hope that parents would have opportunities here to connect with other parents either through discussion groups or chat rooms. But none of these family-friendly support options exist. Parents worried about substance abuse want tips and information about the prevention, symptoms, and possible treatments involved. Unfortunately the one page of facts given here is incomplete and rather clinical. Look elsewhere for more in-depth help and information for this serious concern.

Where To Find/Buy:

On the Internet at the URL: http://www.emory.edu/NFIA.

Overall Rating

★

Concise facts given, but incomplete support for families dealing with substance abuse

Design, Ease Of Use

★★★

Easily navigated, but uninspiring site design

1–4 Stars; N/R = Not Rated

Media:
Internet

Principal Subject:
Critical Issues & Concerns

Internet URL:
http://www.emory.edu/NFIA

IV. Critical Issues & Concerns

Substance Abuse

ADOLESCENT TREATMENT APPROACHES

Overall Rating

★

Explains various treatment programs rather clinically and with little depth

Design, Ease Of Use

★★

Varied footage of teens, professionals, families; highlighted tips would be useful

1–4 Stars; N/R = Not Rated

Media:
Videotape

Price:
$12.50

Principal Subject:
Critical Issues & Concerns

Publisher:
National Clearinghouse for Alcohol and Drug Information (NCADI)

Author:
National Institute on Drug Abuse Videotape Series

Description:

Designed for parents weighing the pros and cons of various substance abuse treatment programs, this 25 minute videotape discusses outpatient family therapy, surrogate family residential treatment programs, and a combination of individual and family counseling day treatment programs. The key to treating substance abuse, say the creators, lies in recognizing that "child development and substance abuse treatment for adolescents go completely hand in hand." Emphasizing that adolescents should not be seen as "little adults," and that adolescents vary from one age to the next, the video includes teenagers' and professionals' testimonials along with group therapy sessions. The importance of including an after-care program in an adolescent's treatment program is stressed. These programs ensure that adolescents continue to feel connected and have an established support system; they may be associated with either outpatient or residential treatment programs, and/or include community-based support groups.

Evaluation:

This tape adequately outlines general factors to consider when treating an adolescent's substance abuse problem, but it manages to leave the viewer confused. Is it intended for parents, professionals, educators, community leaders, who? The tape stresses the importance of understanding adolescent development since, as the tape states, it is difficult to distinguish between typical adolescent behavior and that of drug abuse behavior. To that end, we would hope that the tape would offer some general indicators to let parents know when their child's behavior is questionable. Instead, parents are treated to a rather clinical look at what goes on in residential treatment programs, how they differ from day treatment programs, and how and when family counseling is useful. However, explanations of what to look for, sample questions to ask, and other ways to weigh one program over another would have added more content to a discussion of this topic. Minimally useful, this tape needs considerable back-up for such an important and often life-preserving decision.

Where To Find/Buy:

Bookstores, libraries, videotape dealers, or order direct by calling 1-800-729-6686 or (301) 468-2600.

Sexuality & Pregnancy

IF YOU CAN TALK TO YOUR KIDS ABOUT SEX, YOU CAN TALK TO THEM ABOUT ANYTHING

Terrific Resource For:
Communicating parental expectations and values, especially about sexuality (videotape)

Recommended For:
Critical Issues & Concerns

Description:

Presented in a workshop type format, Roseman's 54 minute videotape focuses on effective ways to communicate with teenagers about general issues, along with discussing sex specifically. Her suggestions are based on her 25 years of experience working with parents and children as a high school Sex Education teacher. The beginning of the tape stresses the need for parents to clarify their own values, or what she terms "early messages," to make sure those are the messages parents want their child to hear. She defines 6 criteria for values, such as "values are chosen freely, from alternatives," "values are publicly affirmed by you," etc. Roseman states that if parents then help children clarify their own values, then when given information, children can responsibly make informed decisions. Next, her workshop participants model four skills to invite teens to talk—be askable, be non-judgemental, find teachable moments, and avoid killer statements. She ends her video by presenting 5 basic communication practices that help facilitate discussions about sex—avoid baby talk, be a sounding board, admit discomfort, and more.

Evaluation:

Parents need to note that the title of this videotape is misleading, it won't direct parents specifically to ways to bring up "the birds and the bees." Instead, Roseman paints a bigger picture to better serve parents than the advice registered in sex-ed resources focusing on the facts of contraception, reproduction, and how to start "the big talk." Roseman believes that sex is more than teaching facts, but instead involves teaching kids about relationships, while ensuring that they feel good about themselves. Children, she states, should feel loved, valuable, and important. Her videotape clearly identifies, both visually and auditorially, how breakdowns can occur in parent-teen conversations. Also included are tips on how parents can recover verbally when they blunder and thereby block communication avenues. She insists throughout her videotape that negotiation and holding one's tongue are necessary skills for parents to practice, but balances this with her "Parents' Rights." Suitable for use by parents on their own, this tape would also be useful as a group discussion lead-in on parent-teen communications.

Where To Find/Buy:

Bookstores, libraries, videotape dealers, or order direct by calling Library Video Company at 1-800-843-3620.

Overall Rating
★★★★
More than "the birds and the bees," this video focuses on general communication skills

Design, Ease Of Use
★★★★
Easy to follow, flows well; major points highlighted in blocks of text; good examples

1–4 Stars; N/R = Not Rated

Media:
Videotape

Price:
$19.95

Principal Subject:
Critical Issues & Concerns

Edition:
1994

Publisher:
East West Media Productions/BMG Video

Author:
Lennie Roseman

**About The Author:
(From Cover Notes)**
Roseman has a Masters in Health, with emphasis on communication and teen issues. As an Advisory Council member, she helped revise New York's public school Sex Education curriculum in 1980. She has been profiled on "60 Minutes" and the "Oprah Winfrey Show."

IV. Critical Issues & Concerns

Overall Rating
★★★★
Excellent essays that highlight the differing viewpoints of sexuality issues

Design, Ease Of Use
★★★★
Well-organized; concise writing; book easily read chapter-by-chapter or in its entirety

1–4 Stars; N/R = Not Rated

Media:
Print

Price:
$16.20

Principal Subject:
Critical Issues & Concerns

ISBN:
1565101022

Edition:
1994

Publisher:
Greenhaven Press

Author:
David L. Bender and Bruno Leone

About The Author:
(From Cover Notes)
The editors created the *Opposing Viewpoints* series to help people attain a higher level of thinking and reading skills concerning different subjects. They hope the series challenges readers to question their own opinions and viewpoints.

Sexuality & Pregnancy

TEENAGE SEXUALITY
Opposing Viewpoints

Terrific Resource For:
Parents seeking to clarify their values regarding sexual behavior in teens

Recommended For:
Critical Issues & Concerns

Description:
The books in the *Opposing Viewpoints* series present many different types of opinions ("well-known professionals," "ordinary persons") in an effort to give readers a deeper understanding of the issues being debated. This book discusses various issues related to teenage sexuality, such as factors that influence teen sexuality, causes and reduction of teen pregnancy, sex education, and teenage homosexuality. Each topic debated involves several viewpoints which illustrate shades of acceptance or denial on the subject. The chapter on sex education, for example, includes essays by authors who feel that sex education is necessary or unnecessary, shouldn't be explicit or should be candid, shouldn't promote abstinence-based programs or should demand abstinence. Each chapter includes a brief introduction, along with a list of questions for the reader to consider prior to reading. The book includes graphs, editorial cartoons, bibliographies, topics for further discussion, a list of organizations to contact, and an index.

Evaluation:
Teenage sexuality is a hotly debated and highly contentious issue. Many oppositional viewpoints are exhibited from those who are confident and passionate in their beliefs and ideals. This intelligent book asks the reader to examine all of them with a clear eye, reading critically and with respect in order to examine their own beliefs and ideals. The chapter prefaces and brief introductions are particularly helpful, in that they provide questions for consideration and overviews for the subject matter. The essays, speeches, and book excerpts are honest and well-written. Parents won't get specific hands-on advice or dialogues on how to communicate with their child about sexuality or how to deal with certain subjects such as pregnancy, suicide, or homosexuality. However, this book is recommended to parents, educators and adolescents alike, because it provides an arena by which parents and their adolescents can discuss their values, and perhaps refine or reestablish their referencing points.

Where To Find/Buy:
Bookstores and libraries.

Sexuality & Pregnancy

I'M PREGNANT, NOW WHAT DO I DO?

 Terrific Resource For:
Pregnant teenagers needing guidance about their options

 Recommended For:
Critical Issues & Concerns

Description:

The authors present three options for teenagers finding themselves in an unplanned pregnancy: giving the child up for adoption, terminating the pregnancy (abortion), or continuing with the pregnancy. The book's intent is to provide up-to-date information so you will be "getting as many facts as you can about your options (that) will help you choose what's best for you." The 11 chapters of this 228 page book include discussions on the following: facts about the reproductive system, brief description of pregnancy (1/2 page+ per trimester), developing support systems, tips on the decision-making process, and the role of your partner in your decisions. The bulk of the book focuses on separate chapters dealing with becoming a parent, considering adoption, and choosing abortion. Each of these chapters present the facts, the pros and cons, how to deal with the changes and associated losses, and "things to consider." Also given are additional chapters that describe case studies of three women who have chosen one of these options and examples of how their lives were impacted. A glossary and list of resources is also given.

Evaluation:

Lack of knowledge about sex, accompanied by the conflicting messages teens get about their sexuality through the media, can result in unplanned teen pregnancies. The U.S. still has the highest rate of adolescent pregnancies in the developed world. Societal avoidance only adds to the denial many teens exercise when they find out they are pregnant. This book presents a fair, unbiased, and factual account of alternatives available to teens. It contains numerous stories from teens that describe their situations, the way they made decisions about what to do, and the effect those decisions made on their lives. These accounts are personal, engaging and supportive. This is a book that isn't just for pregnant teenagers; it would also be of great use for any teen who is considering sexual intercourse. Knowing the consequences and the ensuing decisions that may need to be made would better enable them to make informed decisions.

Where To Find/Buy:

Bookstores and libraries.

★★★★

Overall Rating
★★★★
Sensitive, factual account of decision-making involved with an unplanned pregnancy

Design, Ease Of Use
★★★
Straightforward headings in table of contents; chapter organization sometimes unclear

1–4 Stars; N/R = Not Rated

Media:
Print

Principal Subject:
Critical Issues & Concerns

ISBN:
1573921173

Edition:
1997

Publisher:
Prometheus Books

Author:
Dr. Robert W. Buckingham, P.H. & Mary P. Derby, R.N., M.P.H.

About The Author:
(From Cover Notes)
Buckingham is a professor of public health at New Mexico State University in Las Cruces and author of ten other books. Derby is a maternal child health clinical nurse specialist at Harvard Pilgrim Health Care in Boston and has worked extensively with adolescents.

IV. Critical Issues & Concerns

Overall Rating
★★★
Informative; successfully speaks to both teens and parents

Design, Ease Of Use
★★★★
Highly readable question/answer format; straightforward TOC, index included

1–4 Stars; N/R = Not Rated

Media:
Print

Price:
$14.95

Principal Subject:
Critical Issues & Concerns

ISBN:
1577490347

Edition:
1997

Publisher:
Fairview Press

Author:
Michael J. Basso

About The Author:
(From Cover Notes)
Michael J. Basso, an award-winning instructor, is an active member of the American Association of Sex Educators, Counselors, and Therapists, and was recently voted Teacher of the Year at his high school.

Sexuality & Pregnancy

UNDERGROUND GUIDE TO TEENAGE SEXUALITY (THE)
An Essential Handbook For Today's Teens & Parents

 Recommended For:
Critical Issues & Concerns

Description:
This 12 chapter, 230 page book on sexuality touts itself as "an essential handbook for today's teens and parents." Basso, combining his professional background of teaching health and lifestyle management with personal information he has gathered from many students who have confided in him, presents up-to-date information on sexuality topics of concern to today's teens. His introduction is a compassionate plea of sorts, asking parents to be understanding of teens. The book includes chapters focusing on sexual anatomy, what parents can expect during the teen years, sexually transmitted diseases, contraception and birth control, how to make love, how to say "no" to sex, and more. This book follows a question/answer format. Common questions a teenager may have about health and sexuality are presented, followed by often detailed explanations and definitions. Numerous illustrations are provided.

Evaluation:
This highly informative book on both health and sexuality successfully speaks to teenagers at their level, and at the same time keeps parents informed of today's teens and sexuality. Its question/answer format is very easy to read; the language is kept simple and flows well. Basso writes with an authoritative voice, especially when advising teens on how to be responsible. After all the information is given on health and sexuality, Basso provides a chapter on "How to Say No to Sex" (Chapter 8) and asserts that the teenager absolutely has this right and option, offering a number of sometimes humorous, suggested responses to the initiator. This book keeps teens informed and educated, and also gives them sensible, practical advice regarding potential dangers associated with foolish choices or irresponsible behavior. Void of personal opinion or strong beliefs and having a focus that is teen-centered, this resource will most likely provide parents with a forum from which to converse with their teen about sexuality.

Where To Find/Buy:
Bookstores, libraries, or order direct by calling 1-800-544-8207.

Sexuality & Pregnancy

WHAT EVERY TEENAGER REALLY WANTS TO KNOW ABOUT SEX

Recommended For:
Critical Issues & Concerns

Description:

What Every Teenager Really Wants To Know About Sex is predominately a question and answer book. However, there are two main chapters within Part One that are specifically for parents. These 2 chapters are fact-oriented and are entitled "From Intercourse to Outercourse: The Pleasuring Alternative," and "Just say KNOW." Part Two is more directed toward the teenager (the author even tells teen-readers in her introduction to "skip to page 35"). The chapters in this section address pleasure, love, masturbation, different avenues of sex, STDs, and ways to deal with parents. Each individual chapter generally follows the same format: Hacker briefly explains the issue, then lists questions she has received over the years while teaching adolescents about all the different aspects of sexuality. Questions are concisely and bluntly answered, not taking more than a few paragraphs to get the point across. The reader who wants more will find a list of suggested readings at the end of the book.

Evaluation:

This book will quickly demolish any parent's claim of "MY child doesn't think about sex!" Hacker quickly establishes that adolescents **are** sexually active, mentally and/or physically. She then insists that efforts to change a teenager's hormonal makeup and sexual thoughts are futile. Rather, she suggests teaching adolescents about pleasure. Parents need to remember, though, that Hacker doesn't advocate intercourse. However, she does list a number of other avenues that inquisitive adolescents may choose. The second part of the book truly is designed for teenagers. She even suggests that parents browse the book, and then leave it in their child's room. What is evident in this comment and generally lacking in this book are ways to converse with teens about sexuality. It should also be noted that this book asks parents to be completely open-minded about sexual issues without offering advice on how to attain this attitude. Otherwise explicit and complete, however, this book will serve those parents wanting to broach subjects of sexuality with their adolescent, but unable to find a way to directly discuss it with them.

Where To Find/Buy:
Bookstores and libraries.

Overall Rating
★★★
Explicitly helpful to both parents AND teenagers, however, it lacks discussion how-tos

Design, Ease Of Use
★★★★
Logical order: parents first, teens second; Q & A format has a person-to-person feel

1–4 Stars; N/R = Not Rated

Media:
Print

Price:
$10.95

Principal Subject:
Critical Issues & Concerns

ISBN:
0881849693

Edition:
1993

Publisher:
Carroll & Graf Publishers

Author:
Sylvia S. Hacker, Ph.D. with Randi Hacker

About The Author:
(From Cover Notes)
Hacker teaches human sexuality at the University of Michigan at Ann Arbor. She has lectured widely on the subject and has talked with hundreds of junior high and high school classes.

IV. Critical Issues & Concerns

Overall Rating
★★★
Reinforces how and why parents need to be in charge of teaching about sex and sexuality

Design, Ease Of Use
★★
Generally addresses issues chronologically by child's age; no index; scattered advice

1–4 Stars; N/R = Not Rated

Media:
Print

Price:
$12.95

Principal Subject:
Critical Issues & Concerns

ISBN:
0962946303

Edition:
1991

Publisher:
Preston Hollow Enterprises

Author:
Patty Stark

**About The Author:
(From Cover Notes)**
Patty Stark's work as an educator, media consultant, and writer has brought her in contact with thousands of students and parents for nearly a decade. She lectures and conducts workshops nationally on sexuality and relationships.

IV. Critical Issues & Concerns

Sexuality & Pregnancy

SEX IS MORE THAN A PLUMBING LESSON
A Parent's Guide To Sexuality Education From Infancy Through The Teen Years

Description:

Stark strongly advocates teaching children about sexuality from infancy (touching, cuddling), toddlerhood and early school-age years (talking about human sexual anatomy, answering children's questions in age-appropriate ways), through the preteen and teenage years. Roughly one-third of this 203 page, 12 chapter book is geared toward parent and preteen/teen discussions about sex and sexuality. Stark indicates that parents are the best ones to teach their child about sex. She believes that if parents take time in the early years, refrain from being embarrassed by the subject, and talk openly with their child, then their child will not need to learn about sexuality off the streets or from friends, TV, or other sources when the child is in his teens. The author gives many suggestions on how to speak with your child about sex at the different age levels. Much of Stark's teaching assumes that a good parent-child relationship exists, although she does briefly address strained relationships during the child's teen years.

Evaluation:

Some of Stark's suggestions may appear a bit radical to some parents, such as explaining what a "boner" is when a child asks, talking about masturbation, and discussing other sex-related topics. Although her book focuses primarily on sexuality, Stark also offers parents roundabout advice on how to achieve positive communications with a child starting from an early age. She believes that this foundation is necessary for future parent-child sexuality discussions; she does state, however, that since sexual development is a lifelong process, beginning instruction in the teen years will still benefit one's child. The ultimate goal of Stark's suggestions is to teach children to be responsible when it comes to sex. This is achieved, she believes, only when parents fully educate and inform their children about sex, love, and sexuality. Stark has put much effort toward achieving that goal; there is good insight in her advice, but readers will want to take whatever advice they are comfortable with and filter out the rest.

Where To Find/Buy:

Bookstores and libraries.

VENUS IN BLUE JEANS
Why Mothers And Daughters Need To Talk About Sex

★★★

Description:

This 252 page book, resulting originally from discussions with colleagues, is based on research of 15 mother (or female caregiver)-daughter relationships from focus groups. The girls who participated attended one of two high schools: one a private, prep school, and the other a public school in the inner city. Chapter subtitles (which describe the actual chapter titles) are: "New Times, New Talk," "The Girls of Jefferson and Nottingham High Schools" (the two schools where the girls researched attended), "Nurturing Girls Through Adolescence," "What Adolescent Girls Know about Sex," "Where Girls Get Their Information," "Daughters' Hopes and Fears," "Mothers' Hopes and Fears," "Sexual Desire," "Getting Fathers Involved," "Maternal Strategies," and an Afterword: "Involving the Community." The book also contains a bibliography, as well as extensive end notes.

Evaluation:

The book jacket advertises "sage advice and practical strategies for guiding girls toward womanhood," but doesn't directly provide this. Readers will find that it reads more like a dissertation-turned book, than a practical hands-on guide—it isn't a how-to book at all. In fact, Bartle states that her book "does not profess to offer a set of rules . . . my hope is that we will be able to draw from what these teenagers and their mothers have to say and discover ideas." Thus, parents simply wanting a description of 15 mother-daughter relationships will find their needs addressed here. There is, however, some useful advice sprinkled in, such as a list of 11 signs that a young woman is not prepared for sexual activity, but generally parents will need to hunt diligently to find such advice. Offering interesting perspectives on the nature of sexuality in our culture and the stresses placed on young women, this book is best used as an accompaniment to other resources that include more direct communication tips.

Where To Find/Buy:

Bookstores and libraries.

Overall Rating
★★★
More a report of the 15 studied focus groups than a guide offering "sage advice"

Design, Ease Of Use
★★
Headings within chapters, but not an easily skimmed book

1–4 Stars; N/R = Not Rated

Media:
Print

Price:
$24.00

Principal Subject:
Critical Issues & Concerns

ISBN:
0395841720

Edition:
1998

Publisher:
Houghton Mifflin

Author:
Nathalie Bartle, Ed.D. with Susan Lieberman, Ph.D.

**About The Author:
(From Cover Notes)**
Bartle, mother of 3 children (2 boys and 1 girl) currently teaches at Allegheny University of the Health Sciences in Philadelphia. With a doctorate in developmental psychology from Harvard, she has counseled many adolescents and helped develop sex ed materials.

IV. Critical Issues & Concerns

★★

Overall Rating
★★
Good general information on learning how to talk to kids about AIDS and safe sex

Design, Ease Of Use
★★★★
Bulleted main points and bold highlights with concise coverage of main topics

1–4 Stars; N/R = Not Rated

Media:
Print

Price:
$8.95

Principal Subject:
Critical Issues & Concerns

ISBN:
0941831728

Edition:
1992

Publisher:
Beyond Words Publishing

Author:
Loren A. Acker, Ph.D., Bram C. Goldwater, Ph.D., and William H. Dyson, M.D., Ph.D.

About The Author:
(From Cover Notes)
Drs. Acker, Goldwater, and Dyson are professors at the University of Victoria in British Columbia, and collectively share 45 years of experience in family psychology, medicine, social learning, biochemistry, and AIDS prevention.

Sexuality & Pregnancy

AIDS-PROOFING YOUR KIDS
A Step-By-Step Guide

Description:
This 168 page book is designed to help parents deal with the frightening statistics of the rise of AIDS in the younger population ("20% of all people diagnosed with AIDS were likely infected during their teenage years"). The subject matter is divided into five parts. Part One discusses the importance of discussing AIDS with one's teen, providing tips on how to break the ice, make the teaching easier, etc. Part Two focuses on "Teaching Safer Sex"—using condoms, alternatives to intercourse, and supporting school programs. The main focus of Part Three is "Teaching Alternatives to Interpersonal Intercourse," such as abstinence and masturbation; role-play scripts are also provided for helping kids handle difficult situations. "Medical Considerations," in Part Four, deals with the medical facts of AIDS, its history, how it's transmitted, how it's prevented, treatments, and vaccines. Part Five concludes with a discussion of other benefits derived from AIDS-proofing, a list of further readings, and groups to contact for more information.

Evaluation:
The authors face the difficult challenge of encouraging parents to deal candidly and confidently with the topic of their children's sexuality. Statistics support the importance of the information presented, but the book's strength lies in its clear language and comprehensive treatment of the topics. Although the authors acknowledge that their suggestions may be offensive to some, they advise parents to trust their instincts and moral beliefs when deciding how to approach their children. Well-organized, each chapter begins with a short paragraph or bullets of what will be discussed. Useful role playing scenarios—"AIDS-proofing skills"—are given to help parents and teens get beyond potential embarrassment or discomfort to practice potentially troublesome situations. Parents will find this an effective resource for helping their teens become more aware of AIDS. But other resources which discuss sexual responsibility and making moral decisions along with information about AIDS are also suggested.

Where To Find/Buy:
Bookstores, libraries, or order direct by calling (503) 647-5109 or 1-800-284-9673.

Sexuality & Pregnancy

TALKING ABOUT SEX
A Guide For Families

Description:

The Planned Parenthood Federation of America's 30 minute videotape is part of a kit that "promotes open, honest discussions about sexuality between parents and their children" ages 10–14. Also included in the kit are a Parent's Guide and an Activity Book. The Parent's Guide provides parents with info about sexuality and development, and the Activity Book contains "fun and thought-provoking activities" related to the video's content. Presented in an animated format, the video begins by discussing body changes, and concerns kids have about what is normal and what is not. The differences in male and female anatomy are discussed and illustrated, along with topics such as puberty, hormones, contraception choices, HIV/AIDS, and more. Briefly mentioned topics include sexual orientation, sexual abuse, masturbation, and teen pregnancy choices. PPFA's message is that kids will be exposed to all types of misinformation, and parents will best serve their kids by listening to their kids, and talking about sex and the facts.

Evaluation:

The videotape appears random, but when coupled with the Parent's Guide and the Activity Book, it makes for a dynamic door-opener to discussions of sexuality. The video's lively format will capture any child's attention, and lead uncomfortable parents into useful dialogue. Questions in the Activity Book are eye-openers, such as the "I Thought You Said . . . " activity. Here, parents and kids have the opportunity to separately express their thoughts about issues ("How old should someone be when she or he begins to date? Why?"), and to also predict how the other one thinks. This is especially helpful for clarifying values about sex and relationships. The Parent's Guide contains information parents need to back up a factual discussion, but little advice is offered about discussing the emotional elements of sexuality. On the whole, the video alone is not worth the price, the accompanying guides are useful, but other resources help parents clarify their own values along with ways to inform their children about sexuality.

Where To Find/Buy:

Bookstores, libraries, videotape dealers, or order direct by calling Planned Parenthood Federation of America at 1-800-669-0156, or Library Video Company at 1-800-843-3620.

Overall Rating
★★
Good video for opening sexuality discussions, but mostly centered on factual side of sex

Design, Ease Of Use
★★★
Video is rather random at times; accompanying Parent's Guide and Activity Book useful

1–4 Stars; N/R = Not Rated

Media:
Videotape

Price:
$29.95

Principal Subject:
Critical Issues & Concerns

ISBN:
0934586756

Edition:
1996

Publisher:
Planned Parenthood Federation of America

Author:
Planned Parenthood Federation of America

Internet URL:
http://www.ppfa.org/ppfa

IV. Critical Issues & Concerns

Overall Rating
★★
Great as a starting point for discussing parental expectations & teenage sexual behavior

Design, Ease Of Use
★★
Content is buried deep, but well-organized; site focuses a lot on CFOC public relations

1–4 Stars; N/R = Not Rated

Media:
Internet

Principal Subject:
Critical Issues & Concerns

Internet URL:
http://www.cfoc.org/

Sexuality & Pregnancy

CAMPAIGN FOR OUR CHILDREN

Description:

Incorporated in 1987, this campaign began as a cooperative effort of both the public and private sectors to modify teenagers' sexual behavior thus reducing teen pregnancies. Their materials and underlying message to parents is "talk to your kids about sex before they make you a grandparent." To that end, their homepage supports numerous features such as: "Facts, Figures, & Statistics" (about teen pregnancies), "Success Stories" (from teens), teacher resources, current news events focused on teenage pregnancy, a catalog of the Campaign For Our Children's materials (TV and radio commercials, posters, billboards, bus materials), and more. Three areas are pertinent primarily to parents: "Parents' Resources," "Ask the Experts," and "Sexual Responsibility." Through these areas, parents are given facts about the link between alcohol/drugs and teenage pregnancy, suggestions for how to initiate conversations about sex, tips on how to deal with substance abuse, a list of "talking points," "expert advice," and chat rooms.

Evaluation:

Emphasizing communication, this website is a good starting point for parents facing concerns of their teen's sexuality. We suggest parents and teens begin by participating in the exercise included with the "Talking Points." Use it as a springboard toward a frank discussion of parental expectations, teenager questions, and future concerns. Although parents won't get enough "how-tos" at this site to be able to successfully pass "Sexual Responsibility 101," they will get enough supportive info and tips to boost their confidence as they send their teenagers on their way. Statistical information on the effects of teenage pregnancy is available along with basic information to help those dealing with substance abuse (preventive tips, symptoms, what to do). Particularly disappointing were the segments "Parents' Chat" (within the "Parents' Resources") and "Ask the Experts." No current or past discussions were evident during our visit, and the "Expert" was "out of the office" on several of our visits. This site will help open the door to parent-teen discussions on the subject of sexuality, but parents looking for support from others will need other sources.

Where To Find/Buy:

On the Internet at the URL: http://www.cfoc.org/.

Sexuality & Pregnancy

GROWING UP IN THE AGE OF AIDS

Description:

This 75 minute videotape, hosted by ABC News' Peter Jennings, discusses AIDS, the HIV virus, and teen sexuality. It is filmed before a live studio audience consisting primarily of teenagers with parents and "leading experts" from the Center for Disease Control, Focus on the Family, the U.S. Surgeon General, and more, also present. It also includes call-in questions from viewers and blocks of facts in-between the video's various segments that highlight some of the statistics involved with AIDS. The video covers the medical, social, and psychological facts about AIDS along with teenagers' dilemmas. Topics covered include: the difference between HIV and AIDS; how one gets the disease; ways to protect teens and others from the HIV virus and AIDS (abstinence vs. condoms); the effect of advertising and the media on sexuality; the roles and responsibilities of family, school, insurance, and society; how to communicate about AIDS; and more.

Evaluation:

This video treats a serious problem in a serious well thought-out manner. As many of the experts stated in the video, communication and education are the keys toward combating this disease. Assumably then, this video should offer some how-tos for initiating parent-teen discussions about sexuality so teens can make enlightened sexual decisions. This is where the video falls short. For example, this question was posed several times to Adele Faber (a respected author of books on parenting and communication). Several times, she answered that parents need to learn to listen to their kids, but no constructive advice is offered parents on how to actually **begin** the conversation. Two examples are given about how to deal with finding condoms in a teen's clothes and how to help a daughter deal with sexual pressures by her boyfriend, but nothing more. The participation by the live audience is rather canned and clinical, and many questions are left unanswered. Parents will find this video does a fine job of communicating the urgency of the AIDS epidemic, but it won't help them learn to communicate about sex with their child.

Where To Find/Buy:

Bookstores, libraries, videotape dealers, or order direct by calling Total Marketing Services at 1-800-262-3822.

Overall Rating
★★
Presents the facts, dilemmas of AIDS epidemic, less helpful for parent-teen discussions

Design, Ease Of Use
★★
Well-paced, but advice and information is a bit scattered; feels canned and staged

1–4 Stars; N/R = Not Rated

Media:
Videotape

Price:
$24.98

Principal Subject:
Critical Issues & Concerns

ISBN:
1562782789

Edition:
1992

Publisher:
ABC News/MPI Home Video

IV. Critical Issues & Concerns

Overall Rating
★★
Good for beginning discussions about sexuality, but omits contraceptive information

Design, Ease Of Use
★★
Varied font is distracting throughout, otherwise site is straightforward; no graphics

1–4 Stars; N/R = Not Rated

Media:
Internet

Principal Subject:
Critical Issues & Concerns

Internet URL:
http://www.teenpregnancy.org/

Sexuality & Pregnancy

NATIONAL CAMPAIGN TO PREVENT TEEN PREGNANCY (THE)

Description:

Offering 4 options at their homepage, this Campaign's goal is to reduce the teen pregnancy rate 1/3 by the year 2005 by supporting "values and stimulating actions that are consistent with a pregnancy-free adolescence." One option—"Resources"—has 5 topics specifically for parents: related sites, "Facts and Stats," "10 Tips for Parents," resources, and "Teen In-Site." "Facts and Stats" presents, in a 2 page question and answer format, the rates of teen pregnancy, how teen mothers and their children suffer, ways to prevent teen pregnancy, and when to talk to your child about sex. Each of the "10 Tips" (about 1/2 a page) includes questions and talking points for parents as they begin discussions about sexuality with their teen. A variety of resources (books, pamphlets, videos, websites, etc.) are provided along with contact information for further support and guidance. "Teen In-Site" gives "the real story" with key messages ("it only takes once") supporting the campaign's premise that teen pregnancy doesn't need to be inevitable.

Evaluation:

What do parents really need when they sit down to discuss sexuality with their child? They need support, via resources that can be used as springboards toward parent-teen discussions, or questions to help parents clarify their own sexual attitudes and values. Parents also need to know the advantages and disadvantages of the various birth control available so they can educate their child on ways to protect against teen pregnancy. This website does a fine job of supporting parents' discussions through their extensive resource list, the "10 Tips for Parents," and "Key Messages" (within "Teen In-Site" located under "Teen Pregnancy: The Real Story"). However, the website then leaves parents stranded with no preventive pregnancy information to pass on to their child. This site states the importance of "setting clear expectations . . . and communicating honestly . . . to help teens delay becoming sexually active . . . [And] encourage those who are having sex to use contraception carefully." However, parents will need other resources to help them sort through the pros and cons of various contraception that is available to fulfill this goal.

Where To Find/Buy:

On the Internet at the URL: http://www.teenpregnancy.org/.

Sexuality & Pregnancy

PLANNED PARENTHOOD
Your Uncensored Source

Description:
Believing that "knowledge empowers people to make better choices about their health and sexuality," the Planned Parenthood Federation of America's (PPFA) website approaches teenage sexuality through the "Guides for Parents" and "Teen issues" sections on their homepage. "Guides for Parents" includes 4 different topics focusing on: "Talking About Sex" (what to discuss with kids, how to reinforce parental values, abstinence, sexually transmitted infections, sexual abuse, and "10 Helpful Hints for Parents"), "Talking about Birth Control," "What Parents Need to Know," and a daughter's first trip to the gynecologist. "Teen Issues" also discusses birth control offering information on the advantages, controversies, or cautions of various methods, the bodily changes that occur during adolescence, dating and relationship advice, options for teen pregnancy (keep the baby, adoption, abortion), and more. Various resources are suggested throughout for additional help in dealing with teen sexuality and sexual behavior.

Evaluation:
Parents will find this website disappointing in light of PPFA's goal to empower people with knowledge. Two sections that we did find useful were "Talking About Sex" within the parents' section, and "Birth Control Choices for Teens" within "Teen Issues." The emphasis in these two sections is on mutual respect and sound decision-making skills. By using the advice and the information included here, any parent will be arming their child with enough facts, positive support, and guidance to help them start making confident sexual decisions. More attention should have been paid, however, to the sections on abstinence and "Talking about Birth Control." The first simply states that if 53% are currently sexually active, then 47% are not. More helpful would have been sample dialogues that parents and teens could practice on how to say "no" confidently in various situations. "Talking about Birth Control" states that discussions should be age-appropriate, but then never delivers that necessary guidance. This site is best used with other more exacting resources that bridge the gap between facts and confident sexual behavior.

Where To Find/Buy:
On the Internet at the URL: http://www.plannedparenthood.org/.

Overall Rating
★★
Advice and birth control facts help foster mutual respect when discussing teen sexuality

Design, Ease Of Use
★★
Homepage menu contains buried subtopics; navigation tricky at times with dead-ends

1–4 Stars; N/R = Not Rated

Media:
Internet

Principal Subject:
Critical Issues & Concerns

Internet URL:
http://
www.plannedparenthood.org/

IV. Critical Issues & Concerns

Overall Rating
★★
Thought-provoking modules best for professionals; too time consuming if used by parents

Design, Ease Of Use
★
Cluttered presentation hard on the eyes at times; rather packed with psych discussions

1–4 Stars; N/R = Not Rated

Media:
Print

Price:
$14.50

Principal Subject:
Critical Issues & Concerns

ISBN:
0965364704

Edition:
1997

Publisher:
Summer Kitchen Press

Author:
Janet Ollila Colberg

About The Author:
(From Cover Notes)
Janet Ollila Colberg, a licensed professional counselor in private practice, has worked as a high school nurse in Helena Montana for 18 years. She is involved with the statewide workshops "Families and Youth In Crisis" and "Caring For Kids."

Sexuality & Pregnancy

RED LIGHT, GREEN LIGHT
Preventing Teen Pregnancy

Description:
Written with teenagers in mind, this 120 page book emphasizes ways to prevent teen pregnancy by exploring adolescent social behavior. It is organized into modules intended to be used in small groups of teens and adults. These interchangeable modules are based on counseling techniques and experiences with groups of teens. Each module begins with a vignette or composite sketch, followed by objectives for the unit, methodology for instruction, forms or questionnaires when appropriate, and concludes with questions to consider. Modules 1–4 discuss the topics of sexuality, individual counseling, and group formation. Modules 5–6 use the central theme of the mandala while exploring the importance of building self-worth and making personal spiritual choices. Modules 7–17 offer presentations of serious concerns (assertiveness, substance use, birth control, and more) that impact teen sexuality and discussions of behaviors that prevent teen pregnancy. Module 18 involves group closure. The modules aim to provide safe, honest ways for teens and adults to interact honestly in a safe constructive environment.

Evaluation:
This exhaustive set of seminars on teen sexuality and pregnancy is useful to adults and other teens in that it asks them to validate a teen's sexuality by discussing it openly and honestly. With its straightforward approach to the many intricacies of teenage sexuality and its demand for candid discussion, this book provides outlets for active dialog and positive reinforcement between adults and teens. It discusses everything from confidentiality agreements, to male and female reproductive organs and their functions, and finally to the embarrassment in discussing sex with grown-ups. However, most parents will find this resource difficult to digest. It is loaded with research studies and psychological tenets, bordering more on being a textbook than a friendly parenting companion. This book is best used by professionals looking for a program to use cooperatively with teens. It is only useful for the parent who has ample time to plan and implement the seminars on a regular basis.

Where To Find/Buy:
Bookstores, libraries, or order direct by calling 1-800-418-5237, or contacting Summer Kitchen Press at 314 Chaucer Street, Helena, MT 59601.

Sexuality & Pregnancy

NOT ME, NOT NOW
What Smart Kids Say To Sex

Description:

Reflecting the goals of the "Not Me, Not Now" campaign, this website aims to reduce the rate of pregnancies of 15–19 year old girls in Monroe County, New York. The program focuses on five goals: communicating the consequences of teenage pregnancy, helping teens deal with peer pressure, promoting parent-child communication about sexuality and relationships, promoting abstinence, and raising awareness of the problems of adolescent pregnancy. Their site offers four options—information about the campaign and a list of campaign materials, "teen interactive" (2 quizzes comparing how teens rate themselves vs. actual results from a fill-in Q & A survey), and "talking about sex" (directed toward parents). Here parents will find tips on how to start a conversation about sex, how to help kids say "not me, not now," how to understand adolescents' thoughts nowadays, and more. Each tip is typically 1–2 pages, and concludes with an example of a parent-teen conversation along with "what worked" and "what didn't work."

Evaluation:

The long-term goals of this campaign are quite admirable—to reduce the pregnancy rate for 15–19 year olds by at least 35% by the year 2000, and reduce the onset rate of sexual activity for 15 and 17 year olds. One would hope then that their website would clearly reflect these aims. Unfortunately though, their website lacks the hard facts and detailed tips parents need. It must be assumed, then, that parents will fill in the gaps left by the site's information. For example, no advice is given on how to help teens learn to deal with the peer pressure that accounts for many choices they make. The site does state that parents should "acknowledge peer pressure" by getting to know their child's friends and not making light of peers' influence. But here is where more scripted conversations between parent and teen would be helpful. One **is** offered, but it represents an idealistically open conversation that may not be evident in many households. Preventing teen pregnancy is a concern that needs direct input, not vagueness. Check into other more supportive resources for clearer advice other than "practicing abstinence makes sense for your future."

Where To Find/Buy:

On the Internet at the URL: http://www.notmenotnow.org/.

Overall Rating
★

Actual campaign goals are admirable, but website offers vague tips and little real info

Design, Ease Of Use
★

Many sections can't be printed; examples of parent-teen conversations seem forced

---

1–4 Stars; N/R = Not Rated

Media:
Internet

Principal Subject:
Critical Issues & Concerns

Internet URL:
http://www.notmenotnow.org/

Overall Rating
★★★★
A personal and practical presentation of an important issue

Design, Ease Of Use
★★★★
Clear, simple language; great use of personal stories; many self-reflective questions

1–4 Stars; N/R = Not Rated

Media:
Print

Price:
$13.95

Principal Subject:
Critical Issues & Concerns

ISBN:
09360770903

Edition:
1991

Publisher:
Gurze Books

Author:
Margo Maine, Ph.D.

About The Author:
(From Cover Notes)
Margo Maine, Ph.D., is vice-president of Eating Disorders Awareness and Prevention, Inc. She is also the senior editor of *Eating Disorders: The Journal Of Treatment And Prevention* and is a clinical psychologist.

Eating Disorders

FATHER HUNGER
Fathers, Daughters, & Food

Terrific Resource For:
Understanding how the father-daughter relationship can affect a teen's eating habits

Recommended For:
Critical Issues & Concerns

Description:
Father hunger, according to the author, is "a deep, persistent desire for emotional connection with the father that is experienced by all children." Maine devotes this 254 page book to explaining and analyzing how father hunger can be connected to the development of eating disorders. Part One of three discusses the origins of father hunger. This includes myths about fathers in American culture, the history of fatherhood as an institution, and overviews of the psychological development of males and females. Part Two delves into the emotional impact of father hunger on children. Separate chapters discuss the damage to a daughter's identity and emotions, conflicts around her body image, food, and sexuality, and finally loyalty. The third section provides possible solutions to father hunger, with strategies for fathers, mothers, daughters, and the general public. Four appendices provide strategies for educators, therapists, and physicians. The book intersperses personal vignettes with documented information.

Evaluation:
Maine studies a new angle here in the possible causes of eating disorders. Whereas past theorists would point to disturbed mother-child relationships, Maine focuses on the role of the father in a child's life, and the complications that may arise when his care isn't sufficient. The author succeeds in discussing the problems of father hunger without father-bashing. Her voice is sensitive at all times, and her use of real-life anecdotes provides a personal touch. What is especially impressive about this work is that it goes beyond mere speculation and theorizing. Maine provides strategies fathers, mothers, and daughters can use to ease their father hunger, or at least understand it. The appendices provide an abridged version of these resources for professionals. The scope of this book expands beyond daughters and fathers to include anyone affected by an eating disorder or those mildly interested in the phenomenon of father hunger. It is a must read for families, friends, and professionals needing exposure to the issue.

Where To Find/Buy:
Bookstores, libraries, or order direct by calling 1-800-756-7533 or (619) 434-7533.

Eating Disorders

SURVIVING AN EATING DISORDER
Strategies For Families And Friends

Recommended For:
Critical Issues & Concerns

Description:
The three authors of this 269 page book are all counselors and therapists who have hands-on knowledge of eating disorders. They put together this book as a resource for the friends and family of eating disorder victims. The three main sections of the book are intended to be read in order, and they highlight ways to gain perspective on eating disorders, how to confront the problem, and strategies to deal with the problem. Part One is intended to widen a loved one's knowledge of the disorders. Its three chapters cover the behavioral and psychological aspects of eating disorders, as well as the family context. Part Two gives advice on confronting a loved one, with tips on how to discuss the problem, how to cope with denial, and learning when to get professional help. The final section covers what to do to improve a relationship with a sufferer. This includes dealing with typical questions ("Do I look fat?") to analyzing your relationship with the eating disordered person. A large portion of the book is presented in the form of case studies. Additional resources in the form of books and helpful organizations are included.

Evaluation:
Surviving An Eating Disorder is one of the few books that support those who are personally involved with an eating disordered person as they attempt to understand the disorders, confront their loved ones, and rebuild or evaluate their relationship with them. Overflowing with case studies, the book is highly personal and informative. It never becomes overloaded with psychological terms or statistics. The book focuses on working on relationships involved in eating disorders, which are often a key to healing, more so than food itself. The authors understand that the key to healing is through personal therapy and assessing family and relationship issues. They manage to integrate these core issues with practical, everyday matters, such as how to talk to a sufferer or how to broach the idea of therapy. By reading this book, patients can also gain insight into what those who are close to them are going through. Although they are suffering, they will realize the effect their illness has on those they care about. Overall, this is a wonderful book for anyone personally touched by an eating disorder.

Where To Find/Buy:
Bookstores and libraries.

Overall Rating
★★★★
Necessary reading for friends and family of eating disorder victims

Design, Ease Of Use
★★★★
Excellent organization and integration of case studies

1–4 Stars; N/R = Not Rated

Media:
Print

Price:
$13.00

Principal Subject:
Critical Issues & Concerns

ISBN:
0060952334

Edition:
2nd (1997)

Publisher:
HarperPerennial
(HarperCollins Publishers)

Author:
Michele Siegel, Ph.D., Judith Brisman, Ph.D., and Margot Weinshel, M.S.W.

About The Author:
(From Cover Notes)
Brisman is the director of the Eating Disorder Resource Center, and both she and Siegel were its co-founders. Weinshel is a family therapist. She and Brisman publish, lecture, and present their work nationally.

Overall Rating
★★★★
Thoughtful, helpful insights without provoking undue guilt in mothers and daughters

Design, Ease Of Use
★★★
Very readable and engaging; uses headings, bullets, and graphics; friendly tone

1–4 Stars; N/R = Not Rated

Media:
Print

Price:
$13.95

Principal Subject:
Critical Issues & Concerns

ISBN:
0786882719

Edition:
1997

Publisher:
Hyperion

Author:
Debra Waterhouse, M.P.H., R.D.

About The Author:
(From Cover Notes)
Waterhouse has written 2 other books related to women and diet/food. She conducts seminars and workshops for women and health professionals on weight control, nutrition, and fitness-related issues, as well as on eating disorders.

Eating Disorders

LIKE MOTHER, LIKE DAUGHTER
Breaking Free From The Diet Trap

 Terrific Resource For:
Understanding how the mother-daughter relationship can encourage eating disorders

 Recommended For:
Critical Issues & Concerns

Description:

Based on the idea that most women pursue thinness thereby having unhealthy food relationships, and that women pass on these eating habits, weight-loss behaviors, and body images to their daughters, this book explores ways for all women to "achieve a diet-free, body-accepting lifestyle." This 232 page book is divided into 8 chapters: "The Generation Trap" (patterns of disordered eating and ways to break free), "Mothers Unknowingly Passing the Torch" (how to recognize the influence mothers have on their daughters' behaviors); "Dieting is Dangerous to Your Daughter's Health;" "From Girlhood to Womanhood: The Healthy Biological Passage;" "One Size Does Not Fit All: The Mother-Daughter Body Revolution" (offers ways to reassess one's body image); "Emancipation from Emaciation: The Declaration of Food Independence;" "Rebirth of Healthy Mother-Daughter Food Relationships" (reviews good eating habits); and "Like Mother, Like Daughter: From Generation Trap to Generation Triumph."

Evaluation:

This book is an excellent resource for all parents who want to prevent eating disorders, especially mothers of preteens and teens. It offers informative and thought-provoking chapters, helpful personal assessment questionnaires, a recommended reading list, and an extensive bibliography. The fourth chapter—"From Girlhood to Womanhood" includes a discussion of "biological rights," which is especially useful to help parents understand why girls increase body fat as they mature. Waterhouse recants a theme from her previous book—dieting makes women fat—and suggests helping teen girls to trust their "eating instincts." This book is highly readable, due to a friendly, yet informative style, and by its use of varying headings, lists, short quotes, and graphics. The lists of recommended reading and support organizations are useful. Note that this book deals more with preventing eating disorders than with helping a teen who currently has an eating disorder. Other resources will be necessary for these situations.

Where To Find/Buy:
Bookstores and libraries.

Eating Disorders

BULIMIA
A Guide For Family And Friends

Recommended For:
Critical Issues & Concerns

Description:

As the title states, this is a guidebook for family and friends who wish to understand bulimia and learn what they can do to help those suffering from the disorder. The book is arranged into three parts with nine chapters, and follows a question and answer format. Each chapter ends with a section entitled "What Can We Do To Help," which provides practical suggestions for the reader. Part One is an introduction and overview of bulimia. Part Two discusses possible causes of bulimia, including the role of society, family influence, and individual traits that often put someone at risk for developing the disorder. The third section describes the complexity of the disorder, and goes into the various thoughts, emotions, and behaviors present with bulimia and how these factors interact. Getting into, and going through treatment are discussed in the final chapters, yet, as the authors state, the book is not meant to be a substitute for therapy. The authors include an appendix with additional resources as well as an index.

Evaluation:

This 155 page book is a fine portrayal of the complexity of bulimia. It could be used by friends and family of bulimics as a guidebook, or as a support-book for bulimics. Although the book is not meant to substitute for therapy, patients are often helped by having resources that explain their behaviors, thoughts, and emotions, and that show them they are not alone in their suffering. The book is mostly an informative guide, not a personal account of bulimia or a self-help book, however. Some psychology professors may find it useful for teaching students the basics about the disorder. The layout and structure of the book is excellent. It is very easy to find information, and the question and answer format works well. The sections entitled "What Can We Do To Help," that are included at the end of each chapter, are wonderful resources. They make the book interactive as well as informative. Anyone involved in the life of a bulimic, or studying the disorder, should find this book a solid, practical resource.

Where To Find/Buy:

Bookstores and libraries.

Overall Rating
★★★
Practical advice for friends and family based on solid information

Design, Ease Of Use
★★★★
Question and answer format, index, and appendix work well together

1–4 Stars; N/R = Not Rated

Media:
Print

Price:
$17.95

Principal Subject:
Critical Issues & Concerns

ISBN:
0787903612

Edition:
1990

Publisher:
Jossey-Bass Publishers (Simon & Schuster)

Author:
Roberta Trattner Sherman, Ph.D. & Ron A. Thompson, Ph.D.

About The Author:
(From Cover Notes)
Sherman and Thompson are the authors of *Helping Athletes with Eating Disorders*. They are also the co-directors and founders of the Eating Disorders Program at Bloomington Hospital.

IV. Critical Issues & Concerns

Overall Rating
★★★
Strong discussions of specific behaviors and factors contributing to eating disorders

Design, Ease Of Use
★★★
Bulleted highlights and tips; narratives are easily read with concrete examples

1–4 Stars; N/R = Not Rated

Media:
Internet

Principal Subject:
Critical Issues & Concerns

Internet URL:
http://www.anred.com/

Eating Disorders

ANRED
Anorexia Nervosa And Related Eating Disorders, Inc.

Description:

The table of contents at this website offers 18 bulleted topics including: general information or overview of eating and exercise disorders (definitions, statistics, warning signs, medical problems, psychological complications); background information on who gets these disorders and why; recovery and treatment programs; athletes with eating disorders;, males with eating disorders; eating disorders and diabetes; obesity; ways to help someone with an eating disorder; frequently asked questions; links to other information; and more. Each topic (for example, "Background") is expanded into various subtopics (for example, "Who is at risk?" "What are the causes of eating and exercise disorders?") consisting of bullets questions answered by typically one paragraph of factual information. "Treatment and Recovery" lists, in a bulleted format, various treatment possibilities ("Hospitalization to prevent death, suicide, and medical crisis"), with more extensive narrative advice included on "Binge Prevention Tips."

Evaluation:

The strength of this website lies in its discussion about eating disorder warning signs. Specific behaviors discussed include: "food behaviors," "appearance and body image behaviors," "exercise behaviors," "thinking behaviors," "emotional behaviors," and "social behaviors." Also strong is the website's discussion on "What Causes Eating Disorders?" (within "Background"). Here, biological, psychological, and social factors that produce disordered eating are discussed, along with trigger events. The site's two weakest discussions, however, center on who is at risk and "Treatment and Recovery." For understanding who is at risk, parents should read "What Causes Eating Disorders?;" for advice on treatment and recovery, we suggest parents read "How to Help Someone You Care About" and "Jean's Memo" (the President of ANRED). Parents worried about or those dealing with eating disorders in their family will find this site worth a visit, especially when coupled with other resources addressing treatment options.

Where To Find/Buy:

On the Internet at the URL: http://www.anred.com/.

Eating Disorders

DIARY OF AN EATING DISORDER
A Mother And Daughter Share Their Healing Journey

Description:

Diary Of An Eating Disorder tells the story of Smith and her struggles with bulimia and anorexia. She writes about the time period between Fall of 1992 and Spring of 1995, when she was 16 to 18 years old and suffered from bulimia and anorexia. The 222 pages of this book contain her journal entries, which are interspersed with comments by her mother, Beverly Runyon. The text is broken into three parts, with a prologue and an epilogue. The first part contains journal entries from the time Chelsea was 16–17 years old. Part Two describes her first process of recovery at Remuda Ranch and through letters she sent to her mother. Part Three contains journal entries from Chelsea's 18th year. Each part, including the epilogue, contains a diary entry from her mother, overviewing her perspective on what was happening to Chelsea and revealing her own emotions. Chelsea's wish in writing this story was to provide understanding and insight, and possibly prevent at least one person from falling into the trap of an eating disorder.

Evaluation:

It is very difficult to read this book without feeling profoundly disturbed or distressed by the frequency of eating disorders in American culture. This is most likely the effect Smith and Runyon wanted when they created this work. The diary format reveals the inner turmoil that eating disorder victims go through, and Runyon's comments act as a mirror to reach victims' families. The writing is at all times personal and heart-wrenching, revealing the horror of Smith's eating disorder. The comments from her mother add an interesting twist to the book. The only negative points to this book are the lack of resources to turn to and the lack of an index. Also, some readers may feel turned off by the religious overtones, although spiritual reconnection is part of the therapeutic process at Remuda Ranch. Many parents feel hopeless in the face of eating disorders, and this book shows that most parents do care, but are at a loss for what to do. Coupling the insight gained here with other factual resources, will serve parents well.

Where To Find/Buy:

Bookstores and libraries.

Overall Rating
★★★
Moving, revealing, and disturbing account of the turmoil of a disordered teen and family

Design, Ease Of Use
★★
Diary format makes it easily read, but difficult to relocate parts; no resources or index

1–4 Stars; N/R = Not Rated

Media:
Print

Price:
$12.95

Principal Subject:
Critical Issues & Concerns

ISBN:
087833971X

Edition:
1998

Publisher:
Taylor Publishing Company

Author:
Chelsea Browning Smith with Beverly Runyon

About The Author:
(From Cover Notes)
Smith, still recovering from an eating disorder, is a senior at Texas Christian University and pursuing a degree in Communications and Human Relations. Runyon is the author of *The Overloving Parent* and former director of the Family Guidance Center of Fort Worth, TX.

IV. Critical Issues & Concerns

Overall Rating
★★★
Good starting point for concerned parents of dieting daughters

Design, Ease Of Use
★★
Easy to read, personal voice; no index or common structural theme

1–4 Stars; N/R = Not Rated

Media:
Print

Price:
$19.95

Principal Subject:
Critical Issues & Concerns

ISBN:
0876308361

Edition:
1997

Publisher:
Brunner/Mazel Publishers (Taylor & Francis Group)

Author:
Carolyn Costin

**About The Author:
(From Cover Notes)**
Costin is a recovered anorexic, the director of the Eating Disorder Center of California, and has been treating eating disorder patients for 17 years. She is also director of a six-bed treatment center for women suffering from anorexia, exercise addiction, and bulimia.

Eating Disorders

YOUR DIETING DAUGHTER
Is She Dying For Attention?

Description:

This resource, written by a recovered anorexic, is an overview of eating disorders. The 13 chapters of this 217 page book are written primarily for parents of children with eating disorders (anorexia, bulimia, and compulsive overeating). Costin's prologue is followed by a chapter that discusses how to deal with daughters who diet. The next 2 chapters discuss America's obsession with thinness, and the myths that surround dieting and food. Problems involving exercise addiction are discussed, with tips on how to discern the difference between fit and fanatic. Separate chapters are devoted to mother-daughter and father-daughter relationships. Body image and ways to recognize the various forms of eating disorders (and distinguish them from regular diets) are discussed in Chapters 7 and 8. Pointers are given on how parents can help their daughters, and information is provided on various diets and nutritional needs of girls. The final chapter includes letters from the people the book is written about. A lengthy appendix includes a nutrition guide, recommended daily allowances, and resources.

Evaluation:

Most resources on teens and eating disorders tend to focus solely on anorexia and/or bulimia. This book extends beyond this to include diagnostic criteria and case studies of anorexia nervosa, bulimia nervosa, binge eating, and eating disorders not otherwise specified. Primarily written for parents who have a daughter with an eating disorder, or those who worry about their dieting daughter, it provides guidelines to tell them what is fit or fanatic, and what is a diet or a disorder. Consideration is also given to healthy diets and nutritional guidelines for those who wish to help their daughter maintain a healthy weight. It overviews psychological or emotional problems that are commonly found with eating disorders, and provides suggestions for how parents can help. Where this book is limited is in its lack of an index and in-depth information, except on nutrition. It also is written solely for disordered daughters, neglecting the growing percentage of eating disordered males. However, parents will find it is a fine starting point, written in a clear, personal voice, and it provides solid guidelines and additional resources.

Where To Find/Buy:

Bookstores, libraries, or order direct by calling 1-800-825-3089 or (212) 924-3344.

Eating Disorders

EATING DISORDER SITE (THE)
Hope For The Future

Description:

The Site Map at this website lists 32 bulleted topics for those either suffering from an eating disorder or friends and family "who need an education on the subject to better help and support their loved one." Articles (typically 3–5 pages in length) include a variety of subjects, such as anorexia nervosa, bulimia nervosa, binge eating disorder, and compulsive exercising, along with articles focusing on bodily needs and functions (nutrition, vitamins, fats, etc.). Articles focusing on eating disorders include information in a bulleted format about behavioral signs, physiological signs, attitude shifts, and ways to treat and manage disorders. Advice is given to "Family & Friends" about how to cope with a loved one ("talk about issues other than food," "most of all, hang in there") and what to avoid ("guilt is not the way," "don't get into power struggles over food"). A list of "Treatment Centers" supplies contact information primarily within the U.S. "The Road to an Eating Disorder" offers "diet rules" that may lead to an eating disorder.

Evaluation:

For busy parents concerned about a child's possible eating disorder, this site offers quick facts at a glance to determine whether or not they should seek additional help. The articles focusing on specific eating disorders are well-done, although rather clinically presented. Less useful are the articles meant for "Family & Friends." Here, parents will find short antidotes to a dangerous situation. One paragraph of advice ("Lovingly confront your loved one," or "Listening to your loved one is the best gift you could give") is scant and offers little support for serious problems. The list of treatment centers may help where advice leaves off. The site doesn't specifically address risk factors, but parents will find this information housed within "The Road to an Eating Disorder." Each of the 6 rules ("Fat is evil, diet foods are best") is accompanied by a contradictory explanation. Somewhat simplistic, the explanations do offer supportive health facts for parent-child discussions. This site offers the facts about eating disorders, but parents will need additional support to help them deal with the realities.

Where To Find/Buy:

On the Internet at the URL: http://www.geocities.com/HotSprings/5395/.

Overall Rating
★★
Good quick source of information on the facts of various eating disorders, little support

Design, Ease Of Use
★★★
Site map lists contents; information presented rather clinically, in a bulleted format

1–4 Stars; N/R = Not Rated

Media:
Internet

Principal Subject:
Critical Issues & Concerns

Internet URL:
http://www.geocities.com/HotSprings/5395/

IV. Critical Issues & Concerns

Overall Rating
★★
Useful for a general overview of food disorders with emphasis on family dynamics

Design, Ease Of Use
★★★
Short, to the point w/ numerous self-reflective questions in a workbook style; no index

1–4 Stars; N/R = Not Rated

Media:
Print

Price:
$11.00

Principal Subject:
Critical Issues & Concerns

ISBN:
0805932941

Edition:
1992

Publisher:
Dorrance Publishing Co.

Author:
Laura J. Goodman, M. Ed.

**About The Author:
(From Cover Notes)**
A former high school tennis coach, Goodman is currently a psychotherapist specializing in treating eating disorders. She also speaks and leads in-service training programs on eating disorders and related issues.

Eating Disorders

IS YOUR CHILD DYING TO BE THIN?
A Workbook For Parents And Family Members On Eating Disorders

Description:

The book begins and ends with poems written by Mary, a young woman with bulimia. It is then divided into 15 other chapters, including an introduction. Other chapter headings focus on food and its relationship to disorders, ways to classify disorders (with checklists for parents to evaluate their child, feelings), parents' feelings about their child and the disorder, the eating history of the family, causes, "webbing" to determine a child's losses (intimacy, friends, etc.) and parents' losses (career, family, etc.) due to the disorder, responsibility and blame (also discusses forgiveness and acceptance), hunger (emotional, social, and physical with 3 day worksheet chart), body image (with visuals for self-analysis and discussion), perfection (wishes vs. realistic expectations), sexual abuse (with suggested readings), athletics, nutrition (safe, potential, and unsafe foods for a child), and treatment (uses a team approach with therapists, physician, nutritionist, and support group).

Evaluation:

Rather than focusing solely on the food disorder, this book allows family members to get involved in understanding more about their child, while reflecting upon their own attitudes and behaviors. The book is divided into short segments (a few pages each), which makes it easy to use and absorb. The author uses plenty of examples in each chapter, usually consisting of vignettes of young women with different types of eating disorders and their parents. These narratives really help parents "see" the different behaviors discussed or points being made, rather than simply presenting a clinical description of eating disorders in general. Parents will no doubt find the numerous workbook-type exercises helpful in trying to understand their family's dynamics and perspectives on food. Although this book is not appropriate or thorough enough to provide parents with all the information needed for dealing with eating disorders, it is an excellent resource to help parents deal with the emotions they are experiencing.

Where To Find/Buy:

Bookstores, libraries, or order direct by contacting Dorrance Publishing Co. at 643 Smithfield Street, Pittsburgh, PA 15222.

Eating Disorders

PROBLEM WITH FOOD (THE)

Description:

Presented as an informational segment from a fundraiser drive, this 27 minute videotape focuses on eating disorders, specifically anorexia nervosa, bulimia nervosa, and compulsive overeating. During the course of the program, three individuals are interviewed along with psychiatric nurses, educators, and others. The three individuals' personal stories follow a similar format outlining symptoms of the disorder, examples of typical meals eaten, personal history that contributed to the disorder, problems caused by the disorder, treatment, and current daily life; an on-screen list of symptoms are presented for anorexia and bulimia, not for compulsive overeating. Various professionals (mostly from the Western Psychiatric Institute) discuss how American culture defines attractiveness, nutritional needs, recommended amount of exercise, and more. The tape concludes by stating that support groups are very effective for treatment, combined with medical and psychological treatment for patients, family, and friends.

Evaluation:

Parents won't get specifics on treatment in this tape, and they won't get details of the disorders. What parents will get are firsthand accounts of how eating disorders affect lives, and how those affected proceed with their lives after treatment. The quality of the tape is low, with audio disturbance caused by the background hum of the fundraiser's telephone operators, insensitively distracting from the individuals' stories. At best, this tape grants parents only a general background into the world of those suffering from eating disorders. It does present some issues neglected by other resources, namely, that young men can also be affected by anorexia; the tape discusses athletics, steroids, and other factors that contribute to the rise in male-anorexia. However, only slight mention is given the importance of transitioning from therapy to home. The discussion on treatment is far too brief to be of any help or guidance. Altogether, parents seeking more definitive help, advice, or facts will need better substantiated resources.

Where To Find/Buy:

Bookstores, libraries, or by calling Total Marketing at 1-800-262-3822.

Overall Rating
★★
Recounts stories of 3 individuals affected by anorexia, bulimia, compulsive overeating

Design, Ease Of Use
★
Interview format, segment taken from bustling fundraiser with audio distractions

1–4 Stars; N/R = Not Rated

Media:
Videotape

Price:
$24.98

Principal Subject:
Critical Issues & Concerns

ISBN:
1885538146

Edition:
1993

Publisher:
QED Communications

IV. Critical Issues & Concerns

Overall Rating
★
Provides only a starting point for basic information on eating disorders

Design, Ease Of Use
★★
Easy to navigate; clear separation of anorexia and bulimia sections; no TOC or index

1–4 Stars; N/R = Not Rated

Media:
Print

Price:
$1.95

Principal Subject:
Critical Issues & Concerns

ISBN:
1562461524

Edition:
1998

Publisher:
Johnson Institute—QVS

Author:
Johnson Institute (The)

**About The Author:
(From Cover Notes)**
The Johnson Institute puts together informative pamphlets for parents and teachers about parent-adolescent issues, such as guidelines for teenage parties, STDs, AIDS, tobacco, narcotics, alcohol, handling anger, setting limits, steroids, and more.

Eating Disorders

WHAT TO TEACH KIDS ABOUT EATING DISORDERS
For Parents, Teachers, And Other Caregivers

Description:
What To Teach Kids About Eating Disorders is a very brief pamphlet (12 pages) about eating disorders. It is part of The Parenting For Prevention Information Series, which consists of pamphlets covering a wide variety of critical issues among adolescents. An introductory paragraph overviews possible causes of eating disorders, and urges parents and teachers to help kids form healthier self images. The section entitled "What Is An Eating Disorder" overviews the basic symptoms and differences between anorexia nervosa and bulimia. Common physical complications of each disorder are listed, as are possible causes or triggers for the disorders. Typical traits of eating disorder victims, or those who may be susceptible, are listed. A single page is devoted to treating eating disorders. The authors feel that all sufferers need a physician, individual psychological counseling, and family therapy. This informative brochure is meant to be a resource for parents, teachers, and caregivers—not eating disorder patients.

Evaluation:
For those who know little about eating disorders, this pamphlet gives a starting point, but provides little else. It is simply an overview of eating disorders, stating basic facts and theories, who is susceptible to them, and behavior patterns commonly seen in sufferers; no mention is given for overeating/obesity. The pamphlet's structure is easy to follow, and the sections are clearly marked. The lists of physical complications and characteristics of those susceptible to the disorders are useful for parents or teachers wanting to know the warning signs of eating disorders. One major problem with the pamphlet is that it provides no support resources. It does mention that parents who suspect their child has an eating disorder should call a doctor or mental health clinic, but it doesn't give any other direct resources. Overall, this pamphlet could be used as a quick reference for parents and caregivers. It does not however, as the title states, explicitly tell parents what to teach kids about eating disorders. It is just an overview.

Where To Find/Buy:
Bookstores, libraries, or order direct by calling 1-800-231-5165.

IV. Critical Issues & Concerns—Eating Disorders • 159

Eating Disorders

EATING DISORDERS

Description:

Developed as a public service by the American College of Physicians (through an educational grant from The Upjohn Company), this 27 minute videotape begins by introducing the lifestyle and workday of an internist. The camera follows her around throughout her day as she checks on three of her patients, one with anorexia nervosa, one with bulimia, and one with obesity. Presented in a doctor-patient interview-type format, she delves into each patient's personal history, discusses the past reasons for their eating disorder, and focuses on how they currently handle their food disorder. Also mentioned are some typical forms of treatment each patient has attempted (hospitalization, food models, journaling, group therapy, and more), along with how they try to deal differently with life's stresses. The narrator/internist concludes the tape by stating, "I respect my patients for their guts, their life force."

Evaluation:

Parents wanting serious questions answered, or seeking sincere guidance for their teens with known eating disorders, shouldn't waste a precious moment here. This tape has the feel and script of a movie shown in a health class during the 1970s. For example, it opens with the internist driving through the Civil War battlefields in Tennessee remarking on the "battleground of food disorders." At the conclusion of the tape, she is then found jogging along a trail, commenting that running is like dealing with food disorders, "coming from there to here." Due to denial and secrecy, parents often don't know if they should suspect their child of having an eating disorder. They need a list of symptoms, they need ideas of possible treatments (other than "see a professional"), and they need support. Our advice? Look elsewhere. Eating disorders can be a serious threat and professionals **are** necessary in many cases. This tape would assist parents better if it spent more time addressing the problem and less time profiling the professional.

Where To Find/Buy:

Bookstores, libraries, video dealers, or order direct by calling Library Video Company at 1-800-843-3620 or (610) 645-4000; can also be ordered through the distributor (Karol Media) at 1-800-884-0555.

Overall Rating
★
Presents food disorders through an internist's eyes, no real info on symptoms, treatment

Design, Ease Of Use
★
Outdated, w/ corny visuals/auditory (ex: Civil War field="battleground of disorders")

1–4 Stars; N/R = Not Rated

Media:
Videotape

Price:
$19.95

Principal Subject:
Critical Issues & Concerns

Edition:
1986

Publisher:
American College of Physicians

Author:
American College of Physicians

IV. Critical Issues & Concerns

Overall Rating
★★★★
Well-done expose of gang indicators; up-to-date and relevant

Design, Ease Of Use
★★★★
Graphics, tables of info, bold headings, detailed TOC; gang name and general indexes

1–4 Stars; N/R = Not Rated

Media:
Print

Price:
$12.95

Principal Subject:
Critical Issues & Concerns

ISBN:
1577490355

Edition:
1997

Publisher:
Fairview Press

Author:
Steven L. Sachs

About The Author:
(From Cover Notes)
Sachs has been an officer of the Nineteenth Judicial Circuit of Lake County (Illinois) for over eighteen years, serving as a juvenile probation officer, juvenile detentions counselor, home detention officer, and pretrial bond supervision officer.

Delinquent Behavior, Gangs

STREET GANG AWARENESS
A Resource Guide For Parents And Professionals

 Recommended For:
Critical Issues & Concerns

Description:
The premise of *Street Gang Awareness* is that an informed parent is a better parent, and that signs of gang activity are all around, if parents know what to look for. Consisting of four sections, this 198 page book is written by an experienced juvenile probation officer with a background in home detention and juvenile detention counseling. The first section of the book explains the evolution and history of gang culture, comparing today's gangs with those throughout history. Section Two covers the recruitment process, organizational structures, hierarchical systems, and race demographics which vary from one gang to another. It also explains the "lure of the gang" and why they appeal to kids. The third section explains how to determine whether or not a child is involved with a gang. The various identifiers are highlighted such as clothing, jewelry, hand signs, and more. The final section discusses how communities, organizations, and individuals can respond to gangs, and offers resources for other sources of help.

Evaluation:
This book offers a concise but in-depth analysis of how to tell if a child may be a gang member or is thinking about joining one. Sections Three and Four will be of particular interest to parents and educators. Indicators of gang involvement are presented along with specific advice on how communities, school, and families can combat the problem. For example, in describing hand signs, parents of hearing-impaired children are cautioned about the dangers of gangs who have adopted ASL (American Sign Language) as a method of communicating; there have been reported incidents of deaf people being mistaken for gang members and brutally beaten. Part Four will be particularly helpful to parents, schools, and community leaders seeking advice on how to steer kids away from gangs. This comprehensive book enables parents to not only become aware of gang presence, but also realize that the effects of gang violence are far-reaching and require vigilance to combat.

Where To Find/Buy:
Bookstores, libraries, or order direct by calling 1-800-544-8207.

Delinquent Behavior, Gangs

GANGS
A Handbook For Community Awareness

 Recommended For:
Critical Issues & Concerns

Description:

The aim of this 276 page book about gangs is to educate community leaders and parents about the inner workings and psychology of gangs in the U.S., so that they may learn how to combat the spread of gang influence. This 276 page book is divided into six sections. The first section gives a general background and comprehensive view of gangs, addressing frequently asked questions about street gangs. Section Two highlights various types of gangs, based upon their beliefs, ethnicity, place of origin, and sex. The third section focuses on the violence associated with gangs, including initiation, membership rules, gang signs, and more. Section Four discusses the impact of gangs on everyday life, with chapters dedicated to the influence of gangs in the media, schools and in corporate America. Section Five identifies problem-solving methods, such as community-based anti-gang programs that concerned people are creating in response to gang violence in America. A bibliography and resource guide are provided in Section Six.

Evaluation:

Gangs is a good resource for anyone wanting to learn about the genesis and rise of the gang in today's society. It is full of useful information on how to identify street gangs by the clothes they wear, the graffiti they leave, or the signs they "throw." If anything, it is almost too cluttered with facts and narratives to be read in one sitting or by the casual reader. Rather, it should be read as a reference manual, sifted through for information on gang history or graffiti styles. Of particular interest are the stories at the beginning of each section called "Voices From the Front." These are narratives from gang members, ex-gang members, or people personally affected by gang violence. Also interesting are "Rick's Reports," which are true-life anecdotes and interviews of prisoners conducted by one of the authors. A separate section of 6 pages outlines useful advice for parents on how to recognize signs that their child may be involved with a gang as well as advice on what they can do to prevent gang involvement. Not for the casual reader or busy parent, nonetheless, this book offers an in-depth reference manual to gang awareness.

Where To Find/Buy:
Bookstores and libraries.

Overall Rating
★★★★
Thought provoking, details history of gangs, current practices, and problem-solving tips

Design, Ease Of Use
★★★
Good overall layout, although a bit cluttered at times

1–4 Stars; N/R = Not Rated

Media:
Print

Price:
$22.95

Principal Subject:
Critical Issues & Concerns

ISBN:
0816033595

Edition:
1997

Publisher:
Facts On File

Author:
Rick Landre, Mike Miller and Dee Porter

**About The Author:
(From Cover Notes)**
Landre, senior police officer of the Lodi CA Gang Task Force Unit, has worked as a detective and gang investigator for 6 years. Porter, an award-winning writer, has worked with youth for 25+ years. Miller is an educator in a program for at-risk youth in El Dorado Hills, CA.

IV. Critical Issues & Concerns

Overall Rating
★★★
3-prong approach (family, school, community) toward helping kids stay out of gangs

Design, Ease Of Use
★★
Large print, subdividing chapters would ease readability; should be read in entirety

1–4 Stars; N/R = Not Rated

Media:
Print

Price:
$12.95

Principal Subject:
Critical Issues & Concerns

ISBN:
1879094460

Edition:
1995

Publisher:
Momentum Books, Ltd.

Author:
Mike Knox

**About The Author:
(From Cover Notes)**
Mike Knox is a fifteen year veteran of the Houston Police Department where he helped create the department's Westside Command Divisional Gang Unit.

Delinquent Behavior, Gangs

GANGSTA IN THE HOUSE
Understanding Gang Culture

Description:
The author's approach toward writing this 183 page book was to concentrate on why gangs are popular and what we as a society do to perpetuate their existence. Knox is a 15 year veteran of a police department and helped create their gang unit. Beginning with a prologue, which is a graphic recreation of a drive-by shooting, Knox continues by discussing the mind set of a gangster, the false premises of gangs (e.g., the gang will provide protection, "be there" for the gang member, etc.), the various gang families (Crips, Bloods, Folk Nation, People Nation), girl gangs (traditional, new wave, hybrid), recognizing the "uniforms" of gang members, graffiti, alternative ways to empower youth, the effects of denial by family members and communities, and solutions to gang involvement. Gangs, in the author's opinion, represent family structure and discipline to some kids. If they receive these things elsewhere, there is no need for them to join gangs.

Evaluation:
Many parents may find the prologue of this book difficult to absorb. Knox doesn't illuminate on crimes committed by gang members, or detail their styles of dress and communication. His book examines the reasoning behind the existence of gangs, looking at the ways kids get in over their heads. For example, Knox's depiction of one young man's "jump-in" as though it was a choice of "join or die" is frightening. Using common sense based on his 15 years of experience, Knox describes gangs as failures of our society to respond to the needs of our young people. Knox believes that kids are afraid at school, are often ignored at home, and are looking for something or someone to provide discipline and structure to their lives. He then illustrates ways parents, schools, and communities can collectively combat street gangs. Advocating firm, fair, and consistent discipline, he outlines how gang members respond positively to boot camp environments where they must respect a superior's commands. Parents, teachers, and administrators will gain a general understanding of how they need to work together to combat gang actions.

Where To Find/Buy:
Bookstores and libraries.

Delinquent Behavior, Gangs

BEFORE IT'S TOO LATE
Why Some Kids Get Into Trouble—And What Parents Can Do About It

Description:

Stating that "seeing life almost exclusively as a one-way street is a hallmark of antisocial behavior," this book proceeds to offer both descriptions of children with antisocial behavior, and advice for those who parent them. The author believes that early diagnosis of antisocial behavior is the key to treating this behavioral condition by identifying individuals who have "an agenda for living that is distinctly different" from that of other people. This child typically disregards injury to others, has unrealistic expectations of himself, takes the easy way out, refuses to be held accountable, lies, leads an isolated life, and more. Throughout this book, Samenow paints a picture of how difficult it is to parent these children, and stresses that the child must be held accountable for their actions and forced to deal with consequences. The third and final part of this 225 page book discusses parental errors that interfere with progress, such as denial, lack of consistency, inability to demand accountability, letting the child offer excuses for their behavior, and more.

Evaluation:

The tough tone of this book might put some parents off who are looking for answers on how to deal with their child's difficult behavior, but the discomfort is worth it to get to the messages contained in this book. Parents of antisocial children have difficult hurdles to overcome, especially when trying to instill a sense of responsibility in their child who seems incapable of this expectation. Parents often feel an overwhelming guilt when their antisocial child is acting out, that somehow it is all their fault. Samenow believes that antisocial behavior is a choice that children make, but that parents can take steps to counteract the behavior before it becomes entrenched. The section on early identification is particularly helpful, with its plain language on the emotional development of the antisocial child. This resources does not focus specifically on the teenage years. However, any parent willing to deal with this issue head-on will find this resource offers a "tough love" approach to a child with antisocial behavior.

Where To Find/Buy:

Bookstores and libraries.

Overall Rating
★★
No-nonsense approach might put some parents off; not specifically focused on teens

Design, Ease Of Use
★★
Meant to be read all the way through; combines narrative, research, and anecdotes

1–4 Stars; N/R = Not Rated

Media:
Print

Price:
$23.00

Principal Subject:
Critical Issues & Concerns

ISBN:
0812916468

Edition:
1989

Publisher:
Times Books
(Random House)

Author:
Stanton E. Samenow, Ph.D.

**About The Author:
(From Cover Notes)**
Samenow earned a doctoral degree in clinical psychology from the University of Michigan, and is the author of a three volume work called *The Criminal Personality*. He has served on three presidential task forces on crime and drug issues.

IV. Critical Issues
& Concerns

Overall Rating

★

This book is a good resource for officials, but of little constructive use for parents

Design, Ease Of Use

★★★★

Well laid-out, easy to access; numerous graphics, drawings, photos to illustrate text

1–4 Stars; N/R = Not Rated

Media:
Print

Price:
$25.00

Principal Subject:
Critical Issues & Concerns

ISBN:
0873648447

Edition:
1995

Publisher:
Paladin Press
(Paladin Enterprises)

Author:
Bill Valentine

About The Author:
(From Cover Notes)
Bill Valentine has more than 18 years experience as a correctional officer at Nevada State Prison. For the last five of these years he has served as the prison's gang intelligence officer, identifying, tracking and gathering intelligence on street and prison gangs.

Delinquent Behavior, Gangs

GANG INTELLIGENCE MANUAL
Identifying And Understanding Modern-Day Violent Gangs In The United States

Description:

This 250 page manual provides details about gangs. The first chapter describes general characteristics of gangs and identifiers such as drawings, hand signs, tattoos, graffiti, and more. The remaining 10 chapters individually discuss specific gangs, such as Crips and Bloods, Hispanic gangs, Colombian gangs, People Nation and Folks Nation, the Jamaican Posses, Asia/South Sea Islanders Gangs, The Cuban Marielito, Hell's Angels, White Supremacists and Other White Gangs, and Prison Gangs. A description of each gang's history is included, along with a listing of the known individual gangs within the larger group, ways to identify gang members (i.e. how they dress, what symbols they use, their graffiti, etc.), gang rules and criminal activities, and more. Also discussed is where gangs originated from, why they appeal to young people today, how they recruit and train their members, what tactics they use to issue challenges and threats to other gangs, and how gangs compete for the lucrative drug market.

Evaluation:

The epidemic of gangs in the United States has been on the rise as older, well-established gangs have become highly successful drug organizations. *The Gang Intelligence Manual* clearly and neatly identifies modern gangs, discussing how they operate along with visual identifiers such as the type of clothing, jewelry, hair, and other symbols their members display. The book's numerous graphics, photos, and drawings offer excellent visual signs needed for recognizing gang presence. The author asserts that the only way to stop gangs from getting a better foothold in our society is to become better educated about them. His point is well-taken, but he provides little help for concerned parents who wonder how to address their child's interest or involvement in a gang. Aside from its information on the style of dress, graffiti, slang, and hand signs used by different gangs, this book will serve only as a general resource for parents. It is a far more effective resource for police and school officials on the lookout for gang behavior.

Where To Find/Buy:

Bookstores and libraries.

UNDERSTANDING YOUR TEENAGER'S DEPRESSION
Issues, Insights & Practical Guidance For Parents

Terrific Resource For:
Understanding how depression relates to other serious adolescent problems

Recommended For:
Critical Issues & Concerns

Description:

This 346 page book consists of numerous facts and personal stories that support the author's claim that "depression is a major contributing factor to a host of adolescent problems." These problems include eating disorders, substance abuse, pregnancy, school problems, and suicide. The book consists of 31 chapters which are divided into nine sections. These sections focus on the problems associated with teenage depression, as well as their symptoms and treatments, with a focus in the first three sections on understanding teenage depression and helping one's child cope. Section topics include, "Identifying Teenage Depression—The Signs And Symptoms," "Understanding And Helping Your Teenage Child Through Depression," and "What To Do When Your Teen Is Having School Problems." The author's background in behavioral therapy along with her experience as an editor for Teen magazine contribute to her understanding of teenage depression.

Evaluation:

This book is an in-depth study of the causes, symptoms, and treatments of depression in young people. The author's frank treatment of delicate subjects (sexuality, substance abuse, suicide) contributes to this book's quality. The author primarily focuses on psychotherapy as a treatment for depression, but also includes a section on medical treatments titled "Beyond Therapy: When Your Teen Needs Extra Help." One particularly helpful chapter focuses on common barriers to communication between parents and their teenagers; poor communication obviously slows understanding and delays getting help to adolescents. This resource is directed at parents, but is also a useful resource for all individuals that work with youth, including teachers and school counselors. Originally published as "Coping With Teenage Depression" in 1982, but revised in this edition for the "nineties" teenager, this is a helpful resource for bewildered or concerned parents.

Where To Find/Buy:

Bookstores and libraries.

Overall Rating
★★★★
An invaluable resource for parents of distressed teenagers

Design, Ease Of Use
★★★★
Clearly organized, does not use medical jargon

1–4 Stars; N/R = Not Rated

Media:
Print

Price:
$13.95

Principal Subject:
Critical Issues & Concerns

ISBN:
0399518568

Edition:
(2nd) 1994

Publisher:
Perigee Books (Berkeley Publishing Group)

Author:
Kathleen McCoy, Ph.D.

**About The Author:
(From Cover Notes)**
McCoy is a behavioral specialist and former editor of Teen magazine. She has written ten books and numerous articles for national magazines, newspapers, and journals; she's also the online expert in adolescent psychology for the National Parenting Center.

IV. Critical Issues & Concerns

Overall Rating
★★★
Good resource with understandable descriptions of suicide and depression

Design, Ease Of Use
★★★★
Very readable, chapters end with "Things to Remember," support groups, bibliography

1–4 Stars; N/R = Not Rated

Media:
Print

Price:
$18.95

Principal Subject:
Critical Issues & Concerns

ISBN:
0471621846

Edition:
1995

Publisher:
John Wiley & Sons

Author:
Gerald D. Oster, Ph.D and
Sarah S. Montgomery, M.S.W

**About The Author:
(From Cover Notes)**
Oster has a private practice in clinical child psychology, and is a clinical associate professor at the University of Maryland Medical School. Montgomery is a child and family therapist at the University of Maryland Medical System Department of Psychiatry.

Depression, Suicide

HELPING YOUR DEPRESSED TEENAGER
A Guide For Parents And Caregivers

 Recommended For:
Critical Issues & Concerns

Description:
Meant as a guide to help parents "understand the difference between the 'normal' ups and downs of adolescence and the signs and symptoms of clinical depression," this 184 page book is divided into 3 parts. Part 1, "The Teenage Years," covers adolescence in general terms; the 4 chapters include topics on physical changes, peer influence, achievement, sexuality, resistance, and leaving home. In Part 2, Chapter 5 includes a chart on the symptoms of depression and describes all the effects of the problem; it also discusses models of depression (psychoanalytical, cognitive, and biological). Chapter 6 focuses on questions and answers about depression. Chapters 7, 8, and 9 discuss, respectively, the myths and facts of suicide, intervention and prevention, and family influence. The third part includes 5 chapters on "Treatment Considerations:" evaluation, counseling for the teen, counseling for the family, medication, and hospitalization.

Evaluation:
Each chapter begins with several snapshot descriptions of teens which effectively help parents see teens and the issues/problems being discussed. The sections entitled "Things to Remember" at the end of each chapter provide parents with useful summaries, and makes the book easy to skim. Useful charts, like "Symptoms of Depression" (in Chapter 5) and "Positive Ways to Help" (in Chapter 6) are very effective, as is the author's "what-to-do" approach consisting of a series of "if-this-happens" situations and "try-this" actions for parents. The section on treatment effectively answers parents' concerns, and shows them how to remain active in the teen's life, even when a teen is hospitalized. The lists of resources and support groups are also helpful. A well-organized book, it is thorough in its coverage of the topic—good for parents of teens who have already been diagnosed with depression or for worried parents who want to understand moody teens.

Where To Find/Buy:
Bookstores and libraries.

Depression, Suicide

LONELY, SAD AND ANGRY
A Parent's Guide To Depression In Children And Adolescents

Description:

This book, written by clinical psychologists, aims to offer "accurate and up-to-date information about depression and depressive disorders in children and adolescents." Divided into ten chapters, this 225 page book's intent is to provide a combined approach of scientific research and the authors' combined 40+ years experience working with troubled children and their families. Chapters 1–3 describe symptoms of childhood depression along with related emotional and behavioral problems, such as anxiety disorders, conduct disorder, oppositional defiant disorder, ADHD, and learning disabilities; various diagnostic scales to rate signs of depression are given. The causes of depression are discussed in Chapter 4 while Chapters 5–6 highlight psychological and medical treatments. Chapter 7 offers information on dealing with suicidal behavior and psychiatric hospitalization. Chapters 8–9 presents strategies for parents and teachers on how to help the depressed child. Chapter 10 includes the authors' perspective on societal factors that foster emotional illness and how to address these concerns in the future.

Evaluation:

While some books rely heavily on defining the biological causes of depression, this book offers a more well-rounded proposition, namely that it is a combination of nurture, nature, and environment. To justify this, the authors cite the inherent problems with some research seeking to simply blame the parents' parenting styles or the child's genetic background. In particular, we encourage parents to read Chapters 5 and 8. The pros and cons of the various types of psychotherapy are discussed in Chapter 5 while Chapter 8 focuses on how parents can handle their own emotions, keep their marriage intact, determine positive rewards and negative consequences, and more; appendixes offer parents a list of supportive organizations, ideas for fun rewards, and a depression symptom checklist. To help break up the text, the authors supply the reader with numerous parent-child stories that neatly capture their primary message. Not necessarily an easily read book due primarily to its use of psychiatric terminology, this resource does offer valuable insights warranting parental attention.

Where To Find/Buy:

Bookstores and libraries.

Overall Rating
★★★
Combines research and experience in diagnosing and treating childhood depression

Design, Ease Of Use
★★
Heavy use of clinical terminology at times, useful story vignettes help break it up

1–4 Stars; N/R = Not Rated

Media:
Print

Price:
$11.95

Principal Subject:
Critical Issues & Concerns

ISBN:
0385476426

Edition:
1995

Publisher:
Main Street Books (Doubleday/Bantam Doubleday Dell)

Author:
Barbara D. Ingersoll, Ph.D. and Sam Goldstein, Ph.D.

About The Author:
(From Cover Notes)
Ingersoll, with a Ph.D. in clinical psychology, has treated hyperactive children and counseled their families for 20+ years. Goldstein is a clinical instructor in the Department of Psychiatry and has been in private practice since 1982.

IV. Critical Issues & Concerns

Overall Rating
★★
Basic coverage of clinical depression in 5 unique populations (women, men, teens, etc.)

Design, Ease Of Use
★★★★
Personal vignettes work well; good on-screen visuals listing symptoms, risk factors, etc.

1–4 Stars; N/R = Not Rated

Media:
Videotape

Price:
$24.95

Principal Subject:
Critical Issues & Concerns

ISBN:
076700373X

Edition:
1997

Publisher:
National Broadcasting Company (NBC)

Author:
National Broadcasting Company (NBC)

Depression, Suicide

AMERICAN BLUES

Description:
The goal of this one hour videotape is to "offer ideas on treatments that work as well as strategies for coping with a loved one who's suffering" from clinical depression. Originally presented as a Today show week-long segment, the tape is divided into 5 equal segment addressing the unique depression of women, men, teens, young children, and elderly adults. The teen segment profiles an adolescent who, in his depressed state, attempted suicide before he was given professional help. Several on-screen lists are provided of: symptoms (lack of pleasure, change in behavior, change in sleeping patterns, fatigue, poor concentration, etc.), warning signs (change in personality, self-destructive comments, etc.), risk factors (gender, genetics, biology, environment, depressed parents), and suicidal risk factors (substance abuser, dysfunctional family, limited social network, etc.). Also interviewed along with the teen is Sam Goldstein, coauthor of *Lonely, Sad, and Angry: A Parent's Guide To Depression In Children And Adolescents*.

Evaluation:
Offering a generalized approach to understanding clinical depression, this tape gives parents a good background to determine if their teen is a candidate for professional help. Although each segment is brief (roughly 10 minutes of spotlight time for each depressed population), the on-screen lists serve to inform viewers of signs and symptoms they should be aware of. The individual vignettes help add a personal flavor to the show's rather generalized and clinical discussion. What's missing in this tape is more information on possible treatments and causes of depression. Although risk factors are briefly mentioned (via the on-screen lists), as are each individuals' personal treatment, more elaboration would have been helpful to achieve the tape's stated goal. The term "brain chemistry" is brought up several times with no explanation to enlighten viewers unfamiliar with the causal relationship between biology and depression. Not useful by itself, this tape is best used in conjunction with other resources.

Where To Find/Buy:
Bookstores, libraries, video dealers, or order direct by calling 1-800-420-2626, or through Library Video Company at 1-800-843-3620 or (610) 645-4000.

Depression, Suicide

WHEN LIVING HURTS

Description:

Gordon approaches the problems people face, and the depression that may ensue by sharing his view of the world as a terrible place, but illustrating that it can also be a wonderful place. He advocates reaching out beyond one's pain and being helpful to others as a means to learn to deal with depression. Gordon provides more immediate suggestions for getting out of a depressive state (write a letter, daydream, bake cookies from scratch, etc.), along with more extensive advice for understanding the sources of the depression (get a medical exam, seek therapy). Other topics covered include: what to do if you or someone you know is suicidal, issues of sex and love, problem parents and problem children, spiritual concerns, and finding the purpose of life. Throughout the book, Gordon suggests books to read on specific topics. Throughout this 127 page book, photos and artwork are included as inspiration for the reader to look for the beauty in everyday life.

Evaluation:

Gordon writes with compassion and love to those suffering with depression. His book reinforces his view of the world as an imperfect place, where perfect happiness doesn't exist. The trick, according to Gordon, is to reach out to others, and be of service. Learning to let go of blame and move beyond childhood pain is key; he believes that the best revenge is living well. For parents' use, he lists warning signs of serious depression and suicidal behavior, providing alternatives for turning away from thoughts of harm. Sexuality issues are discussed honestly and with warmth, and spirituality is seen as a key for inner transformation. One of the book's most moving passages is a letter from a bereaved mother of a child who committed suicide; she asks people to promise that they won't do anything to harm themselves. Although directed primarily at the depressed individual, this book offers comfort and understanding. Armed with the information in this book, however, parents and professionals may approach depression with compassionate acceptance and honesty.

Where To Find/Buy:

Bookstores and libraries.

Overall Rating
★★
Compassionate, yet realistic reference directed at the depressed individual

Design, Ease Of Use
★★★★
Bulleted points of interest, beautifully illustrated

1–4 Stars; N/R = Not Rated

Media:
Print

Price:
$10.00

Principal Subject:
Critical Issues & Concerns

ISBN:
0807405051

Edition:
2nd (1994)

Publisher:
UAHC Press

Author:
Sol Gordon

**About The Author:
(From Cover Notes)**
Dr. Gordon is a lecturer, author, educator, and professor emeritus of Child and Family Studies at Syracuse University. As a consultant for films and filmstrips on young children and adolescents, he has also appeared on many TV talk shows and radio interviews.

IV. Critical Issues & Concerns

Overall Rating
★★
Painful but valuable insights into teenage suicides; more observation than help, though

Design, Ease Of Use
★★★
Gripping narratives; index helpful

1–4 Stars; N/R = Not Rated

Media:
Print

Price:
$12.00

Principal Subject:
Critical Issues & Concerns

ISBN:
0393313921

Edition:
1994

Publisher:
W. W. Norton

Author:
Andrew Slaby, M.D. & Lili Frank Garfinkel

**About The Author:
(From Cover Notes)**
Slaby is a psychiatrist specializing in depression, as well as techniques in crisis intervention in New York. Garfinkel is a parent educator and resides in Minneapolis.

Depression, Suicide

NO ONE SAW MY PAIN
Why Teens Kill Themselves

Description:
This 12 chapter, 207 page resource offers guidelines on identifying and working with depressed and potentially suicidal adolescents. Chapter 1 is about the impact of depression; its physiological and emotional effects. Chapter 2 addresses parental denial in terms of realizing depression in their child. Chapters 3, 4, and 5 contain information on listening to and understanding your relationship with your child, acceptance, and the effects of alcohol and other drugs on depression. Chapter 6 focuses on the reasons surrounding teen suicide; Chapters 7 and 8, address the behavioral symptoms of depression, parents' unanswered questions after a child commits suicide, and the impact of guilt, respectively. The final chapters, 10, 11, and 12, explore the topics of suicide notes, ways to begin the road back to recovery, and how to interact with suicidal youth.

Evaluation:
This book is a sad, but very useful resource. Based upon eight real-life case studies, it attempts to help us understand why these teenagers killed themselves (or attempted to). These are compelling stories, graphically and explicitly narrated to help readers understand the problem of adolescent depression. The author explores personal journals and conversations with families to help the reader better anticipate and help prevent this potentially deadly outcome of depression in teenagers. Also valuable are the final chapters which describe others' reactions as "survivors" and how an adolescent's decision and ensuing consequences threaten the physical and mental health of those left behind. Also discussed is how adults need to work proactively with seriously depressed teenagers to help them work through their depression without having them resort to suicide as a viable option. This is a worthy resource, if only read by just one parent who winds up helping a child in turmoil avoid suicide.

Where To Find/Buy:
Bookstores and libraries.

Depression, Suicide

A PARENT'S GUIDE FOR SUICIDAL AND DEPRESSED TEENS
Help For Recognizing If A Child Is In Crisis And What To Do About It

Description:

Williams wrote this 234 page book as a guide for parents, to help them get healthier emotionally so that they may better help their children. Part One deals with recognizing the signs of depression or suicidal tendencies. Part Two discusses ways of taking action: finding support, self-education, giving support, and more. Part Three covers "adolescent issues," such as coming of age, stress, grief, loss, anger, depression, caretaking of others, and gender pressures. Part Four deals with how to face difficult situations in life, such as divorce, choices involved with sexuality, adoption, and "birth secrets" (difficult birth, etc.). Part Five discusses the difficulty of making recovery a daily habit and ways to create a "manageable family life." This book includes an index, a notes section, a list of recommended reading, and appendices on suicide warning signs, an self-inventory on one's "lifestyle profile," and a quiz to tell when drinking has become a problem.

Evaluation:

Williams shares her story with honesty and love, and without apology. Her prescription of hard work and self-care for parents acknowledges the toll that a child's depression and thoughts of suicide have on the family as a whole, opening the door for parents to work on their own issues and challenges. Williams' writing style is confessional and her brutal honesty about her limitations will make it easier for parents to be open to their own personal challenges. Part Two of the book is well done, providing information on finding a therapist, recognizing emergencies, finding support, showing courage, fighting against the "romance of death," chemical dependency and anti-depressant treatments, and ways to break the negative family cycle of depression. The majority of the book, however, is rather choppy and seemingly haphazard. However, if parents wade through this resource, they will find basic advice on how to determine if their child needs help, along with the steps they need to take to get help as a family.

Where To Find/Buy:

Bookstores, libraries, or order direct by calling 1-800-328-0098 (outside U.S., call (612) 257-4010), or by FAX at (612) 257-1331.

Overall Rating
★★
Excellent reference for parents to help them deal with their own emotions and recovery

Design, Ease Of Use
★★
Journalistic style, choppy chapters; bulleted highlights; referral organizations needed

1–4 Stars; N/R = Not Rated

Media:
Print

Price:
$11.95

Principal Subject:
Critical Issues & Concerns

ISBN:
1568380402

Edition:
1995

Publisher:
Hazeldon

Author:
Kate Williams

About The Author:
(From Cover Notes)
Williams (a pseudonym) wrote this book as a mother of a depressed teenage girl. Williams found very few family-oriented resources that provided her with any helpful information on dealing with the "storm of emotions and daily hurdles of her daughter's depression."

IV. Critical Issues & Concerns

Overall Rating
★★★★
Good overview of an important, seldom discussed topic

Design, Ease Of Use
★★★
Sensitive, clear voice; sometimes dense text; good index and layout; various contributors

1–4 Stars; N/R = Not Rated

Media:
Print

Price:
$14.00

Principal Subject:
Critical Issues & Concerns

ISBN:
0807023078

Edition:
1995

Publisher:
Beacon Press

Author:
Earl A. Grollman

**About The Author:
(From Cover Notes)**
Rabbi Earl Grollman has written 22 books on death and coping with loss. In 1995 he worked with children following the Oklahoma City bombing.

BEREAVED CHILDREN AND TEENS
A Support Guide For Parents And Professionals

 Recommended For:
Critical Issues & Concerns

Description:
This 238 book investigates death and bereavement in children and adolescents. The book is divided into three main parts and fifteen chapters, each written by a different contributor. Part One focuses on how to talk to children about death at various developmental stages, with emphasis on young children and adolescents. It also gives overviews on talking to siblings about death, explaining the meaning of terminal illness, and discussing disenfranchised grief. The differences between various cultural and religious viewpoints on death is discussed in Part Two. Separate chapters are devoted to African-American children's coping styles, as well as those of Catholic, Protestant, and Jewish children. Part Three offers specific treatments and therapies to help children cope with grief; one chapter focuses on taking care of the dying child. Also included in this part are film, story, and drama resource tools to help children get in touch with, and vent, their feelings. Each chapter includes a brief abstract about the contributor and footnotes.

Evaluation:
Rabbi Earl Grollman, a founder of a crisis intervention program that provides guidance when family members or close friends die, compiled this overview of death and bereavement in children and adolescents. The book is meant to be a support guide for professionals such as teachers and counselors, but it provides guidance for parents or caregivers as well. On the whole, the chapters are written in a clear, knowledgeable voice, with some variation existing among the contributors. Some chapters, however, are a bit dense, reading more like professional psychology journals or term papers than a parenting book. Nonetheless, personal accounts and research findings are delicately intertwined affording readers a well-rounded understanding of this sensitive subject. Especially remarkable is this resource's ability to discuss such a universal issue, yet take time out for religious and cultural differences. Recommended for teachers, counselors, and parents, this resource sheds light on how children view death, and how they can be helped.

Where To Find/Buy:
Bookstores and libraries.

Divorce, Death

GROWING UP WITH DIVORCE
Helping Your Child Avoid Immediate And Later Emotional Problems

 Recommended For:
Critical Issues & Concerns

Description:
Growing Up With Divorce focuses on how to help parents identify and deal with the challenges their children encounter as a result of divorce. This book describes three stages of divorce—the immediate crisis stage, the short-term adjustment stage, and the long-range aftermath—and how each stage affects children in different phases of their development. Each of the five age phases of child development rates a chapter (infancy, preschool, early elementary school, later elementary school, and adolescence), including discussion of the typical divorce experiences at each phase. Each age-specific chapter is followed by a related chapter on how to best help the child cope with his/her divorce issues. The author uses several examples of families from his research to further illustrate and relate divorce's effects on families and children. Among the other topics covered are communicating with children, recognizing distress in children, the psychological defenses a child may engage in, and the effects of parents' dating on children.

Evaluation:
This resource thoroughly covers children's needs and responses through the stages of divorce. The author has a strong knowledge of child psychology and applies it within the context of divorce and its effects on children. Despite the book's clinical subject matter, it is well-written and understandable, presenting information in an easy-to-follow, sequential manner. The case studies and analysis are helpful and realistic; the children mentioned are not emotionally disturbed, but rather typical of children in their age group. Although lengthy (400 pages, small type, no figures or illustrations), the book is accessible to most readers. Parents can go straight to the relevant age group and find helpful tips and background. This book has an especially good chapter on communicating with children. The sections on how children adapt to the presence of a significant other or stepparent should be helpful to parents making this adjustment. Overall, this is an excellent guide for adults seeking to understand the impact that divorce may have on children of various ages.

Where To Find/Buy:
Bookstores and libraries.

Overall Rating
★★★★
Comprehensive coverage of the stages of divorce and child development

Design, Ease Of Use
★★★
Easy-to-follow format, though quite dense

1–4 Stars; N/R = Not Rated

Media:
Print

Price:
$12.95

Principal Subject:
Critical Issues & Concerns

ISBN:
0449905632

Edition:
2nd (1991)

Publisher:
Fawcett Columbine (Ballantine Books)

Author:
Neil Kalter

About The Author:
(From Cover Notes)
The author is Director of the Center for the Child and Family at the University of Michigan, and Associate Professor of Psychology and Psychiatry at the University of Michigan.

IV. Critical Issues & Concerns

★★★★

Overall Rating
★★★★
A valuable resource for teenagers and parents

Design, Ease Of Use
★★★
Easy reading in a well-organized, attractive package

1–4 Stars; N/R = Not Rated

Media:
Print

Price:
$11.00

Principal Subject:
Critical Issues & Concerns

ISBN:
0380779579

Edition:
1996

Publisher:
Avon Books

Author:
Beth Joselow & Thea Joselow

About The Author: (From Cover Notes)
This mother-daughter team experienced the effects of divorce in their own household. Beth Joselow is an assistant professor at the Corcoran School of Art in Washington, D.C. Thea Joselow was a student at Oberlin College when she wrote this book.

Divorce, Death

WHEN DIVORCE HITS HOME
Keeping Yourself Together When Your Family Comes Apart

 Recommended For:
Critical Issues & Concerns

Description:
Written for children with divorced parents, this book provides tips, anecdotes, and real-life accounts. It examines the various aspects of divorce from a teenager's perspective, and discusses some of the feelings he/she may encounter during this traumatic time. Though the children of divorce are the target audience, the authors encourage divorced parents, teachers and other adults to read this book for insight into young people's thinking. The book is comprised of 50 chapters, all roughly four pages-long. Each chapter presents a self-explanatory topic (e.g. "It's Not Your Fault," "Don't Be Afraid to Ask Questions," "Holidays Will Be Strange," "Most Divorces Cause Money Problems"). Chapters conclude with a three-point summary, as well as a few first-hand accounts from teenagers relating their own experiences. Each chapter begins with a reflective quote from authors such as Thurber, T.S. Eliot, and others.

Evaluation:
Books aimed at helping children of divorce grapple with their feelings are of critical importance, and this book is a good attempt at helping teenagers come to grips with their new situation. The authors have focused on providing empathetic insights rather than a psychological treatise, and present realistic feelings and situations that kids can relate to. Written from the teenager's point of view, it provides a sensible approach to feeling better about oneself and parents. The book should be helpful for teenagers struggling with their parents' breakup. It is well-organized, appealing in appearance, written with a light touch, and unimposing. We highly recommend this resource for teenagers, parents, counselors, and teachers.

Where To Find/Buy:
Bookstores and libraries.

Divorce, Death

VICKI LANSKY'S DIVORCE BOOK FOR PARENTS
Helping Your Children Cope With Divorce And Its Aftermath

Description:

The author wrote this book after her own experience with divorce and bringing up children as a single parent. A wide variety of topics pertaining to children and divorce are covered here, with guidelines to follow at each stage of the process, from the decision to separate to living in a restructured family. Chapters 1–4 cover the initial stage of parental separation, including the typical reactions of preschoolers, teens, and young adults, how to talk to your kids sensitively about a departing spouse, and possible communication problems that can arise. Chapters 5–7 provide information on the "technical" aspects of custody and shared parenting, including money matters, options for parenting arrangements, and sole/joint custody issues. The final chapter, "Looking Down the Road," discusses the long-term adjustments of children and parents, and the special difficulties of holidays, dating and remarriage, and children of divorce in the classroom. Suggested readings on selected topics are provided throughout.

Evaluation:

This book provides a good general introduction to the subject of children and divorce. It covers a lot of ground, and manages to touch upon just about every issue encountered in helping your kids adjust to divorce and its aftermath. The advice offered here is sound, practical, and even creative, such as in the section describing how a long-distance parent can stay connected with children by providing them with self-addressed stamped envelopes or postcards, keeping a special journal, or by sending "coded" messages for younger children to decipher. Other particularly useful sections are those discussing the problems of shared parenting (joint custody) in which the author shares her own experience. Specific details offered here should make shuttling between homes far smoother. Because this book covers so much ground, it does not delve as deeply as one would like into any one topic, although the author does provide lists of suggested readings on certain topics. However, parents searching for an introduction to the subject of children of divorce and shared parenting will find this a good place to start.

Where To Find/Buy:

Bookstores and libraries.

Overall Rating
★★★
A good overall introduction to issues affecting children of divorce

Design, Ease Of Use
★★★★
Easy-to-read style

1–4 Stars; N/R = Not Rated

Media:
Print

Price:
$5.99

Principal Subject:
Critical Issues & Concerns

ISBN:
0916773485

Edition:
1996

Publisher:
Book Peddlers

Author:
Vicki Lansky

**About The Author:
(From Cover Notes)**
Lansky has written over 30 books on parenting and household advice, including the best-selling *Feed Me! I'm Yours, Games Baby Play, Practical Parenting Tips*, and *It's Not Your Fault, KoKo Bear* on divorce (1998).

IV. Critical Issues
& Concerns

★★★

Overall Rating
★★★
Written to teens, offers parents explanations of common reactions

Design, Ease Of Use
★★★
Good mix of personal vignettes and informative text

1–4 Stars; N/R = Not Rated

Media:
Print

Price:
$19.95

Principal Subject:
Critical Issues & Concerns

ISBN:
089490633X

Edition:
1995

Publisher:
Enslow Publishers, Inc.

Author:
Beth Levine

About The Author:
(From Cover Notes)
Levine has written articles for adults and younger people. Her articles have appeared in *Redbook*, *Seventeen*, and *Woman's Day*.

Divorce, Death

DIVORCE
Young People Caught In The Middle

Description:
This relatively short text provides an overview of issues affecting young adults from divorced families. The author states in a brief introduction that the book contains theories and speculations, and that it is up to the reader to formulate their own opinions and methods of coping. The text begins with a comparison of two sisters' reactions to the divorce of their parents. Chapters Two and Three deal with the periods before and during a divorce. Topics include feelings of anger, guilt, and abandonment in youth, and technical issues such as separation, custody, and visitation rights. The financial aspects of divorce are discussed, as are the emotions of the children. Chapters Five and Six discuss "disappearing fathers" and how young adults adjust emotionally to divorce. Other chapters go into stepfamily arrangements, as well as the future of children of divorce. Levine includes a list of organizations helpful for youth, along with resources for future reading, an index, notes, and a bibliography.

Evaluation:
When a couple gets a divorce, their children are affected in a multitude of ways. Often, parents and children do not know how to cope with the divorce, or they don't realize that their feelings are normal. *Divorce: Young People Caught In The Middle* gives both parents and young adults a resource to understand what children of divorce are going through. It doesn't provide a direction, or much advice for change, but it does give theories and information that may soothe the hurt. The author shows that different children handle divorce in different ways depending on their age, birth order, gender, and general emotional background. Her writing is accessible to both teenagers and adults. She uses real-life examples interchangeably with informative text, giving the book a more personable feel. This book would be a fine resource for children and parents of divorce, school and family counselors, or students of developmental psychology or counseling. The author includes several organizations of use to teens looking for additional help.

Where To Find/Buy:
Bookstores and libraries.

Divorce, Death

HELPING TEENS WORK THROUGH GRIEF

Description:

The author's stated hope for this 143 page guide is to "encourage adults to reach out and provide a safe place for young grieving persons to be with the turmoil of grief and allow new life to emerge." She believes that teens unable to process or deal with the grieving process need to be guided through the cycle of grief by adults who can provide a supportive atmosphere for teens to deal with the process in their own time. This book contains background information as well as activities designed to help the teen talk about their feelings. A wide variety of activities is introduced (sculpting, drawing, painting, movement, writing, listening to music), using both group situations and talking in pairs. The book provides instruction on initiating, organizing, and leading a group of teens, specific kinds of structured activities (connecting, learning about grief, creating balance, dealing with pain, remembering the person who died), and a process of evaluation and follow-up. A list of resource materials and an index are included.

Evaluation:

Teenagers in pain over the loss of a loved one would benefit greatly from having a trusted adult lead them through the ideas and exercises in this book. It offers a means of reaching out to the grieving person and helping them deal with the stages of grief and accept the reality of death. The varied exercises will appeal to kids who may have a difficult time finding words at the beginning of the grief process. The author provides a clear vision of how the workshop should progress, giving tips on how to approach the grieving adolescent and ways to make them feel comfortable discussing and processing their pain. The illustrations and poetry are well done and will be a help for working through grief. The section on remembering the person who died is especially helpful, in that it uses compassion and sensitivity to help kids work through their feelings of loss. Although it is best used in a workshop or group setting, this is an excellent reference to help a young person through the pain of losing a loved one.

Where To Find/Buy:

Bookstores and libraries.

Overall Rating
★★
Excellent resource to help teens through the grieving process, best used in a group setting

Design, Ease Of Use
★★★★
Simple layout aids comprehension; activity sheets direct and helpful

1–4 Stars; N/R = Not Rated

Media:
Print

Price:
$18.95

Principal Subject:
Critical Issues & Concerns

ISBN:
1560325585

Edition:
1997

Publisher:
Accelerated Development (Taylor & Francis Group)

Author:
Mary Kelly Perschy, M.S.

About The Author:
(From Cover Notes)
Perschy has worked with grieving teens for over 10 years. She is currently Bereavement Coordinator at Hospice Services of Howard County in Columbia, Maryland. She has served as teacher, administrator, and counselor.

IV. Critical Issues & Concerns

IV. Critical Issues & Concerns

Overall Rating
★★
A decent amount of information, but more useful to the parent of young children

Design, Ease Of Use
★★
Straightforward TOC; would help to have a section dedicated entirely to teenagers

1–4 Stars; N/R = Not Rated

Media:
Print

Price:
$10.95

Principal Subject:
Critical Issues & Concerns

ISBN:
1557041814

Edition:
3rd (1993)

Publisher:
Newmarket Press

Author:
Dan Schaefer & Christine Lyons

About The Author:
(From Cover Notes)
Dan Schaefer's 25+ years as director of a New York funeral home thrust him into the role of a "front-line counselor" to families in crisis situations. He organized his concerns into a looseleaf notebook, consulted a variety of professionals, and the result became this book.

Divorce, Death

HOW DO WE TELL THE CHILDREN?
A Step-By-Step Guide For Helping Children Two To Teen Cope When Someone Dies

Description:
This book discusses children's emotions when confronted with death. The 5 chapters in this 172 page book are a compilation of Schaefer's experiences, notes, and consultations with professionals during his 25 years as the director of a funeral home. Chapter 1—"What Children Think About Death"—is divided into age groups (2–6, 6–9, 9–12, teenagers); the discussion for teenagers encompasses 1 page about teenagers' emotions. Chapter 2 details how to explain death to children; it offers scenarios for different people, i.e., sibling vs. grandparent death, etc. Chapter 3 explains the grief and healing process of a child, and attempts to prepare parents for certain problems which may arise. The next chapter's—"The Funeral"—is designed to help parents prepare their children for the occasion. Chapter 5, an addendum to this new edition, deals with talking to children (including mentally retarded children) about AIDS, pet deaths, and more. A "Crisis Section" is included as a quick-reference for the anxious parent.

Evaluation:
Dealing with death is a difficult topic to address. Young children need to be carefully informed when someone close to them is dying, or has already passed away. In terms of its usefulness to parents of small children who really need some advice on how to approach their kids, this book is an excellent resource. To a lesser degree, if a parent doesn't know how to tell a teenager about a death this book may help. It is important to note that there IS NOT a wealth of literature available that specifically helps parents of teens discuss death. In fact, this book may actually say all there is to say in one page. Essentially, the author tells the reader that teenagers understand the concept of death, understand how people die, and understand that they've done nothing wrong. The difficult part for teenagers dealing with death is the grief, which may be well-hidden and manifest itself in different ways. This book offers a few ideas on determining if there is hidden grief within teens, but for the most part this book is designed for those parenting younger children.

Where To Find/Buy:
Bookstores, libraries, or order direct by contacting Newmarket Press at 18 East 48th Street, New York, NY 10017.

General Overview

HELPING THE STRUGGLING ADOLESCENT
A Guide To Thirty Common Problems For Parents, Counselors, & Youth Workers

 Terrific Resource For:
Christian parents needing guidance for dealing with minor to serious teenage problems

 Recommended For:
Critical Issues & Concerns

Description:
The author's experience as a counselor and psychotherapist are coupled with experiences of his colleagues in this two-part, 320 page book. Taking both the perspective of a Christian and a clinical psychologist, Parrott cites psychological research along with numerous Biblical references. Part One targets parents, counselors, and youth workers on ways to help adolescents through tough times. It focuses on helping a concerned parent or youth worker learn to listen to the child, rather than simply offering input. Part Two offers specific information about 30 problems ranging from everyday headaches like anxiety and school work to the more serious problems of abuse, depression, drugs and alcohol, and suicide. A case example is included for each problem along with descriptions of the symptoms, possible causes, suggested treatment/solutions, and a "when to refer" section (life-threatening, etc.). Suggestions for more in-depth reading are offered at the end of each issue's discussion.

Evaluation:
For the counselor or youth worker who wants to help a teenager with a specific problem, this book is an excellent resource. Parrott's framework is based on his "thorough review of hundreds of scientific studies" proven to be most therapeutic and "consistent with Christian understanding." Therefore, some parents may find some chapters one-sided; for example, the section on homosexuality focuses primarily on reversing the tendency. Other sections, however, are very objective and informative; the section on eating disorders, for example, offers parental "Dos and Don'ts" along with warning signs—valuable information given the lack of accurate knowledge available. Because much of the advice and information focuses on counseling the child or referring the child to other professionals, this book may be less useful to parents. In addition, some suggested techniques may be too complicated, such as changing a teenager's thought processes. An excellent resource, but mainly for the Christian counselor or psychologist.

Where To Find/Buy:
Bookstores and libraries.

Overall Rating
★★★
Good coverage of teen issues w/ a Christian perspective; some chapters lack objectivity

Design, Ease Of Use
★★★★
Well-organized w/ worksheets, examples, questions; logical consistent layout of topics

1–4 Stars; N/R = Not Rated

Media:
Print

Price:
$14.99

Principal Subject:
Critical Issues & Concerns

ISBN:
0310578213

Edition:
1993

Publisher:
Zondervan Publishing House (HarperCollins Publishers)

Author:
Les Parrott III

**About The Author:
(From Cover Notes)**
Les Parrott III received his Ph.D. from the Fuller Graduate School of Psychology. He is an assistant professor of clinical psychology at Seattle Pacific University, and an experienced psychotherapist and psychologist.

IV. Critical Issues & Concerns

★★★

Overall Rating
★★★
An authoritarian guide that addresses serious and less serious problems succinctly

Design, Ease Of Use
★★★★
Well-organized and logical presentation; excellent index for cross-referencing

1–4 Stars; N/R = Not Rated

Media:
Print

Price:
$10.00

Principal Subject:
Critical Issues & Concerns

ISBN:
0684807777

Edition:
1995

Publisher:
Fireside (Simon & Schuster)

Author:
Gregory Bodenhamer

About The Author:
(From Cover Notes)
Bodenhamer, nationally renowned as an expert on parenting difficult children and a former probation officer, is a consultant/trainer for schools, police departments, and court agencies. He directs the Back in Control Center in Portland, Oregon, and wrote *Back In Control*.

General Overview

PARENT IN CONTROL

 Recommended For:
Critical Issues & Concerns

Description:
This 191 page book shows parents how to regain parental authority over their children. Its 10 chapters address common, less serious problems such as not doing chores around the house, as well as serious problems such as participation in crime and parent abuse. The author prefaces his book with an apology for offensive language used and writes, "it is important to portray the real-life situations . . . as accurately as possible . . . many children use highly offensive language." Bodenhamer defines parents as authority figures over their children, and states that there have been many anti-authority and anti-parent activists who seek to undermine parents' role of raising their children and having influence on them. The author stresses throughout the book that consistency, specific and detailed rules, supervision, and "being there" for your child are key to restoring order in the home and creating a loving parent-child relationship. An appendix of questions and answers addressing specific problems is provided.

Evaluation:
As this book defends strong parental authority, it is not for the fainthearted or for those parents who wish to give their children equal authority with them. However, it calls for a second look by parents who hold this belief and who are struggling to regain order in their homes. It becomes clear early in the book that Bodenhamer believes that he knows best how to parent difficult teens. His very authoritative writing style and tone compels the reader to keep reading from the onset. Bodenhamer's experience as a probation officer is evident as he presents his no-nonsense approach while not being tyrannical. He is simply establishing boundaries—boundaries necessary to raise adolescents, particularly "temperamentally difficult" children, if parents do not want to continue to live with chaos. This book is a "must read" for parents who want to take a stand as parents, and who are serious about not wanting to get pushed around mentally, emotionally, or physically by their controlling adolescent children.

Where To Find/Buy:
Bookstores and libraries.

General Overview

YOUR CHILD'S EMOTIONAL HEALTH: ADOLESCENCE

Recommended For:
Critical Issues & Concerns

Description:

This 143 page resource is essentially a compilation of the Center's 73 years of experience. There are 11 major topics covered—sexuality, popularity, school, depression, discipline, divorce, substance abuse, running away, overeating, planning for the future, and psychotherapy. Within each chapter are teen-centered facts about the selected topic; for example, the chapter on substance abuse states, based on the Center's research, that the main reason adolescents use drugs/alcohol is to fit in with peers. Each chapter also offers parents bulleted tips and advice about how to help their child, or in some cases, how to let the child make their own decisions. Advice such as "educating rather than dictating," and "punishing in an appropriate fashion" are typical examples of some offerings. Being involved in the child's life is highly advocated, although the reader is cautioned about too much restriction. Plenty of distinctions are made between what is normal and what is "unhealthy" teenage behavior. A comprehensive index is given.

Evaluation:

If the parent is ready for no-nonsense, fact-filled advice about their child, this book will be extremely helpful. It is important to note, though, that parents aren't going to want to hear much of the information in this book. The introduction minces no words, explaining that behaviors such as driving a car without a license, lying, abusing drugs, running away, and skipping school, while destructive, are behaviors "common among teenagers." There are few parents who will be able to keep their jaw from dropping. Nevertheless, this book is a realistic look at reason and fact. For example, they point out that kids use substances FOR FUN. An amazing concept, but one rarely noted by other resources. Also, parents are told to "accept as much as possible in [their] child's behavior, even if [they] can't approve." In other words, pick battles wisely. Written from the jaded, honest view mirroring 73 years of child observation and care, this book has the tone of authorities who can't beat around the bush. This book will be an invaluable tool to the parent who can accept reality and move on.

Where To Find/Buy:

Bookstores and libraries.

Overall Rating
★★★
Honest and straightforward information; realistic advice; excellent knowledge base

Design, Ease Of Use
★★★★
Quick & to the point; no trouble quickly finding desired information

1–4 Stars; N/R = Not Rated

Media:
Print

Price:
$9.95

Principal Subject:
Critical Issues & Concerns

ISBN:
0028600037

Edition:
1994

Publisher:
MacMillan (Prentice Hall Macmillan Company)

Author:
Philadelphia Child Guidance Center with Jack Maguire

About The Author:
(From Cover Notes)
Founded in 1925 by Frederick Allen, M.D., the Philadelphia Child Guidance Center has an international reputation as a foremost center for child and adolescent psychiatry in the U.S. The staff of 230 professionals provides comprehensive care for children and families.

IV. Critical Issues & Concerns

Overall Rating
★★★

Friendly book that speaks to Christian teenagers about today's issues

Design, Ease Of Use
★★★

Easy reading; simple language directed toward a teenage audience

1–4 Stars; N/R = Not Rated

Media:
Print

Price:
$10.99

Principal Subject:
Critical Issues & Concerns

ISBN:
0310208084

Edition:
1997

Publisher:
Zondervan Publishing House (HarperCollins Publishers)

Author:
Ron Hutchcraft

About The Author:
(From Cover Notes)
Hutchcraft is an author, speaker, and international radio host of such programs as "A Word With You" and "Alive! with Ron Hutchcraft," a widely circulated Christian youth broadcast. A 34 year veteran of youth and family work, he has spoken around the world.

TEN TIME BOMBS
Defusing The Most Explosive Pressures Teenagers Face

Description:

This 10 chapter (one chapter for each of the ten time bombs), 199 page book is written for teenagers. It also can be used by adults to gain "knowledge and understanding so [they] can provide help to a young person [they] know." This book is a product of Hutchcraft's 34 years of experience working with teenagers on what has hurt or destroyed their lives. The author states that his book is a teen's "personal 'Bomb Squad' manual, showing . . . some very practical ways to avoid life-wrecking explosions." The "ten time bombs" are pressures or issues that teenagers are faced with, including premarital sex, peer pressures, family relationships, suicide, anger, loneliness, suicide, "the dark side of the supernatural," music, and more. Hutchcraft gives personal anecdotes and analogies from his own life as well as from his encounters with others to illustrate these different "bombs." He provides advice, much of which is rooted in biblical principles and Scriptural passages, for teens to handle these pressures, their feelings, and choices.

Evaluation:

Strong biblically based messages run through the veins of *Ten Time Bombs*. It reads like a collection of essays, anecdotes, and advice from a wise big brother writing to his teenage sibling. Hutchcraft relates to teens at their level, although not condescendingly, and speaks their language. The book's biblically based contents are directed specifically toward Christian teens or teens who may be seeking life's answers from a spiritual perspective. Some of Hutchcraft's advice may be far-fetched for teens who are in the midst of rebellion or seeking their identities; for example, he suggests writing parents a letter telling them "I love you," or "thank you for . . ." as a way to build family relations. Also, some of Hutchcraft's advice requires a fair amount of discipline and self-control from teens. The goals of his book, to speak to teens as their friend and to show them practical ways to avoid "life-wrecking explosions," are valuable. This book is easy reading that Christian parents can feel offering to their teens.

Where To Find/Buy:

Bookstores and libraries. An audiotape version (1997) of this book is also available for $14.99 (ISBN No. 0310211905).

General Overview

ROMANCE OF RISK (THE)
Why Teenagers Do The Things They Do

Description:

Divided into three parts, this 13 chapter, 307 page book is stamped with the author's very personal, first-person narrative of 16 adolescent case studies. Through this approach, the reader is drawn into Ponton's world, allowing a close glimpse of not only her patients, but also the author as a professional. The types of "unhealthy" risk behaviors or situations discussed includes: running away, eating disorders, gang participation, dysfunctional parent-child dynamics, and alcohol abuse. The second section focuses on the dynamics existing between father and teen, and mother and teen. Ponton asserts that risk-taking is a means for adolescents "developing and defining themselves," that "to risk is to grow." The author, a clinical psychiatrist and psychoanalyst, describes her own experience with individual adolescents and their families, intermingling diagnoses of the problem with treatment for improving the home life. She then promotes alternate "healthy" risk-taking that can replace the "unhealthy."

Evaluation:

Ponton's dramatic style of writing invites the reader to step into her world, viewing her as a psychiatrist who bows down, although not condescendingly, to meet adolescents at their level. Rather novel-like, this book offers a refreshing approach to dealing with difficult adolescent problems, while still cutting to the core of the problems. Ponton combines artistry in her writing and a voice of authority in her presentation of individual cases. She addresses the specifics of those cases, then pans across the page with general information relevant to each type of unhealthy risk behavior. She then wraps up her discussion with solutions that were applied to the specific case discussed, but which could be assimilated in turn into the reader's life. For a different twist on understanding the backgrounds and causes of adolescent problem behaviors and alternative ways to work with teens, this book is riveting, warm, and offers hope for the weary parent.

Where To Find/Buy:

Bookstores and libraries.

Overall Rating
★★★
Unique approach to presenting case studies, this resource is refreshing and warm

Design, Ease Of Use
★★
Reads like a novel, so doesn't offer a system of problems-solutions; index is helpful

1–4 Stars; N/R = Not Rated

Media:
Print

Price:
$25.00

Principal Subject:
Critical Issues & Concerns

ISBN:
0465070752

Edition:
1997

Publisher:
Basic Books
(Perseus Books, L.L.C.)

Author:
Lynn E. Ponton, M.D.

About The Author:
(From Cover Notes)
Ponton is a practicing clinical psychiatrist and psychoanalyst, and also a professor of psychiatry at the University of California, San Francisco. World-renowned teacher and lecturer on adolescent development, she is the mother of two teenagers.

IV. Critical Issues & Concerns

Overall Rating
★★★
Unusual contributors, succinct articles make research an interesting and rewarding task

Design, Ease Of Use
★
Graphics absent; can't rely on site's listed features to fully access articles, use "search"

1–4 Stars; N/R = Not Rated

Media:
Internet

Principal Subject:
Critical Issues & Concerns

Internet URL:
http://www.kidsource.com/

General Overview

KIDSOURCE ONLINE

Description:

This online community, created by a group of parents with varied backgrounds, aims to find "the best of the healthcare and education information . . . and deliver it . . . in new and innovative ways. . . ." General options on their homepage offer articles under the headings of "Education," "Health," "Recreation," "Parenting," "Guide to Best Software," and "New Products." Specific options address four given age groups—newborns, toddlers, preschoolers, and K–12. Within these age groups are articles found under subtopics such as safety, learning, health & medicine, growth & development, toys & recreation, and more. Most of the articles within this website are ranked using a 5 star system with 5 stars being "best, in depth and most helpful overall." A list of articles is presented along with a brief synopsis of the article's contents and its rating; generally articles average 2–3 pages. Also listed within these sections are online forums specific to each age grouping. Links are also provided to other related articles.

Evaluation:

This site's primary benefit is that it hosts numerous articles from unusual but well-respected contributors—the U.S. Department of Education, National Institute of Mental Health, child-related organizations (child abuse consortia, etc.) and associations (learning disabilities), and others. The articles' succinct nature, convenient rating system, positive tone, and friendly voice can be easily handled by any busy parent. Although graphics are intentionally absent from the site, the creators say this is because "most of (their) visiting parents do not have time to wait for extensive graphics to download." The main problem with this site, however, is its organization. Articles seem to have arbitrarily fallen within "Health," "K–12," and other categories, with many related articles not apparent. Use the site's "search" feature to find specific articles on particular subjects such as "teen pregnancy," "substance abuse," "eating disorders," and more. Here you will find the site's treasure chest and you won't be disappointed. Although this site is a good informational site, other sites will need to be used for parent-to-parent "conversation."

Where To Find/Buy:

On the Internet at the URL: http://www.kidsource.com/.

General Overview

BRIDGES
15 Sessions To Connect Teenagers & Adults On Drugs & Alcohol, Decision-Making, Communication, Character, Independence, Sexuality

Description:

Bridges is a 94 page book designed to help kids and Christian adults communicate. DeVries & Russell have designed fifteen games and hands-on activities along with discussions to help connect teenagers and adults. Each of the fifteen "chapters" starts with a stated purpose. For example, the session dealing with character explains that its purpose is "to encourage youth and their parents to identify significant people who model for them what it means to be a Christian and to appropriate specific faith models for their own Christian growth." Following the purpose is a session overview, in which the general content of the activity is explained; there is also a list of materials that will be needed. Each session is concisely outlined, offering the group leader specific guidelines and suggestions; also included are estimates for how long each session will take. Included at the end of each chapter are workbook exercises, which are to be photocopied and handed out for use during the session.

Evaluation:

This resource will be most useful to the leader of a church youth group, a neighborhood association of Christian families, or a counselor of a Christian family camp. The content of the chapters, the authors' trial experiences with the chapters' activities, and the guide's logical layout will prove helpful in exposing teenagers to a cadre of Christian adults. These activities are not intense sessions, making the guide atypical compared to others focusing on the same objective. The underlying premise is that if teens feel comfortable with adults by relating to them on a playful level, then teens shouldn't have a problem opening up, talking about their feelings, and asking questions about some "taboo" subjects. Providing an excellent overview with concise guidelines, any Christian group leader will applaud its value. However, more than one family is required for the activities to effectively achieve their goals, making this guide useless for a single family unless they intend on inviting other families to join.

Where To Find/Buy:
Bookstores and libraries.

Overall Rating
★★
Great value for Christian youth group leaders, but limited value for individuals

Design, Ease Of Use
★★★★
Excellent, concise organization of activities; easy language and fun writing

1–4 Stars; N/R = Not Rated

Media:
Print

Price:
$12.99

Principal Subject:
Critical Issues & Concerns

ISBN:
0830811680

Edition:
1996

Publisher:
InterVarsity Press

Author:
Mark DeVries & Nan Russell

**About The Author:
(From Cover Notes)**
DeVries is associate pastor for youth and their families at First Presbyterian Church and has led Young Life Clubs. Russell is a teacher at Oak Hill School. With DeVries, she has written and refined family-based youth ministry curriculum.

IV. Critical Issues & Concerns

Overall Rating
★★
Provides parent-to-parent succinct advice on issues facing today's teenagers

Design, Ease Of Use
★★★★
Bulleted, tabbed, well-designed layout makes this book easy to read and understand

1–4 Stars; N/R = Not Rated

Media:
Print

Price:
$9.95

Principal Subject:
Critical Issues & Concerns

ISBN:
0963104918

Edition:
2nd (1995)

Publisher:
Parents' Pipeline

Author:
Sheila Fuller & Leigh Rudd

About The Author:
(From Cover Notes)
Rudd wrote this book as a result of her own child's substance abuse problem. She has testified in Washington on adolescent substance abuse and has produced radio shows on the subject. Fuller is the past President of the Greenwich Council on Youth and Drugs.

General Overview

PARENTS' PIPELINE GUIDE (THE)
Plain Talk About Teens And Alcohol, Drugs, Sex, Eating Disorders And Depression

Description:
Beginning by stating that "kids have not changed, but the times have," *The Parents' Pipeline Guide* contends that American culture has undergone a radical change over the last 30 years. Kids today have much more opportunity to engage in negative and sometimes life-threatening behavior. The authors are parents themselves and are concerned with the world their children are growing up in. They created this guide to give parents "a clear picture of the dark side of the adolescent world . . . [To] have a better idea of how to deal with it." This book is divided into three sections. Part One deals with "Prevention," describing parental and community approaches to head off trouble before it starts. Part Two—"Problems"—provides specific facts about the sources of trouble facing teens, with a discussion of the reasons why a teen might want to indulge in destructive behavior. Part Three provides help for parents, discussing in detail the recovery process. The Guide is tabbed to help locate subjects of interest more easily.

Evaluation:
This is a great general book for parents. The authors define themselves as mothers first and foremost, and provide facts and information that they think other parents should have in their quest to keep their children safe. Their book provides clear directives and guidelines that rely on the authors' experiences and those of other parents. It gives parents starting points and ideas on how to become actively engaged in their children's lives. The main premise, that the best parent is one who is present for their child, assumes that anyone who reads this 159 page book is willing and able to take the time to get to know their child and learn about their world. The authors provide basic statistics and trends, profiles of various drugs including signs of addictive behavior to look for, and a discussion of addiction and other related teen problems. This book is best used as a "check-in" reference for parents, with other resources used as back-up for more in-depth coverage of the issues.

Where To Find/Buy:
Bookstores, libraries, or order direct by contacting Parents' Pipeline, Inc. at P. O. Box 11037, Greenwich, CT 06831.

General Overview

FACTS FOR FAMILIES
To Educate Parents And Families About Psychiatric Disorders Affecting Children And Adolescents

Description:
This website contains information for parents and families on the effects of various situations, influences, and disorders on children and adolescents. It provides a list of diverse topics, including: normal adolescent development, sexuality, sexual abuse, alcohol, drugs, eating disorders, suicide, violent behavior, teenage pregnancy, and more. Each topic is briefly discussed (typically 1–2 pages) and a recommendation for seeking further professional help is always included. The website contains scores of pages of up-to-date information, available in English, Spanish, or French. It also provides a list and URL addresses of about 40 other organizations that deal with the issues affecting today's children. This site includes much background on the American Academy of Child & Adolescent Psychiatry itself (the organization's involvement in research, training, and legislative issues). Abstracts from the past two years of the *Journal of the American Academy of Adolescent Psychiatry* are also given.

Evaluation:
AACAP claims that between 7 and 12 million American youth suffer from mental, behavioral, or developmental disorders at any given time. Their website is an excellent starting point then to glean a quick understanding of the complexities facing today's youth. If parents have concerns about a particular issue, they're sure to find it among the list provided. Simply click on the topic that concerns you (60+ topics) and a concise fact sheet is given that outlines basic information often followed by a list of trouble signs to watch for. Unfortunately, the site doesn't link you directly from the topic you're exploring to sources of additional information—you'll have to do that additional research yourself. The AACAP website does provides parents with a good general overview of issues concerning teenagers, but use this site in conjunction with other more in-depth resources or professional advice.

Where To Find/Buy:
On the Internet at the URL: http://www.aacap.org/web/aacap/factsfam/

Overall Rating
★★
Provides the basics on many problems that children and teenagers face

Design, Ease Of Use
★★★
Simple, effective design; easy to maneuver around; absence of graphics

1–4 Stars; N/R = Not Rated

Media:
Internet

Principal Subject:
Critical Issues & Concerns

Publisher:
American Academy of Child & Adolescent Psychiatry

About The Author:
(From Cover Notes)
The AACAP is the leading national professional medical association dedicated to treating and improving the quality of life for children, adolescents, and families affected by mental, behavioral, or developmental disorders.

Internet URL:
http://www.aacap.org/web/aacap/factsfam/

IV. Critical Issues & Concerns

★★

Overall Rating
★★

Provides information and resources for a variety of important teen issues

Design, Ease Of Use
★★

Chapters organized by topic, but question-answer format makes for a choppy read

1–4 Stars; N/R = Not Rated

Media:
Print

Price:
$8.95

Principal Subject:
Critical Issues & Concerns

ISBN:
0944176038

Edition:
1992

Publisher:
Terra Nova Press

Author:
Nancy Keltner

About The Author:
(From Cover Notes)
Nancy Keltner is the editor of a teen newspaper column called "FYI." She has a background in English, mental health, and publicity, and is the mother of three grown sons.

General Overview

IF YOU PRINT THIS, PLEASE DON'T USE MY NAME
Questions From Teens & Their Parents About Things That Matter

Description:
This text grew out of a question-and-answer newspaper column ("FYI") for teenagers and parents. It is a compilation of several questions that were asked by parents and teens, with responses given by "experts" in many fields. The ten chapters in this 227 page book cover many topics at the forefront of teenagers' minds. These include dating, loneliness and suicide, family differences, and problems that arise at school. Other areas discussed are friendships and groups, health, physical and mental abuse, drinking, smoking, and sex. For each issue discussed, additional resources are provided, as well as places or people to go to for help. Using a question-and-answer format, the book's chapters also include a page or two devoted to quotes from teens about the issue at hand. An index is included at the end along with information about each professional contributor. As stated in the introduction, this book is meant to be a starting point for dealing with tough problems rather than a resource that will solve every parent-teen conflict.

Evaluation:
This question-and-answer book for teens and their parents discusses many topics that may be too touchy to bring up in family conversations. The questions cover territory ranging from drugs and sex to relationships with family and friends. The responses given by professionals don't necessarily provide easy answers to the questions, but they do let the reader know they aren't alone, and that others have similar problems. Also, the resources provided (additional books and organizations) give the reader another outlet in case the book can't answer their questions. At times the question-and-answer/"Dear FYI" format makes the book a very choppy read. The chapters are clearly marked, though, and the index helps find specific information. This book would be useful to teens with questions they are afraid to ask, or parents wanting to know what topics are prevalent in teenagers' minds. Teachers and counselors needing quick answers to kid's questions or additional resources to suggest will also find it useful. Those looking for an in-depth discussion of critical issues in teens' lives, however, should look elsewhere.

Where To Find/Buy:
Bookstores, libraries, or order direct by calling (916) 753-1519, or by FAX at (916) 753-6491.

General Overview

VIOLENCE IN THE LIVES OF ADOLESCENTS

Description:

Strauss, a clinical psychologist, details the many ways violence has become commonplace for today's teenager. This 238 page book provides and discusses case studies of suicidal adolescents, runaways, delinquents, adolescent sex offenders, and physically abused adolescents. Strauss gives violence faces and names, providing real examples of the effects of sexual abuse and neglect on young people in our society. She illustrates how families can break the cycle of violence from an ecological perspective. "In a violent world, adolescents can be buffered immeasurably by someone who will love them irrationally." The author believes that four levels of understanding must be addressed to determine the extent to which violence affects adolescents' lives, whether they are perpetrators or victims. These four levels that must be analyzed include the individuals' development (parents, adolescent), the family system (interactions, communication), community, and social policy.

Evaluation:

Stating that individual therapy alone is not sufficient for stopping the violence in adolescence, Strauss continues this argument throughout her book by providing examples of how family, community, and social influences need to also be included in therapy. Of primary importance to Strauss is the belief that treating the adolescent requires treating the family as a unit. Strauss also analyzes the need for community involvement and political/social action to stem the violence that surrounds today's children. Of use for many will be her discussions on self-help groups and programs such as 12-step groups, ToughLove, and others. Although mostly succinct, the text sometimes sings the laurels of the author's therapy work to distraction. On the whole, though, this is a good reference for any parent who has questions about how therapy works or what to expect from the therapeutic process. Better suited for therapists, however, this resource offers solutions to breaking the cycle of violence within families.

Where To Find/Buy:

Bookstores and libraries.

Overall Rating
★★
Case studies give theories and opinions human definition, best for the professional

Design, Ease Of Use
★★
Well laid-out; can read chapters individually; narrative case studies illustrate points

1–4 Stars; N/R = Not Rated

Media:
Print

Price:
$27.00

Principal Subject:
Critical Issues & Concerns

ISBN:
0393701867

Edition:
1994

Publisher:
W. W. Norton

Author:
Martha B. Strauss Ph.D.

**About The Author:
(From Cover Notes)**
Martha B. Strauss, Ph.D., is a clinical psychologist in private practice with University Associates in Psychology in Keene, New Hampshire. She specializes in problems of adolescence, family violence, family development, and women's issues.

IV. Critical Issues & Concerns

GENERAL
OVERVIEW
OF RAISING
TEENAGERS

INTRODUCTION

Anxiety, fear of the unknown, mood swings, depression, risky behavior, living in the present, irritability, instantaneous changes in behavior and perspectives, and so on. These all sound like the symptoms of a mentally ill individual. Yet, as any parent of a teenager will attest, it also describes normal adolescent behavior. However, when describing an adolescent, one must also consider the flipside of their behaviors—their keen and intense articulation as they argue their viewpoint when wanting to drive the family car, their clear sense of value and morality when defending what they consider to be right, their clear sense of how things should be, and their incredible sense of wonder and promise at what the world still holds for them. These are all part of the adolescent experience.

Many adults fear adolescence and adolescents. A teenager's emotional imbalance and their radical departure from conventionality scare adults. For parents, gone are the days of being the "center of their universe." Instead, parents are now faced with serious issues, such as sexuality and AIDS, the use of drugs and alcohol, choices involving violence and destruction, and the worship of dubious idols. Parents must now completely acknowledge that their child is growing away from them. Parents' ability to comfort, protect, and guide their child begins to take a form that is alien to them. Those same children who sought them out for these things suddenly see their parents as the "other side," the harbinger of danger and discomfort, and a threat to their freedom and individuality.

During adolescence, parents become greatly concerned about their teenager's:

- Feelings of indestructibility

- First experiences

- Intense highs and lows

- Struggle for identity

Feelings Of Indestructibility

Thinking back on their own adolescence, parents may remember a time when they felt like nothing could hurt them, that anything was possible, and that they would live forever. Now they fearfully see that in their son or daughter. This is the gift, and yet the curse of adolescence. The innocence of this frame of mind allows for great possibilities . . . anything IS possible and dreams WILL be realized . . . it's just a matter of time. This underlying perception of indestructibility, however, can also translate into the physical realm. Often, adolescents feel as if they can't be hurt physically, and they lack a sense of their own mortality. This in turn can, of course, translate into risky, and at times, dangerous behavior.

First Experiences

The life of an adolescent may be filled with firsts. First date, first girlfriend or boyfriend, first kiss, first sexual experience, first heartbreak. No doubt there may be the first solo drive, first traffic ticket, or possibly first accident. It may be the first time an adolescent will be faced with making long-range decisions such as "What do I want to do with the rest of my life?"

But, perhaps the most difficult thing parents face is the feeling that this child, whom they have nurtured for so many years, no longer respects their parents' advice, support, or input. Where family was once so all-important, now peers take on the roles once held solely within the realm of the family. In their drive for independence, adolescents take these first steps away from their family, and try to gain acceptance by "the group." Parents may receive solace in the fact that this is generally a short-term journey . . . most likely their child will reenter the family sphere as young adulthood takes hold. Yet, this temporary exit from the family aegis can be sad, frustrating, and scary for parents who suddenly feel a loss of control. For the adolescent, it's perhaps their first experience at risking their ego, forming an identity separate from their family, making decisions about drug and alcohol use and other serious concerns, and becoming responsible about their sexual behavior. It may also be the adolescent's first time to see life on a continuum that extends beyond the next weekend or party.

Intense Highs And Lows

To parents and teenagers, adolescence seems to be a time of extremes. Emotional outbursts are often coupled with calm deliberation as both teens and their parents begin to explore new arenas, clarify their beliefs, and make decisions for their behaviors. How teens and parents deal with this intensely emotional time will be encapsulated in young people's lifelong memories. Teenagers learn, either positively or negatively, how they can influence others and change the world around them through their encounters at home and with their peers. Teenagers' successes (and failures) and conquests (and losses) are empowering and ego-forming.

This is also a time of contradictions. Parents see this while watching their adolescents transition between concrete thinking and abstract thinking—sometimes in mid-sentence. This is where the emotional roller coaster of adolescence sees its greatest flux. Parents become perplexed and agitated that there doesn't seem to be much ground between love and hate, fascination and boredom, engagement and isolation. Added to these intense emotions is the affirmation that a teenager's emotions are constantly vulnerable to instant change, influences, and outside factors.

Struggle For Identity

Identity and acceptance are perhaps a hallmark of adolescence. Though rarely articulated, the age-old question of "who am I?" reverberates through literally every aspect of being a teenager. Unfortunately coupled with that question is the teenager's sense of not liking what they see. It is the "too" syndrome—too tall, too short, too big, too small, too smart, too awkward, and so on. For example, physical looks rarely live up to desires, and teenagers often express this conundrum through identity anchors. These are visual cues, such as the clothes and hats teens wear, their ways of walking and talking, and tattoos or pierced body parts. Ironically, as an adolescent expresses and projects their "own" identity, the more that adolescent identifies with their peer "group," in effect losing this individuality.

What, then, is adolescence all about? Is it a phase, is it a parenting nightmare, is it avoidable? Typically, the word "individuality" is the one underlying answer used to identify the main outcome of adolescence. Until recently, most adolescent development theorists believed that the turmoil of adolescence centered on the teen's drive to become independent, separate from others, and in particular separate from their family. Now, however, many educators and researchers believe that what the adolescent seeks is not strictly independence, but is instead trying to redefine their already existent relationships. And, most parents would attest that total independence is not what they want for their children, nor what they believe their children really need. We live in a society with communities that require connection and relationship to others, not isolation. What parents really want for their children is that they become effective people.

How then do parents help their teenagers achieve this outcome? Certainly the answers are as cloudy and complex as the question, but one thing is clear, parents need help. Given the complexities and eccentricities of this "life syndrome," parents want the best resources that can help them better understand the intricacies of how to parent effectively during these tumultuous years. They want a resource that can become their "24 hour companion" to explain what to expect as their teen grows, inform them of their available choices, and assuage their worries. Perhaps most of all, parents need reassurance that they **are** doing their best and **are** doing a great job. They need a resource that will educate them about options, possibilities, and consequences. In other words, parents need an "all-inclusive" manual or resource that affords them a general overview of adolescence and teenagers. But what type of information should be present to make this resource a worthwhile investment of time and money?

As we developed this guidebook, we looked for resources that would offer parents a full perspective of adolescence, including information on adolescent development, the importance of teenage relationships, how to effectively communicate, and how to handle crises. Since effective parenting often does not rely on one authority's opinion, resources that offer a general overview of these areas should strive to remain objective, allowing parents to understand other parenting styles while developing and refining their own.

We have identified some of the best general overview resources in the following pages. These resources address topics ranging from what to expect during puberty to how to deal with "letting go." You'll find resources that offer advice and information on how to effectively talk with your teen, along with how to help your teen communicate with others and develop good peer relationships. These resources offer tips for dealing with daily issues, like getting your teen to do their chores or obey their curfew. And you'll also discover preventive measures to ward off problems such as substance abuse, along with ways to deal with a full-blown addiction. Please take the time to carefully read our full-page review of each recommended resource so that you can choose those that are best for you. Remember that all-inclusive guides, by their very nature, are useful in presenting the big picture, but usually don't offer in-depth information in any one area. Whenever you find you need further help, read our recommendations for specific topics we've identified.

As parents, it can be difficult to remember that these are the best of times as well as the worst of times. For when parents are in the throes of a "you're-not-being-fair" argument, they must constantly remind themselves of the significance and wonder of this unpredictable, and borderline psychotic, syndrome called adolescence.

General Overview

COMPLETE IDIOT'S GUIDE TO PARENTING A TEENAGER (THE)

★★★★

Overall Rating
★★★★
Great general resource for most parents' questions; strength lies in its communication tips

Design, Ease Of Use
★★★★
Bulleted highlights; general & detailed table of contents; icons of tips; easily read

1–4 Stars; N/R = Not Rated

Media:
Print

Price:
$16.95

Principal Subject:
General Overview

ISBN:
0028612779

Edition:
1996

Publisher:
Alpha Books (Macmillan General Reference/Simon & Schuster Macmillan Company)

Author:
Kate Kelly

About The Author:
(From Cover Notes)
Kelly has written several books on home and family. Her work has appeared in *Harper's Bazaar, Glamour, Parents,* and *Working Woman.* She is the mother of three children, including one teenager.

 Recommended For:
General Overview

Description:
Based upon the premise that "you have to give your children both roots and wings," this 294 page book is divided into 6 parts. Part 1 presents topics involving the "Home and Family"—communication tips, family obligations and chores, and teenagers' bedrooms. Teenagers' development (physical, emotional) is discussed in Part 2 along with the importance of teenagers' self-esteem. "School Life" is the focus of Part 3 with advice on transitions into middle and high school and later into college; also discussed are issues involving homework management, learning problems, extracurricular activities, and more. Part 4—"Special Interests, Special Privileges"—deals with TV and telephone limits, video games and computers, sports, and teenagers driving privileges. Creating an atmosphere that promotes good health and then what to watch for if your teenager gets involved with drinking, drugs, smoking, and sex is the focus of Part 5. Part 6 concludes with advice on teaching money management to your teenager along with tips on jobs.

Evaluation:
Neat, concise, and informative are words that best describe this book in the Complete Idiot's series. The book's main strength lies in its discussions of how to communicate effectively with a teen in various situations from handling family chores to dealing with body piercing. Lighter treatment, however, is afforded the topics of substance abuse, depression, suicide, etc.; useful lists of danger signs are provided for each critical issue, however, along with a fairly comprehensive list of who to contact for additional help. The book is well-organized with each chapter beginning with highlights of what the chapter covers and ending with a summary or "the least you need to know." Major points are bulleted throughout along with iconic text blocks providing additional information—warning signals, hard facts/ statistics about an issue, and insights for connecting with your teen. Parents will find this a good general resource for answering basic parenting questions, but one that is best accompanied by other more specific resources.

Where To Find/Buy:
Bookstores and libraries.

YOU AND YOUR ADOLESCENT
A Parent's Guide For Ages 10–20

Recommended For:
General Overview

Description:

This 18 chapter, 431 page guide/reference book covers topics ranging from A to Z—from finding the right therapist to changes in puberty, family communications, teenage pregnancy, drug and alcohol use, and more. The book starts off by introducing the reader to a positive outlook on adolescence ("Relax! The horror stories you have heard about adolescence are false."). The authors then lay the groundwork for the book with "The Basics," which are general topics applicable to all ages from 10 to 20—attributes of good parenting, family communication, problem-solving, etc. The book is then divided into sections by age group: The Preteens—10 to 13; The Teens—14 to 17; and Toward Adulthood—18 to 20. Each age-group section includes the physical health and development, psychological and intellectual growth, and the adolescent's school and social world relevant to that age group. A list of resources is provided at the end of chapters where additional information on a topic may be warranted.

Evaluation:

The goal of *You And Your Adolescent* is lofty. The author states it was written in the "spirit of those baby books" parents used when their child was younger to get a preview of what lay ahead, and then later referenced for reassurance. It is an all-encompassing "owner's manual" and encyclopedia of sorts, addressing the biological, physical, social, educational, mental, and emotional aspects of the adolescent. The purpose of this book is to provide introductory information and general guidance, as well as to serve as a reference; to that end it does an excellent job. However, because the book covers an expanse of topics, it generally does not address specific issues in great detail. It does offer a list of related resources at the end of many chapters to address this inherent dilemma. Most parents will find this book is a valuable general resource to have in one's personal library—one that will be visited and revisited many times over many years.

Where To Find/Buy:

Bookstores and libraries.

Overall Rating
★★★★
Contains a wealth of information on physical, emotional, and social topics

Design, Ease Of Use
★★★★
Organized by age groups and age concerns; breadth mandates an index, which is given

1–4 Stars; N/R = Not Rated

Media:
Print

Price:
$15.00

Principal Subject:
General Overview

ISBN:
006273461X

Edition:
2nd (1997)

Publisher:
HarperPerennial
(HarperCollins Publishers)

Author:
Laurence Steinberg, Ph.D. and Ann Levine

**About The Author:
(From Cover Notes)**
Steinberg, professor of psychology at Temple University and director of Graduate Studies in Psychology, is an expert on adolescent psychological development and family relations. Levine's work includes psychology, sociology, and anthropology college textbooks.

Overall Rating
★★★★
Delightful, appropriately humorous book inspiring hope and comfort for all parents

Design, Ease Of Use
★★★
Detailed table of contents offers quick guidance; clear writing; no index

1–4 Stars; N/R = Not Rated

Media:
Print

Price:
$11.00

Principal Subject:
General Overview

ISBN:
0374523223

Edition:
1991

Publisher:
Noonday Press (Farrar, Strauss, and Giroux)

Author:
Anthony E. Wolf, Ph.D.

About The Author:
(From Cover Notes)
Wolf is a practicing clinical psychologist, and has worked with children and adolescents for the past 20 years. He is also the author of *It's Not Fair, Jeremy Spencer's parents let him stay up all night!: A Guide to the Tougher Parts of Parenting.*

GET OUT OF MY LIFE, BUT FIRST COULD YOU DRIVE ME AND CHERYL TO THE MALL?
A Parent's Guide To The New Teenager

 Recommended For:
General Overview

Description:
Composed of three main sections, this book is directed at parents who are looking for an anchor in the stormy sea of adolescence. The author explains that his resource "is a guide to adolescents–how to understand them, cope with them, and . . . direct their turbulent lives." Wolf supports this goal with 11 chapters, 3 parts. Part One explains adolescence—what it is, what kids do, and general guidelines for parents. Part Two—"Communication and Trust," "Controlling Your Teenager," and "Conflict"—discuss the parent-teen relationship. The last five chapters in Part Three deal with "Reality and the World Outside," highlighting important issues for teens. Divorce, school, sex, drugs and drinking, and suicide are each given about ten pages of attention. In the preface, Wolf writes that "much of this book is funny . . . much that goes on between teenagers and their parents is funny." His main purpose is to help parents gain a new perspective about their "daily travails," instead of viewing them as "deadly serious issues."

Evaluation:
Although Wolf has an amazing knack for demonstrating a sense of humor about virtually every parenting situation, this book deserves serious recognition, too. Even the title imitates life—the parents and teen have an earthshaking fight, and twenty minutes later the child is asking for a ride somewhere. What the author really advocates is a parenting stance which is far too often pushed to the side—moderation. He asks parents to recognize that they cannot control their children like they used to be able to. The balance of power is delicate, and battles need to be picked. The humor in this book is perfectly placed; for example, when the parent denies the child the right to stay out past curfew, the teen yells "you LOVE ruining my life, don't you?" It's the funny comments that make this book so valuable, comforting, and enlightening to parents. It is also vital to note that parents having **serious** problems with their child will also be comforted by some of the facts, insights, and suggestions offered in *Get Out of My Life.*

Where To Find/Buy:
Bookstores and libraries.

SAFEGUARDING YOUR TEENAGER FROM THE DRAGONS OF LIFE
A Parent's Guide To The Adolescent Years

 Recommended For:
General Overview

Description:

This book aims to provide parents with information and advice to help their children "come closer to the true meaning of fulfilled adulthood." There are 6 parts in this 292 page book. The first part describes changes evidenced today compared to parents' youth, along with "today's dragons" (suicide, drop-out rates, runaways, abuse, drugs, alcohol, pregnancy, etc.). Chapter topics include the following: the importance of a good marriage, various family dynamics, the function and profile of adolescence and puberty, developmental stages of adolescence, assessing family stress, depression in adolescence, communication guidelines, discipline, sexuality, alcohol and drugs, issues of physical and emotional well-being, and the school experience. The book also includes appendices on how to find a therapist, where to go for help if needed, and a list of suggested readings. The table of contents lists all subheading, and there is no index.

Evaluation:

This thoughtful guide provides parents with a general overview of ways to nurture and support their children through adolescence. Striking a good balance between the clinical and personal, this approach presents various exercises and questions to help parents learn to help their children deal with the "dragons" of drug and alcohol abuse, issues of sexuality, low self-esteem, and other concerns. The author places emphasis on the home, believing that teenagers now, more than ever, need the stability of a loving, concerned family. She offers advice to help teens deal with stress, an area not often included in resources; she is considered an "authority in the field of personal and professional wellness." Although much of the advice is not presented in-depth, Youngs provides (in Part Five) a good communication blueprint through which parents can assess, improve, and stimulate parent-child discussions. This book is recommended to parents looking for a good general resource, but they should also realize that more specific guides will offer better in-depth advice.

Where To Find/Buy:
Bookstores and libraries.

Overall Rating
★★★★
Excellent resource providing good, concrete advice to parents of teenagers

Design, Ease Of Use
★★★
Detailed TOC, bold subheadings, no index; can be randomly accessed

1–4 Stars; N/R = Not Rated

Media:
Print

Price:
$11.95

Principal Subject:
General Overview

ISBN:
1558742646

Edition:
1993

Publisher:
Health Communications

Author:
Bettie B. Youngs, Ph.D., Ed.D.

About The Author:
(From Cover Notes)
The author is an international lecturer, author, counselor, and consultant. She is also the author of 14 books. Youngs is a former Teacher-of-the-Year and university professor.

Overall Rating
★★★★
This book offers a warm and upbeat style of parenting based on choices and consequences

Design, Ease Of Use
★★
Authors' run-on commentary/dialogue style makes advice appear rather randomly

1–4 Stars; N/R = Not Rated

Media:
Print

Price:
$18.00

Principal Subject:
General Overview

ISBN:
0891096957

Edition:
1992

Publisher:
Pinon Press

Author:
Foster Cline, M.D. and Jim Fay

About The Author:
(From Cover Notes)
Cline, a physician and adult and child psychiatrist, specializes in working with difficult children, and founded Evergreen Consultants in Evergreen, Colorado. Fay, with 31 years of experience as an educator and school principal, is an educational consultant.

PARENTING TEENS WITH LOVE & LOGIC
Preparing Adolescents For Responsible Adulthood

 Recommended For:
General Overview

Description:
This 269 page, 3 part, 8 chapter book presents a "love-and-logic" approach to parenting teenagers. The authors explain that love is "essential to parenting" but does not mean "hovering around . . . to protect them from all the rocks flung at them . . . " nor "tolerating outlandish, disrespectful, or illegal behavior." "Logic" centers on allowing teenagers to make decisions (and mistakes) and to learn from the consequences as part of growing up. Part 1 teaches parents how to be love-and-logic parents, discussing effective and ineffective parenting styles. Part 2 addresses the challenges of parenting teenagers and offers practical guidelines and encouragement for parents. Part 3 consists of 33 love-and-logic parenting "pearls," which are short essays on a number of everyday issues and problems, some of which are "Acne," "Back in the Nest: If an Older Child Needs to Move Home," "Grades," "Mood Swings," "Sex," "Drug or Substance Abuse," "Video Games," and more.

Evaluation:
Parenting Teens With Love & Logic is an upbeat book that exudes the authors' positive parenting attitude. Its tone is warm, teaching parents how to apply firmness and guidance along with the essential—love. What Cline and Fay have to say may appear practical and common sense to many parents. However, it is their presentation and illustrations that make this book stand out. Vacillating back and forth from their own experiences and those of other parents, they provide a rich tapestry of personal narratives that parents will be able to relate to. Although many of the issues and problems addressed in their "parenting pearls" are difficult ones, the authors' authoritative and friendly tone have turned much of it into enjoyable reading. Parents should note that these "pearls" do not explore issues at great depth, but they do offer some basis that parents can apply to their situation. Cline and Fay have honed in on and fine-tuned the practical and common sense logic of parenting in this book.

Where To Find/Buy:
Bookstores, libraries, or order direct by calling 1-800-366-7788. An audiotape version (1997) of this book is also available for $24.95 (ISBN No. 0944634419).

ADOLESCENCE
The Survival Guide For Parents And Teenagers

Recommended For:
General Overview

Description:
Designed for both parents and teenagers, this 286 page book presents the different outlooks of adolescents and parents on various issues. The main text of the book is written mostly for parents and is organized into short separate articles "so that it can be read like a magazine." The book contains two table of contents. One lists chapters within the book's four parts (adolescent milestones, family dynamics, peer group/outside world, crises); the other lists "box contents" (organizational tools presented within each of the book's chapters of case histories, dialogues, etc.). Each chapter topic includes issues for parent-teen discussions, questionnaires, sample dialogues, case histories, and more. For example, the chapter on "boosting morale" defines the topic, then provides a case history in which a parent handles a teenager's haircut badly, followed by issues focusing on teens' appearances, and ending with a section for parents about adolescent shyness and unsociability along with a section for teens on how to cope with shyness and blushing. A list of organizations' addresses and phone numbers are also provided.

Evaluation:
This book provides good, albeit brief, information on the physiological, emotional, and mental changes that take place during puberty and adolescence. While the book claims to be written for both parents and teens, the style of writing and topics discussed are less focused on adolescents' perspectives, however, and will hold more interest for parents. Written in a textbook-like fashion, the book begins each chapter with a discussion of the issue, including statistics and quotations. Especially helpful are the case histories, which present potentially difficult issues and situations that have been handled poorly; the participants' own words are included in these scenarios. Then, the authors explain different ways to handle similar situations, including questions parents should ask themselves before reacting. Although the authors recommend that the book should be read in its entirety, the book doesn't need to be read in one sitting to be understood or utilized. Indeed, it would be better used as a situational reference.

Where To Find/Buy:
Bookstores and libraries.

Overall Rating
★★★
Good balance of statistics and personal narrative

Design, Ease Of Use
★★★★
Precisely laid out, includes a guide for how to use the book, can be referenced randomly

1–4 Stars; N/R = Not Rated

Media:
Print

Price:
$14.95

Principal Subject:
General Overview

ISBN:
0789406357

Edition:
1996

Publisher:
D K Publishing

Author:
Elizabeth Fenwick and Dr. Tony Smith

About The Author:
(From Cover Notes)
Fenwick and Smith wrote *Adolescence* from their perspective as parents, backing up their personal experience with the knowledge of those who are academic experts in the field.

Overall Rating
★★★

Honest, in-depth coverage of a wide range of issues; helpful workable advice, solutions

Design, Ease Of Use
★★★★

Topics arranged alphabetically backed up with an extensive index, cross-referencing

1–4 Stars; N/R = Not Rated

Media:
Print

Price:
$12.95

Principal Subject:
General Overview

ISBN:
0449909964

Edition:
1997

Publisher:
Fawcett Columbine (Ballantine Books/Random House)

Author:
Karen Renshaw Joslin & Mary Bunting Decher

About The Author:
(From Cover Notes)
Karen Joslin, a schoolteacher, with a master's degree in Education, is the author of *Positive Parenting from A to Z.* Mary Decher, a clinical social worker and affiliate instructor at the University of Washington, has worked extensively with teens and their families.

POSITIVE PARENTING YOUR TEENS
The A To Z Book Of Sound Advice And Practical Solutions

 Recommended For:
General Overview

Description:
Written for parents seeking a reference type guide for the various problems of adolescence, this 412 page guide is organized alphabetically, beginning with "acne" and ending with "worry." Over 100 problems, such as alcohol and tobacco, sex, sneaking out, cliques, lying, and more, are addressed. The introductory sections discuss what happens during the teen years to parents and their adolescents, the positive parenting philosophy (based on Adler, Dreikurs, and others), and the "tools of the trade" (techniques to maintain open channels of communication); a section also explains how the entries of the book are organized. Each problem is divided into sections: "Understanding the Situation," "What to Say and Do," "Preventive Tips," and "When to Seek Help." Sample dialogues, alternative strategies, and advice by other parents are included within each discussion. When appropriate, cross-references to related topics within the book are also given. A reference section and an index conclude the book.

Evaluation:
Although no single resource can perfectly address all the issues faced by teenagers and parents, this guide makes a valiant effort. Each issue is logically organized, and readers will feel as if they are having a conversation with a wise, advice-giving neighbor. The authors use easy-to-read language, and don't mince words. They insert their own values into their work at times, but readers will not feel as if they are being lectured on how to raise their children. Too often, resources suggest only one angle by which parents should approach their teenager about an issue. This book offers more, succeeding where others fail. For example, on the issue of hygiene, the authors suggest one of two approaches: 1) buy your teen deodorant and congratulate her on her "graduation" to adult hygiene, or 2) tell your teen that it doesn't matter how he looks, as long he smells decent. Parents looking for support and guidance while dealing with teen issues, will find that this book maintains the balance between humor and seriousness that is absolutely necessary while raising teens.

Where To Find/Buy:
Bookstores and libraries.

TEEN TIPS
A Practical Survival Guide For Parents With Kids 11 To 19

Recommended For:
General Overview

Description:

Geared to parents of 11–19 year olds, this 241 page book is divided into 16 chapters. The first chapter introduces the cognitive, psychological, and "identity" development in adolescents. Other chapters cover the following: the transition into parenting a teen, communication, responsibilities, friendships, school and learning, leisure activities and curfews, discipline, values, sexuality and dating, driving, drugs and alcohol, "promoting a healthy self-concept," relationships within the family, divorce and step-parenting, and planning for the future (college and careers). Each chapter begins with background information, including data from surveys and research. All chapters consist primarily of other parents' "secrets of success" that were shared with the author during his 3 years of research. The book also includes tips by teens and 15 "Skill Builders" (quick lessons on parenting skills). Many chapters include a list of recommended reading and other resources such as hotline numbers.

Evaluation:

This book's strength lies in its varied, proven tips collected from "the real experts"—parents and teens. Accordingly, the advice contained within this resource comes from parents with a variety of values and parenting styles. For some readers, however, this may also be the book's weakness. While each chapter begins with a short introduction, including up-to-date research, the variety of solutions may cause some confusion. Little information is provided on teen development; other resources are needed for this. The book is highly readable and easily skimmed, making it a good reference; topical bibliographies list additional resources. In the front-matter, McMahon provides a list of questions inviting parents to reflect on their own teen years. This exercise may help parents gain perspective and lead to interesting discussion. This resource is full of practical advice, but parents must choose which advice to use—similar to how they sorted through the advice they were given when parents first brought their new baby home.

Where To Find/Buy:

Bookstores, libraries, or order direct by writing to Mail Order Department, Simon & Schuster, Inc., 200 Old Tappan Road, Old Tappan, NJ 07675.

Overall Rating
★★★
Varied tips provided on many topics from friendships and school to dating and drugs

Design, Ease Of Use
★★★★
Organized by topic, summary of each tip in bold; easy to skim; parent "skill builders"

1–4 Stars; N/R = Not Rated

Media:
Print

Price:
$12.00

Principal Subject:
General Overview

ISBN:
0671891065

Edition:
1996

Publisher:
Pocket Books
(Simon & Schuster)

Author:
Tom McMahon

**About The Author:
(From Cover Notes)**
McMahon, who spent 20 years as a professor of counseling and psychology, writes a weekly newspaper parenting column, and has appeared on national talk shows. This is his second parenting book. He has 2 children.

★★★

Overall Rating
★★★
Good general book on
Christian parenting and
parent-teen communication

Design, Ease Of Use
★★
Somewhat random design;
each chapter presents
scenarios, suggestions,
discussion topics

1–4 Stars; N/R = Not Rated

Media:
Print

Price:
$5.75

Principal Subject:
General Overview

ISBN:
1562120093

Edition:
1991

Publisher:
CRC Publications

Author:
Jacob P. Heerema

**About The Author:
(From Cover Notes)**
Jacob Heerema is the
"pastor of Bethany Christian
Reformed Church, Holland,
Michigan, and former chaplain
to troubled adolescents at
Pine Rest Christian Hospital,
Grand Rapids, Michigan."

CALL ME WHEN YOU'RE 20!
A Parent's Guide To Living With Teens

Description:

This 87 page book on Christian parenting looks at "some of the
issues that trigger teens' tempers and bring parents pain." The book
"is part of *Issues in Christian Living,* a series of six-session study guides
that present a Reformed, biblical perspective on life issues Christians
face as they try to live out their Christianity in a society that teaches
and models contrary values." Its six chapters present numerous
scenarios dealing with such issues as drinking and drugs, sex, church,
faith, family, and abuse. *Call Me When You're 20!* describes ways
parents can acknowledge that their children are growing up, so they
can emancipate their teens, and love and affirm them through the
difficult process. A "Suggestions for Group Session" section at the
end of each chapter provides suggestions for opening prayer, many
topics for group discussion, and Scripture readings relevant to the
chapter. A list of suggested readings is presented at the back of the
book.

Evaluation:

Although this book was designed for use in a group setting, it can,
by all means, be used by individuals. This book's design as a group
study guide in itself presents a good idea: that parents need not go
it alone—they can draw from others and get support in the task of
raising teenagers. Heerema presents a realistic array of contemporary
issues and problems parents of teenagers face and draws on Bible-
based answers to lead their teens "to grow up as servants of Christ."
The "Suggestions for Group Session" section at the end of each
chapter holds the book true to its "study guide" design, offering much
food for thought. These sections are designed to prompt parents to
think hard and look inwardly as well as to the Bible for answers.
The book's somewhat random fashion makes it difficult to access
specific advice on parenting; it is therefore best read cover-to-cover.
Modeling strong Christian values, this book not only offers parents
guidance and support, but calm understanding of the ups and downs
of parenting teens.

Where To Find/Buy:

Bookstores and libraries.

HELPING TEENS IN CRISIS

★★★

Description:

This 240 page book is an all-inclusive resource for parents of teens. Neff's goal is to help parents understand, from a mild Christian perspective, the changes and crises which teens experience. She offers guidelines for dealing with teens along with advice on when to compromise. Her expertise is based upon her work as a counselor through which she has dealt with "hundreds of young people, moms, and dads." The target audience for the book is "any caring adult who knows or lives with a teenager in crisis." Accordingly, the chapters (14 total) cover a diverse range of topics, ranging from family dynamics to hospitalization, and each chapter is between 15–20 pages. Some of the specific issues include drugs and alcohol, adoption, family purposes, male/female differences, legal trouble, and proper helping behavior. Many of the chapters offer a large number of statistics (e.g. "90% of high-school seniors have used alcohol") about their topics of focus. There is no index.

Evaluation:

On the whole, Neff delivers an excellent piece of work. Many books written from a Christian perspective tend to offer only one point of view, and parents sometimes feel lectured. In contrast, Neff's views are moderate, and she encourages parents to make their own rules, choose their battles wisely, and know when to compromise. For example, Neff gives a list of possible issues which parents and teens are sometimes forced to deal with, including "booze," school activities, entertainment, tobacco, etc. Parents and their teenager are asked to categorize each topic—teen decision, teen/parent compromise, or parental wisdom. After this exercise, discussion may ensue. This example is just one of the pieces of advice offered to help parents and their child deal with the issues before problems occur. Our only criticism is the book's lack of focus; parents looking for help on specific issues will want to look elsewhere. However, parents seeking hope-inspiring advice and information will be well-served by this book.

Where To Find/Buy:

Bookstores and libraries.

Overall Rating
★★★
Compassionate, understanding writing; helpful advice for the concerned parent

Design, Ease Of Use
★★
Numerous parent-teen stories; table of contents lists issues of interest; index would help

1–4 Stars; N/R = Not Rated

Media:
Print

Price:
$9.99

Principal Subject:
General Overview

ISBN:
084236823X

Edition:
1993

Publisher:
Tyndale House Publishers

Author:
Miriam Neff

About The Author:
(From Cover Notes)
Neff (M.A., Northwestern University) is a counselor at a large pubic high school near Chicago. She is the mother of four, all of whom are in their teens or twenties. She is also the author of *Women and Their Emotions* and *Devotions for Women in the Workplace.*

Overall Rating
★★★
Broad, but shallow subject coverage typical of AOL will appeal to some

Design, Ease Of Use
★★
The AOL interface seems slow and clunky compared to the best websites

1–4 Stars; N/R = Not Rated

Media:
Online Service

Principal Subject:
General Overview

Publisher:
Moms Online

MOMS ONLINE (AOL)

Description:

The Moms Online community on AOL (Keyword "Moms Online") is a popular one, and with good cause: it's a place to go (if you're an AOL subscriber) for advice and feedback on parenting kids of all ages. The "Teen Center" portion of the site is hidden is a scrollable list on the first page, but once you've found it, coverage is reasonably broad. A small variety of live chat rooms are always available. Most comprehensive is the message board, consisting of hundreds of postings on dozens of teen-related subjects. Sub-directories are available for "Teens & Investing," "Teen-Related Essays By Moms," and a variety of short articles (written by members of their "Guidance Council," a group of professionals and interested lay persons ranging from experienced Moms to a nurse in an inpatient adolescent psychiatric unit). The article of the day in this area responded to a Mom's concern about her 13-year old son's practice of using the computer to have "sex chats" with his girlfriend.

Evaluation:

The AOL "model" is focused on interactivity among its subscribers; thus chat rooms and message boards are found virtually everywhere—AOL does this well and it's a well-deserved foundation for its popularity. And while this kind of focus is obviously appealing to their millions of subscribers, we nonetheless find it a bit "light" in those cases where an adult is making a serious effort to find a comprehensive treatment of a subject of concern. For example, talking to teens about sex is covered in a 2–3 page "article" from their "Guidance Council," but is more conversational than serious in its coverage. And, while the subjects addressed by their message board are many in number, content consists of a half-dozen sentences shared by a parent. This can be valuable, of course, but it's just not very thorough and it's not based on professional experience or training. If AOL is your favorite place online, then this area is OK, but we'd recommend you look elsewhere for more studied responses to some of the more critical issues.

Where To Find/Buy:

On America Online, using the Keyword "Moms Online."

REBEL WITHOUT A CAR
Surviving And Appreciating Your Child's Teen Years

Description:

This 250 page book presents adolescence as a "syndrome" that every parent and child must pass through. Focusing on the trials and tribulations of everyday teens, the text consists of 11 chapters and includes an introduction, conclusion, notes, list of recommended resources, a bibliography, and an index. The subjects covered include adolescence as a syndrome and contradiction, parenting, sex, morality issues, and risky behaviors. Risky behaviors include such issues as gangs, suicide, and eating disorders. Others chapters focus on young women finding their own voice, issues of difference and equality, the education system and teens, and motivating adolescents. Most chapters introduce the mood of the section with humorous quotes. The writing is a compilation of Mednick's experience with teenagers, "thousands" of interviews, and research findings. His point is not to provide answers to major problems in adolescent's lives, but to present a clear, entertaining portrayal of their culture.

Evaluation:

This book paints a picture of teen culture as seen through the eyes of a high school principal. Describing what he has seen in schools and what he knows of adolescent life, Mednick characterizes this time period as a "syndrome" that everyone must go through. The book is very engaging, with Mednick's use of humor and numerous examples making the book an easy, fast, and entertaining read. He doesn't provide a lot of advice, but Mednick does point parents in certain directions allowing them to make up their own minds based on details he provides within each chapter. Additional resources are also provided for those parents who wish to know more about a particular subject. The book is not meant to be a cure-all to the teen "syndrome," but it will help parents have a better idea of what happens to their kids at school every day, and how life for their teen is different than when parents were teenagers. This book provides a fine starting point for parents who wish to understand adolescence.

Where To Find/Buy:

Bookstores, libraries, or order direct by calling 1-800-544-8207.

Overall Rating
★★★
Humorous, engaging overview of the "syndrome" of adolescence

Design, Ease Of Use
★★
Entertaining tone; table of contents a bit vague, subtopics would help; index adequate

1–4 Stars; N/R = Not Rated

Media:
Print

Price:
$12.95

Principal Subject:
General Overview

ISBN:
1577490142

Edition:
1996

Publisher:
Fairview Press

Author:
Fred Mednick

About The Author: (From Cover Notes)
Mednick has worked with adolescents for twenty years and is married with two children. He has been a high school principal for ten years, and is director of the Bush Upper School in Seattle, WA.

★★★

Overall Rating
★★★
Child psychology mixed with anecdotes provide framework for this general resource

Design, Ease Of Use
★★
Well-structured, but few subheadings and bulletted main points; question-driven

1–4 Stars; N/R = Not Rated

Media:
Print

Price:
$14.00

Principal Subject:
General Overview

ISBN:
0890877491

Edition:
1995

Publisher:
Celestial Arts

Author:
Michael Riera, Ph.D.

About The Author:
(From Cover Notes)
Riera has worked with teens for 15 years; currently he is the Dean of Students for a prep school in California. He speaks nationally and writes a monthly internet column for ParentsPlace.com called "Dr. Mike About Teens." He has one daughter.

UNCOMMON SENSE FOR PARENTS WITH TEENAGERS

Description:

Written for parents of high school students, this 222 page book responds to sample parent questions so that parents can "design solutions appropriate" to their situations. Three initial chapters detail "The Parent-Adolescent Relationship," "The Adolescent World," and "The High School Experience." In the next 18 chapters Riera discusses adolescent development in relation to a specific topic, and then he cites examples a parent can use as they work toward a solution. These chapters cover: graduation; limits and structures; natural consequences; alcohol, drugs, and parties; academics, grades, and motivation; sex and romance; being gay; television, music, and computers; sports and extracurricular activities; making friends; the driver's license; eating modifications and eating disorders; adolescent grieving; divorce; remarriage and blended families; single parenting; parent mental health; and when to seek professional help. Topical chapters average 6 to 10 pages in length.

Evaluation:

This informative book covers a broad range of teen issues—from common issues like sports, driving, and friendships, to heavier issues like being gay, eating disorders, and grieving. Also included are parental issues that have a direct impact on teens, such as divorce, blended families, single parenting, and mental health of parents. The initial 3 chapters (almost a third of the book) provide a good overview of the physical, cognitive, and psychological development in high school students. The variety of topics covered make this a useful resource. The author has provided not only a table of contents, but also a table listing the parent questions addressed in this "question-driven" book. Although this book is well-structured, the individual chapters are not easily skimmed and would be most beneficial for those who like to read from beginning to end. Parents looking for a general translation of adolescence, without how-tos or specific advice, will get a good start here.

Where To Find/Buy:

Bookstores and libraries.

MAKING SENSE OF YOUR TEENAGER
Understanding Your Teenager's Changing Body, Mind And Spirit

Description:

This quick-reference manual is a collection of ideas from Lawrence Kutner's experience as a psychologist, as well as the interviews he has done as a journalist for *The New York Times* and *Parents* magazine. Therefore, a large number of parental concerns are presented in this 224 page book. The nine chapter topics cover broad issues; subsections within each chapter breakdown the issue into smaller concerns. Different topics covered include: teens' self-image, parent-child communication, emotional development, friends/peer pressure, dating, risky behaviors, career aspirations, college, and letting go. A typical subsection is about 3–5 pages, in which Kutner explains the issue, gives insight as to why the teenager may be engaging in the behavior, and then offers different tips parents may use to eliminate, modify, or encourage certain behaviors. There is a detailed table of contents for readers to quickly locate an issue, and a 9 page index.

Evaluation:

Written by a professional who is used to writing for a large audience, the writing style of this resource maintains an identifiable journalistic tone. The broad array of topics covered illustrate the author's attempt to touch upon ALL the possible parental concerns and issues which many teenagers face. The only problem is that there are simply too many topics; no single issue quite receives the attention it deserves. For example, the section on "decisions about alcohol" is the same length as "visiting a child at college." While it is noble to dedicate equal amounts of attention to the subjects, it inevitably shortchanges some issues which do deserve serious discussion. Another aspect in which this book falls below par are the blocks of parenting tips within each chapter. They seem a bit trite and outdated, especially given the circumstances and serious pressures facing teenagers nowadays. For the parent, though, who wants a little background on everything their teen is experiencing, this book does offer a quick-reference overview.

Where To Find/Buy:

Bookstores and libraries.

Overall Rating
★★
Vast spread of issues covered, many topics given light treatment

Design, Ease Of Use
★★★★
Easy-to-read; user-friendly vocabulary; helpful table of contents, extensive index

---

1–4 Stars; N/R = Not Rated

Media:
Print

Price:
$11.00

Principal Subject:
General Overview

ISBN:
0380713551

Edition:
1997

Publisher:
Avon Books (Hearst Corporation)

Author:
Lawrence Kutner, Ph.D.

About The Author: (From Cover Notes)
Kutner is a respected psychologist and child development writer. For seven years, he wrote the nationally syndicated "Parent and Child" column for *The New York Times.* He currently writes the "Ask the Expert" column on child development for *Parents* magazine.

Overall Rating
★★
Basic coverage of light and serious issues with one page's worth of advice

Design, Ease Of Use
★★★★
"Problem-solution" format at times; can be read randomly; good use of italics & bullets

1–4 Stars; N/R = Not Rated

Media:
Print

Price:
$12.00

Principal Subject:
General Overview

ISBN:
0688131964

Edition:
1996

Publisher:
Hearst Books (William Morrow & Company)

Author:
Judi Craig, Ph.D.

About The Author: (From Cover Notes)
Craig has counseled teens and their families for 20+ years, has consulted for schools and agencies, and gives national seminars to mental health professionals and parents. She is the author of four other books, and writes the nationally syndicated column "Family Matters."

YOU'RE GROUNDED TILL YOU'RE THIRTY!
What Works—And What Doesn't—In Parenting Today's Teens

Description:

This Good Housekeeping Parent Guide provides 9 chapters of strategies for dealing with parent-teenage concerns. The author offers advice on how to deal with common issues such as homework, phone time, spending sprees, skipping school, and breaking curfew. Also discussed are the more serious issues of depression, sexuality, date rape, eating disorders, and substance abuse. Using a "problem/solution" format, Craig provides hypothetical situations as dilemmas and illustrates her points by giving advice on how to handle each situation. Part One of this 196 page book provides "Some Basics" on the process of becoming an adolescent (body changes, emerging sexuality, etc.), parental responses to the adolescent changes, and discussion of how to talk to a teen. Part Two discusses friendships; house rules; school and work; sex, love, and dating; alcohol and drugs; and warning signs for potentially serious problems. The book includes a list of suggested readings and an index.

Evaluation:

This book provides one page's worth of basic advice on parent-teen issues. Craig provides general suggestions on the many facets of change experienced by teenagers: body changes, early vs. late bloomers, independence, peers, emerging sexuality and sexual orientation, teenage love, and higher education. The book is aimed at busy parents, looking for immediate relief, thus most of the advice is general, rarely in-depth. Some of the advice is wishy-washy, such as that offered for a teen returning from college who wants to sleep with his girlfriend—"It is your home . . . however . . . your son might visit you less often until he's married!" The advice offered for finding birth control pills in your teen daughter's room, discusses how to converse with her about her reasons for sex, but no mention is made about her behavior and AIDS protection. This is an adequate general reference for busy parents, but others looking for more discussion, useful advice, and better guidance will be best served with a more in-depth reference.

Where To Find/Buy:
Bookstores and libraries.

CARING FOR YOUR ADOLESCENT AGES 12 TO 21
The Complete And Authoritative Guide

Description:

Developed by physicians under the direction of an editorial board for the American Academy of Pediatrics, this 326 page book covers a range of topics. Part I, discusses communication and discipline, as well as diverse family types. Part II covers physical growth, specifically, puberty; Part III covers psychological growth, including alcohol, drugs, depression, suicide, coping with death and dying, as well as more information on communication and discipline. Sexual growth is the focus of Part IV: communicating about sex, influencing your teen's values, and specific information on contraception, pregnancy, homosexuality, and sexual abuse. Friends, dating, loneliness, manners, and the need to belong are covered in Part V on social growth. Part VI deals with education (goals, motivation, and learning problems), while the last section, Part VII covers many medically-related topics: nutrition, eating disorders, obesity, sports, STDs, gynecological problems, common medical disorders, and chronic illness.

Evaluation:

While written by a number of physicians, this book is very easy for a lay person to understand. Even the most technical chapter, "Signs of Puberty," is easy to read, with many terms defined and a chart supplied to help parents identify where their teen is at in the maturation process. Some chapters, like the one previously mentioned, and the one on nutrition contain very specific information, but other topics, like rape, substance abuse treatment, and other topics, are covered in just a few paragraphs/pages. Because the book tends to be a very general resource, it needs bibliographies or lists of other supportive resources; unfortunately, none are provided. While the book includes a few cross-references for the topics of sexuality, learning disabilities, weight loss, and substance abuse, as a whole, it is sadly disappointing. This book comes with a substantial set of credentials, but parents seeking a general reference guide would most likely be better served using other resources that offer additional supportive cross-references.

Where To Find/Buy:

Bookstores and libraries.

Overall Rating
★★
Covers most topics in a very general way; a good resource as a starting point

Design, Ease Of Use
★★★
Short, succinct; ample index, general TOC; needs cross-referencing resources

1–4 Stars; N/R = Not Rated

Media:
Print

Price:
$24.50

Principal Subject:
General Overview

ISBN:
055307556X

Edition:
1991

Publisher:
Bantam Books (Bantam Doubleday Dell Publishing)

Author:
Donald E. Greydanus, M.D., F.A.A.P.

About The Author:
(From Cover Notes)
Greydanus, Professor of Pediatrics and Human Development at Michigan State University is editor-in-chief; in addition, 5 other pediatricians/professors served on the editorial board, and more than 30 specialists in adolescent medicine contributed to the book.

Overall Rating
★★
Sparse paragraph descriptions and advice on teen development, family, and issues

Design, Ease Of Use
★★★
Logically organized with good chapter overviews; writing style dense at times

1–4 Stars; N/R = Not Rated

Media:
Print

Price:
$10.00

Principal Subject:
General Overview

ISBN:
0345386795

Edition:
1993

Publisher:
Ballantine Books
(Random House)

Author:
David Elkind, Ph.D.

About The Author:
(From Cover Notes)
Dr. David Elkind is a Professor of Child Study at Tufts University, and is the author of more than ten books, most notably *The Hurried Child*. He is also a consultant to government agencies, mental health centers, and private foundations.

PARENTING YOUR TEENAGER

Description:
This book is a compilation of monthly columns which Elkind wrote for *Parents* magazine from 1987 onwards. The book is organized into five chapters, each covering a specific aspect of adolescent development. Within each chapter are thirteen or so of Elkind's columns specific to the chapter topic. An overview introduces each chapter and at the end of each column, there is a section entitled "what parents can do." The columns have been revised to make them "as current and cohesive as possible." The first chapter contains articles on emotional and psychological development—self-esteem, stress, anxiety, etc. Chapter 2 moves into friendships and dating, and addresses peer groups and teen sexuality. The next chapter deals with family matters, such as letting go, power struggles, privacy, divorce, and respect. Chapter 4—Education—includes topics ranging from homework and religion to decisions about college. The last chapter deals with the more serious problems of adolescence—alcohol, violence, suicide, and more.

Evaluation:
Parenting Your Teenager is for the parent who wants a brief look at the wide range of issues that arises during the adolescent years. The book is organized in a logical fashion with the subheadings relevant to each chapter. The language is mildly academic, which is natural given Elkind's educational and professional background; therefore, the reader must be prepared to tolerate a bit extra in the overviews to each chapter. There are two problems with this book. The first is the fact that each subheading was originally published in a magazine and targeted at an incredibly diverse group of people. Therefore, the language used may not always be on the same level as the reader; sometimes you feel as if you're being lectured. Secondly, each topic is given quick coverage, and topics which deserve far more attention, such as "drugs and alcohol," are given the same amount of discussion as "grandparents and teenagers." Anyone who wants a paragraph of advice, though, on over 65 issues will be well-served by this book.

Where To Find/Buy:
Bookstores and libraries.

YOUTHINFO

Description:

Developed by the U.S. Department of Health and Human Services (HHS), this website provides "the latest information about America's adolescents." The five options on their homepage include: "What's New" (upcoming events, grants, etc.), a profile of America's youth (from a 1998 HHS publication), recent reports and publications (divided by subject matter—substance abuse, violence, health), "Resources for Parents," and transcripts of speeches by federal officials on youth-related topics. The section "Resources for Parents" features website links to various agencies and organizations (National Institute on Drug Abuse, Food and Drug Administration, Centers for Disease Control and Prevention, American Academy of Pediatrics, etc.). Provided through these links are various HSS online publications and fact sheets focused on substance abuse, teen pregnancy, violence, teen safety at work, and more. The website also hosts their own publication "Supporting Your Adolescent: Tips for Parents."

Evaluation:

Primarily focusing on substance abuse, this site offers a compilation of publications helpful for busy parents. Here they can access the latest (1992–1996) information surrounding substance abuse along with several online publications (also offered free through the mail) from the National Institute on Drug Abuse and other HSS branches. The HSS's own publication "Supporting Your Adolescent: Tips for Parents" is a 6+ page article detailing the challenges youths face today, tips for parenting adolescents, what to do when adolescents need help, resources, and more. Although rather dry and broad-based ("Educate yourself about adolescent development," "Think about taking a course on good parenting," etc.), parents nonetheless can get a quick overview of what's involved with parenting adolescents. It would have been even more parent-friendly to have these "tips" linked to other sites offering detailed advice for those seeking further help. This site grants parents a general overview, but other resources can offer more depth.

Where To Find/Buy:

On the Internet at the URL: http://youth.os.dhhs.gov/.

Overall Rating
★★
General overview of how to parent adolescents, especially in regard to substance abuse

Design, Ease Of Use
★★★
Straight-forward; synopsis of each link would aid parents looking for appropriate info

---

1–4 Stars; N/R = Not Rated

Media:
Internet

Principal Subject:
General Overview

Publisher:
U.S. Department of Health and Human Services

Internet URL:
http://youth.os.dhhs.gov/

Overall Rating
★★
Christian perspectives
on how to communicate
values; some ambiguous
recommendations

Design, Ease Of Use
★★
Sometimes difficult to find
the main points; no index

1–4 Stars; N/R = Not Rated

Media:
Print

Price:
$10.99

Principal Subject:
General Overview

ISBN:
0802463916

Edition:
1997

Publisher:
Moody Press

Author:
Tim Smith

About The Author:
(From Cover Notes)
Smith, M.A., is the author
of several books including
The Relaxed Parent and *Hi,
I'm Bob and I'm the Parent
of a Teenager*. Trained in
psychology and education,
Tim is a family life pastor
and conference speaker.

ALMOST COOL

Description:

Smith, a pastor, writes from a Christian perspective as he explains the "how-tos" of parenting teenagers; his aim is to help parents become "almost cool." Within the book's 12 chapters, 217 pages, Smith addresses what he sees as the "real world" of teenagers—their development process and what they feel. He also offers Christian advice for discussing sex, dating, puberty, values, and love. There are two chapters, entitled "Dealing With An Angry Teen" and "Dealing With A Hurting Teen," for parents with special concerns. Two related chapters address the topics of empowering a child to make his/her own decisions, and helping them make wise choices. The last chapter is designed to assist the parent in giving their child "An Emotional and Spiritual Legacy." Provided within the book are nine charts which display answers given by teens in a nationwide survey (both church and non-church goers); topics such as "things teens want most from life" and "feelings teens may experience" are listed.

Evaluation:

This book will benefit the Christian parent who wants information on communication, as well as some ways to talk to their child about values. These parents will also glean the author's interpretation of what it's like to be a teenager. He includes some funny anecdotes from his own experience, and he makes good overall recommendations. The main difficulty parents will have with this book, however, is its ambiguity. Smith tends to float around a bit. Although his humor IS funny, it seems as though it is a substitute for real information. When Smith does have a strong opinion on something, his advice seems a bit trite. For example, his directive to parents when disciplining their children is to "have a consequence for the behavior, and stick to it." Uh-huh—but what if the child isn't listening? All in all, Christian parents may be comforted by reading this book, and they may learn something about adolescent development, but it's doubtful that they'll be prepared if their teenager pushes them.

Where To Find/Buy:

Bookstores and libraries.

MOTHERING TEENS
Understanding The Adolescent Years

Description:

Each chapter of this 314 page book is written by a different female professional specializing in a certain area. *Mothering Teens* is organized into three main parts. Part One, entitled "Basic Issues," addresses general concepts and development of adolescents. Specific chapters deal with gender, self-image, spirituality, sexuality, and family life. Part Two introduces the reader to "Teens in the World," offering chapters (of about 15 pages each) that focus on drugs and alcohol, racism, schooling, socioeconomic influences, family breakups, and grief. The last major part of the book, "Parenting Different Kids," is dedicated to parents of: activist teenagers, lesbian or gay teens, adolescent mothers, children with a chronic illness, and daughters with developmental delays. The contributor of each individual essay offers a bibliography at the end of her piece. The editor, Kaufman, is responsible for the introduction and the opening chapter, "Change is the Essence: Adolescent Development."

Evaluation:

The approach this book uses is nontraditional compared to others of its type, almost creating a new category of parenting books. Kaufman, in her introduction, explains that this "is not a parenting book in the traditional sense . . . Its purpose is not to tell you how to parent, but to help you understand the process of adolescence." She expresses her belief that, because every child is different, "cookie-cutter approaches to parenting" do not work. The book does a fine job explaining complicated issues to parents. The chapter on sexuality, for example, teaches parents all about teenage sexuality—what, why, with whom, and how parents should react. It outlines ways parents can assess their parent-teen communication practices, encouraging **extremely** open lines of communication. Assuming that parents believe that knowledge is power, this book demands then that parents accept today's facts so families can progress. Open-minded parents will find this is an excellent book for learning ways to communicate effectively.

Where To Find/Buy:

Bookstores, libraries, or order direct by contacting: gynergy books, P.O. Box 2023 Charlottetown, PEI, Canada C1A 7N7.

Overall Rating
★★
A wealth of information; a new approach to parenting advice

Design, Ease Of Use
★★
Lack of index is unfortunate; written as a compilation of essays; sometimes rather dense

1–4 Stars; N/R = Not Rated

Media:
Print

Price:
$16.95

Principal Subject:
General Overview

ISBN:
0921881460

Edition:
1997

Publisher:
gynergy books

Author:
Miriam Kaufman, M.D.

About The Author: (From Cover Notes)
Kaufman is a pediatrician at the Hospital for Sick Children in Toronto, and associate professor in the Dept. of Pediatrics at the Univ. of Toronto. She has worked with teens with chronic conditions, teen mothers, and young women who have been sexually abused.

Overall Rating
★★
Good succinct info, although inconclusive at times, necessitating additional research

Design, Ease Of Use
★★
Merging homepage options would help ease access to info, otherwise well-organized

1–4 Stars; N/R = Not Rated

Media:
Internet

Principal Subject:
General Overview

Internet URL:
http://www.parent.net/

PARENT NEWS
A Unique Opportunity For Parent Information

Description:
Nine options are available at the Parent News' homepage. "Articles" allows parents access to a weekly article; the archive is divided into 9 categories (positive parenting, self-esteem, etc.); an article on substance abuse treatment was the topic when we visited. Similarly, "Family Facts" offers a weekly information sheet (typically 1–2 pages) along with an archive of 8 categories (from abuse, development, etc.); facts were presented on various topics such as teen drugs and alcohol, teen pregnancy, eating disorders, teen suicide, and more. The "Health" option presents past articles concerning eyes. "Movies" highlights weekly a movie, and rates it in 15 categories, such as the extent to which the movie included alcohol/drugs, blood/gore, disrespectful or bad attitudes, guns/weapons, and so on; an archive is also available. "Homework" links to other sites for help with various school subjects. Archives in "Tips" and "News" offer parenting advice and current events, respectively. Suggested books and resources are also given.

Evaluation:
Much valuable information can be found at this site, but parents will need to go deep into some of the archives to find it. The site's information would be better accessed if the "Articles" section and the "Family Facts" section were merged thereby allowing for quick and comprehensive searches. For example, parents looking for advice about helping children during a divorce will find that information, but it's separated under "Divorce" (within "Articles") and "Abuse" (within "Family Facts"); some valuable information may be missed by hurried parents. Information is good, some of it is from AACAP's "Facts for Families" website. Some areas are treated briefly though, for example, "adolescent development" consists of a mere one page of bulleted tidbits. A list of suggested resources for additional reading at the end of each article would better serve parents' needs. This site offers busy parents good information, but those looking for implicit how-tos in dealing with serious parent-teen problems will need to look elsewhere.

Where To Find/Buy:
On the Internet at the URL: http://www.parent.net/.

PARENTTIME

Description:

Access to this site's features starts with selecting a child's age which ranges from pregnancy, baby, toddler, and preschooler ages to school-age, "middler," and teen. Five departments at their homepage feature advice from "experts" along with information on a child's growth and health, parenting issues (family relationships, behavior, finance, education, practical parenting), fun and games for children, and more. Within these departments, numerous articles, sub-articles, book excerpts, and experts' advice can be accessed. The site's team of "experts" include Dr. William Sears, Dr. Benjamin Spock, Dr. Ruth, and numerous authors of *PARENTING* and *Baby Talk* magazines. A live chat room is available along with a list of parenting topic discussions that can be accessed through the "Bulletin Boards." One may also subscribe for free to their weekly magazine that reports on "new and interesting articles," along with highlights of the site's upcoming chat talks and ongoing debates.

Evaluation:

Users of this site will find a wealth of information here to answer many of their questions and concerns, however, much of it is tailored for parents of younger children. Some parents will enjoy the chat room, others will find the online live forum fun. But one needs patience and time because most of the information is buried deep within the various departments. Even though you select a child's age to access information, unfortunately the articles aren't focused solely on that age. You must weed out what's not pertinent and hunt for what is. The section containing "Expert Advice" includes book excerpts, frequently asked Q & As, and the experts' perspectives on topical parenting issues, and should not be missed. Even though this website's database of articles largely comes from *PARENTING* magazine, parents will generally get an array of opinion to help them weigh alternatives for various parenting issues. Although a visit here will prove interesting, use other sites for more specific advice and information.

Where To Find/Buy:

On the Internet at the URL: http://www.pathfinder.com/ParentTime/Welcome/.

Overall Rating
★★
Access to abundant info, other online parents on selected topics, and "experts"

Design, Ease Of Use
★★
Most info is buried deep, but fairly well-categorized; graphics slow down the process

1–4 Stars; N/R = Not Rated

Media:
Internet

Principal Subject:
General Overview

Publisher:
ParentTime LLC (Time, Inc. and Procter & Gamble Productions, Inc.)

Internet URL:
http://www.pathfinder.com/ParentTime/Welcome/

Overall Rating
★★

Exhaustively illustrates the components of successful programs for youth in society

Design, Ease Of Use
★★

Well-written, but facts and statistics are overwhelming; should be read in its entirety

1–4 Stars; N/R = Not Rated

Media:
Print

Price:
$27.50

Principal Subject:
General Overview

ISBN:
0195112563

Edition:
1998

Publisher:
Oxford University Press

Author:
Joy G. Dryfoos

**About The Author:
(From Cover Notes)**
Joy G. Dryfoos is an independent researcher and writer whose work is supported by the Carnegie Corporation. She is the author of *Adolescents At Risk* and *Full Service Schools*.

SAFE PASSAGE
Making It Through Adolescence In A Risky Society

Description:

As outlined throughout this book, "safe passage" for a young person is contingent on them finding a place of value in a constructive group. It is in these groups that adolescents learn how to form meaningful human relationships, feel worth as a person, and discover ways to respect and be responsible for the world they live in. Dryfoos has examined hundreds of programs and current research, analyzing the ways in which various institutions and individuals have responded to the increasing epidemic of at-risk youth. By sifting through the wreckage of programs which have failed and those that have succeeded, Dryfoos highlights ways in which people are applying real-world solutions to working with at-risk youth. She believes that investing in successful programs is of vital importance, and families can not do it alone; community involvement is more important than ever. Dryfoos feels that by bringing together the school restructuring movement and caring individuals from the public and private sectors, we can effect beneficial changes for our youth.

Evaluation:

By dealing with the world as it is and not as we think it should be, this 292 page book provides a compelling call to action for our society. Dryfoos dissects field-tested programs purporting to provide energizing atmospheres in which young people can grow and develop. The facts and statistics in this book, however, can be overwhelming at times. With her common sense and realistic approach, Dryfoos's suggestions and analysis might help communities and schools find solutions that really work in the lives of adolescents. Less in-depth is her presentation of "Safe Passage Parents" in Chapter 11 (10 pages). She sprinkles implications for parents throughout her book, but this chapter specifically aimed at parents is broad and vague (regarding teen sexual discussions—"communication of that message has to start early . . ."). This resource is important for those interested in positively concerning themselves with the lives of adolescents, but parents will need to read the book in its entirety to get specific advice for their family.

Where To Find/Buy:
Bookstores and libraries.

SURVIVING YOUR ADOLESCENTS
How To Manage And Let Go Of Your 13–18 Year Olds

Description:

This 152-page, six-part book focuses on getting parents through this period of their child's life (ages 13 to 18) using the author's how-to methods. Phelan first advises parents to "size up" the situation by stepping back and taking an objective look at the child, the parent, and the child-parent relationship. He offers a 1 to 5 rating system to rate "how well you and your adolescent get along." The parent is to apply this numerical value to real-life problems and decide accordingly what role to assume: observer, advisor, negotiator, or director. Phelan defines each of these roles in ensuing chapters, dedicating a chapter to each role. He also encourages parents to sort out "minor but aggravating" (MBA) behavior and ways to choose their battles wisely. Phelan's analytical approach addresses minor problems while leading up to more serious problems in Part Five. Here he suggests how to handle these problems, along with advice on what role parents should take. Also discussed are the needs of children with attention deficit disorder (ADD).

Evaluation:

Phelan's knowledge and wisdom from his 25 years as a clinical psychologist are reflected in this book, but in a pedagogical, structured way which may be objectionable to some families' parenting style. Others will find his ideas good, practical, and useful. His methods will be most attractive to those who like to analyze people and relationships, and those who like rating systems. The book's logical format of addressing minor issues and leading up to serious problems makes it easy to follow. Phelan offers suggestions for resolving specific problems in Chapter 15, but the discussions are generally too brief or inconclusive. For example, in discussing sex, Phelan advises giving the teen "The Sex Test," listen to their definitions of sexual terms while not laughing, and understand that parents "may still be stuck with some unsettling differences." He devotes a chapter to an important parenting topic that other resources often overlook—"Taking Care of Yourself," but on the whole, parents wanting to take care of their parent-teen relationship will need other resources too.

Where To Find/Buy:

Bookstores, libraries, or order direct by calling 1-800-442-4453. An audiotape version (1997) of this book is also available for $24.95 (ISBN No. 1889140066)

Overall Rating
★★
Good, informative resource, with light treatment of serious problems

Design, Ease Of Use
★★
Step-by-step, analytical style with scenarios; an adequate table of contents, no index

1–4 Stars; N/R = Not Rated

Media:
Print

Price:
$12.95

Principal Subject:
General Overview

ISBN:
0963386107

Edition:
2nd (1994)

Publisher:
Child Management

Author:
Thomas W. Phelan, Ph.D.

**About The Author:
(From Cover Notes)**
Phelan, a registered Ph.D. Clinical Psychologist, has worked with children, adults, and families for 25 years and has raised two teenagers. A renowned expert and lecturer on child discipline, Phelan is the author of *1-2-3 Magic* and *All About Attention Deficit Disorder*.

Overall Rating
★★
Many opportunities for discussions (170+), but minimal opportunities for information

Design, Ease Of Use
★
Vague feature headings make navigation confusing; site "tour" does little to help

1–4 Stars; N/R = Not Rated

Media:
Internet

Principal Subject:
General Overview

Internet URL:
http://www.parentsoup.com/

PARENT SOUP
An iVillage Community

Description:

Six features are offered at Parent Soup's homepage to address parents' needs from prepregnancy through their child's teenage years. At "Education Central," parents may access a library of articles by selecting any age ranging from preschool to high school along with 6 focus areas that offer information from "home schooling" and the "school yard" to "parent-teacher relations" and "standardized testing;" many articles are reprints from various educational institutions and the American Academy of Child and Adolescent Psychiatry's "Facts for Families." Six "experts" (pediatrician, counselor, early education, summer camp, college, breastfeeding) will answer 10 questions a week from parents via email, but parents have the option of browsing previously asked Q and As. Visitors can access chat rooms, the "Boards" (discussion groups of 170+ different topics), and "Resources" (including "Parents' Picks" about items such as books, movies/videos, websites, etc.). A free weekly newsletter is also available through email. Also available on AOL (Keyword "PS Teens").

Evaluation:

The vague feature headings here will lead visitors to many dead ends. Most of the factual information is housed within "Education Central." Here parents will gain the basics about parenting adolescents, but with little depth. For example, a one page article focusing on teens and substance abuse offers brief warning signs with a disclaimer that these signs can also indicate other problems—certainly not the information that will guide or reassure parents. Also, the expert panel offers few choices for parents of teens. However, if parents seek discussions, this site may be paradise with live chats (free software must be downloaded), 170+ discussion groups, or connections with other members; a search facility is supplied to locate others in the "Soup family" by name, location, or parenting issue (divorce, disabilities, adoption, ADD/ADHD, etc.). Better suited for parents of young children, Parent Soup offers minimal information for parents of teenagers. Use better sources for more in-depth understanding and guidance.

Where To Find/Buy:

On the Internet at the URL: http://www.parentsoup.com/.

FAMILY.COM
Disney.Com

Description:

Coordinated with Disney, this site boasts an "online parenting service that offers comprehensive, high-quality information and a supportive community for raising children." Ten options are available at their homepage, six of which pertain to parenting interests. Those seeking information about teenagers will most likely find it within the "Parenting" option. Here, they will find a drop-down list of topics (16) ranging from behavior, development, and discipline to eating and siblings; they will also find a drop-down list of age choices ranging from birth to "12 and Over." Then, parents may customize their searches, for example, for all the information about behavior of a "12 and Over" aged child. Links to articles (abstracts are provided) can be pursued for further investigation. A Q & A segment is offered with advice from the "Experts" (Leach, Schmitt, Faull, and the Prices). The "Boards" lists forums for parent discussions, and a "Chat" segment is available from 1 pm. to 5 p.m. (EST) Monday through Friday.

Evaluation:

Although this site is comprehensively dedicated to parenting concerns, it primarily addresses the needs of parents of younger children, not teens. Parents of teenagers will find information, but they'll have to conduct numerous searches to locate it. Their best bet is to use the "keyword" search feature available at the site, avoiding the searches via the drop-down lists altogether. Parents looking for others to share ideas and tips will find the "Boards" to be the most well-organized of any website. However, the possibilities for parents of teens are also lacking here with basically one avenue available for parents—within "Boards ("Parenting"/"teens"); the listings are fairly active with the capability of reading postings from either a year ago or just the most recent ones. This saves busy parents from wasted time and effort responding to discussions that are no longer current. The site is easily navigated, concise, and visually appealing, but recommended for parents of younger children, and not those of teenagers.

Where To Find/Buy:

On the Internet at the URL: http://family.disney.com.

Overall Rating
★
Site hosts articles on various parenting concerns, mostly geared toward younger children

Design, Ease Of Use
★★★★
Easily navigated, very well-organized for speedy access; customized searches

---

1–4 Stars; N/R = Not Rated

Media:
Internet

Principal Subject:
General Overview

Internet URL:
http://family.disney.com

Overall Rating
★
Information and advice from "authorities" too succinct and simplistic

Design, Ease Of Use
★★★★
Good access to discussion forums/bulletin boards; headings make for easy navigation

1–4 Stars; N/R = Not Rated

Media:
Internet

Principal Subject:
General Overview

Internet URL:
http://www.tnpc.com/

NATIONAL PARENTING CENTER (THE)

Description:

Programmed and hosted by ParentsPlace.com, this website was founded in July 1989 to provide parents with "comprehensive and responsible guidance from 9 of the world's most reknowned [sic] child-rearing authorities." Features at their homepage include articles, a mall, chat facilities, and a daily feature. Articles, presented through the "ParenTalk Newsletter," are written by their panel of 9 parenting authorities (bios include parenting authors, a psychologist, pediatrician, and more). Information is grouped by: pregnancy, newborns, infancy, toddler, preschool, preteens, and adolescence; various subcategories are then presented along with names of the respective authors. Articles typically range from 1/2 a page to 1 page in length. "Chat" leads you to ParentsPlace.com's discussion rooms with 20+ topics along with numerous parenting "bulletin boards." TNPC's "Mall" houses award-winning products from their Seal of Approval program organized by age groups and available for purchase online.

Evaluation:

Visitors to this site will be initially impressed by the discussion forums available here. The topics are more numerous than most sites, they're clearly labeled for access, and the participants are active. The articles, however, were very inadequate, sidestepping serious issues involved with such topics as suicide, sexuality, drugs and alcohol, etc. The advice given is too succinct and too simplistic to be helpful to any struggling parent or teen. For example, advice about sexuality states that parents might say, "Sex is best enjoyed by those who are grown up, emotionally as well as physically." However, this type of approach will not invite communications between parents and teens, but most likely will be seen as yet another parent lecture from the teen's perspective; the teen in question probably feels grown up enough to take on this responsibility, thus the advice will be perceived as demeaning and non-respectful. Other sites provide more in-depth follow-through and situational help than this one does. Use them instead.

Where To Find/Buy:

On the Internet at the URL: http://www.tnpc.com/ or by calling 1-800-753-6667.

13 TO 19
A Parent's Guide To Understanding The Teenage Years

Description:

This 167 page, 15 chapter book covers a sweeping range of topics, including the physical and emotional changes taking place during puberty, types of school teens might attend, learning difficulties, friends, rules, contraceptives and sex, homosexuality, sexual impotence, money matters, drugs and alcohol, and more. Preceding the text is a "Teenager-Parent Questionnaire" designed to be answered by the teenager and parent as a tool to invite communication and understanding between the two. The author, a hypnotherapist and psychotherapist, also offers some new age techniques (mental/relaxation exercises) for dealing with stress for both the parent and teen. A chapter is also dedicated to "Family Problems," including advice for divorced and single-parent families, "no dad at all," stepchildren, new parents in a family, bereavement, and grandparents moving in. "Tips For Your Survival," "Organizations Offering Advice and Support," and "Recommended Reading" are listed at the back of the book.

Evaluation:

Although the author makes a valiant attempt to give advice to parents of teens, she has tried to discuss too much in her book's 167 pages. This leaves the reader wondering what the book's focus really is, since it often fails to address topics adequately. In her discussion of problems parents face with teens, Grant often does not provide solid answers—a typical solution advises parents to " . . . deal with the problem. If [they] can't, seek help." Some of her suggestions seem superficial or impractical; for example, if a child is spending a lot of time and money at amusement arcades, parents are advised to give him access to a home computer. Solid guidance is lacking in many cases, and Grant seems to believe that if parents have tried talking it out with their teen, or tried counseling with no success, it eventually will work out. There is a prevailing tone of "whatever happens, it is good to remember that others have had similar problems." Unfortunately, this light and fluffy attitude won't offer hope for parents in the midst of turmoil.

Where To Find/Buy:

Bookstores and libraries.

Overall Rating
★
Attempts to cover too much, resulting in insufficient treatment of certain topics

Design, Ease Of Use
★★★
Straightforward, logical organization of topics presented; meager index

---

1–4 Stars; N/R = Not Rated

Media:
Print

Price:
$12.95

Principal Subject:
General Overview

ISBN:
1852308621

Edition:
1996

Publisher:
Element Books

Author:
Wendy Grant

**About The Author:
(From Cover Notes)**
Wendy Grant, a hypnotherapist and psychotherapist, lectures and writes on "emotional and behavioral problems and the unconscious mind." She is also the author of *Are You In Control* and *Dare!*

Overall Rating

★

Informative guide, but too concise and too generalized to be of any real benefit

Design, Ease Of Use

★★

Table of contents format wieldy with all questions listed; index not comprehensive

1–4 Stars; N/R = Not Rated

Media:
Print

Price:
$12.95

Principal Subject:
General Overview

ISBN:
1577490053

Edition:
1995

Publisher:
Fairview Press

Author:
Gerald Deskin, Ph.D., M.F.C.C., and Greg Steckler, M.A., M.F.C.C.

About The Author: (From Cover Notes)

Deskin, Ph.D.,M.F.C.C., is a licensed psychologist and licensed marriage, family, and child therapist. Steckler, M.A., M.F.C.C., is a marriage, family, and child therapist and is founding director of the Halcyon Center for Child Studies, Inc.

PARENT'S ANSWER BOOK (THE)
Over 101 Most-Asked Questions About Your Child's Well-Being

Description:

Divided into five sections, this 216-page answer book centers on offering advice and suggestions on 100+ child and adolescent development issues. The first section answers questions related to family development. Some of these issues include: how to tell if your child is ready to drive, dealing with sibling rivalry, what to do when your child wants things that you can't afford, how to tell if your child is over-scheduled, and more. The second section answers questions about school and learning problems. The next two sections offer advice on social and emotional development, and the final section deals with physical development. A sampling of issues in these last three sections address subjects such as depression, weight problems, dealing with stress, sleep disorders, etc. Questions are listed in the table of contents, delineated in bold within each section, and follow-up, explanatory subtopics are also given in bold. An index is also included.

Evaluation:

Ask a question, any question, and this book is sure to have an answer—at least on most of the more frequently addressed issues for school-aged child and adolescents. This book does an adequate job of answering significant questions, such as what to do if your son has impregnated a girl, what to do if you find out your child has been sexually involved or abused, how to get your child to attend religious services, how far away should you live from your ex-spouse, how to find out if your child is in a gang, and more. The authors answer all questions in a concise, no-nonsense manner, with a "Recommendations" section included that highlight the authors' main points on each question. The book's candor is refreshing, and parents of adolescents will find themselves referring to it time and time again for background information regarding basic issues. Parents wishing in-depth, well-thought out answers to some of the tougher questions, however, will end up turning to other better resources.

Where To Find/Buy:

Bookstores and libraries, or order direct by calling 1-800-544-8207.

TERRIFIC
RESOURCES FOR
SELECTED TOPICS

INTRODUCTION

During the course of our ongoing research, we've determined several other "views" of the resources we've reviewed. This section, then, provides you with our recommendations for **unique and helpful resources** as you parent your teenager. These specific resources will help you:

- Improve parent-and-teen communications and dialogues

- "Let go" of your child into adulthood

- Deal directly with peer pressures using explicit, hands-on techniques

- Guide your pregnant teenager as they decide upon their options

- Clarify your values regarding your teen's sexual behavior

- Communicate your expectations/values, especially about sexuality (videotape)

- Approach substance abuse using reenacted parent-teen scenarios (videotape)

- Understand how a mother-daughter relationship can encourage eating disorders

- Understand how a father-daughter relationship can affect a teen's eating habits

- Understand how depression relates to other serious adolescent problems

Specific recommended resources that offer a **Christian perspective** while parenting a teenager, include those resources that will help you:

- Strengthen your parent-child relationship

- Deal with minor to serious teenage problems

- Prevent or treat substance abuse in your teen

Be sure to also read other full-page reviews of resources we recommend within Sections II, III, IV, and V. Here, you will find additional resources that focus on similar general subjects (understanding adolescents, parent-teen relationships, critical issues and concerns, general overview). Take some time to read the full descriptions and evaluations for each recommended resource carefully; we're certain that you will discover the right resources to best serve your needs.

Assisting parents in "letting go" of their children into adulthood

Title:	**Give Them Wings**
Author:	Carol Kuykendall
Overall Rating:	★★★★
Media Type:	Print

Short Description:

■ **Read The Full Review Of This Resource On Page 57.**

In this 15 chapter book, Kuykendall reflects on the feelings experienced as she let go of her own children. She advises parents gently on how to think of the different processes, and how to react to certain issues or problems that may arise. The time period is essentially from 16–22, and she delves deeply into all the feelings parents may experience during these years. The book is 232 pages, and there are a number of biblical references.

Christian parents needing guidance for dealing with minor to serious teenage problems

Title:	**Helping The Struggling Adolescent**
Author:	Les Parrott III
Overall Rating:	★★★
Media Type:	Print

Short Description:

■ **Read The Full Review Of This Resource On Page 179.**

Designed for the parent or counselor, this two-part book offers various techniques for helping, listening to, and directing teenagers. Part One deals with the "How-Tos" of dealing with teenagers. In Part Two, 30 issues, which Parrott cites as being "common teenage problems," are discussed in detail (symptoms, causes, treatment, etc.). Issues range from minor to highly serious problems. Suggestions for further reading on each topic are offered.

Christian parents wanting to prevent or treat substance abuse in their teen

Title:	**Drug Proof Your Kids**
Author:	Stephen Arterburn and Jim Burns
Overall Rating:	★★★★
Media Type:	Print

Short Description:

■ **Read The Full Review Of This Resource On Page 105.**

This "drug-proofing" approach uses scriptural passages and personal narratives to discuss ways to help kids stay off drugs. This 222 page book includes 13 chapters about facts of illicit drug use, why kids take drugs, ways to intervene, how to obtain treatment, how to deal with relapse, and more. A 40 page chapter-by-chapter study guide, and discussion leader's guide are also included.

Christian parents wanting to strengthen their parent-child relationship

Title:	**Seize The Moment, Not Your Teen**
Author:	Bill Sanders
Overall Rating:	★★★★
Media Type:	Print
Short Description:	*Seize The Moment* is a 178 page, 9 chapter book rooted in biblical principles of parenting and daily living. Discussions, stories, and advice on teen issues are presented, along with some of the author's personal experiences. Chapter titles include "Kids Hear Best with Their Eyes," "We Do One Thing; They Learn Another," "Classic Mistakes and the Walls They Build," and more. Each chapter includes a parent self-evaluation and scriptural references.

■ **Read The Full Review Of This Resource On Page 59.**

Communicating parental expectations and values, especially about sexuality (videotape)

Title:	**If You Can Talk To Your Kids About Sex, You Can Talk To Them About Anything**
Author:	Lennie Roseman
Overall Rating:	★★★★
Media Type:	Videotape
Short Description:	Within this 54 minute videotape, Roseman uses values as the foundation that "gives direction to our lives." She outlines criteria for values, along with four parenting skills to invite teens to talk, and five practices that specifically address how to communicate about sex. Roseman believes that sex is not just teaching kids facts, but instead involves teaching them about relationships, while ensuring that they feel good about themselves.

■ **Read The Full Review Of This Resource On Page 133.**

Hands-on techniques to deal with peer pressures

Title:	**Peer Pressure Reversal**
Author:	Sharon Scott
Overall Rating:	★★★★
Media Type:	Print
Short Description:	This 235 page resource teaches parents and teachers how to protect children against negative peer pressure. Scott's program called "peer pressure reversal" is outlined in this step-by-step guide which includes ways to reinforce the skills learned. Consisting of six chapters, this book includes examples of how teens can deal with uncomfortable situations, along with additional supportive resources.

■ **Read The Full Review Of This Resource On Page 87.**

Improving parent-teenager communications

Title:	**Art Of Talking With Your Teenager (The)**
Author:	Paul W. Swets
Overall Rating:	★★★★
Media Type:	Print
Short Description:	Claiming that the best way to communicate is to "become an expert on your teen," this 211 page book highlights several ways parents can listen to, observe, and learn from their teenager. Swets provides parents with techniques to communicate more effectively, improve listening skills, keep their cool in difficult situations, respond to problems, and get to know their teenager better.

■ **Read The Full Review Of This Resource On Page 51.**

Parent-teen role-played scenarios concerning substance abuse issues (videotape)

Title:	**Drug Free Kids**
Author:	Legacy Home Video
Overall Rating:	★★★★
Media Type:	Videotape
Short Description:	This one hour videotape explores the how-tos of parent-teen communication along with specific ways parents can address their concerns about their adolescent's substance abuse. Consisting of numerous role-played scenarios by actors such as Jane Alexander, Ned Beatty, Melissa Gilbert, and others, this tape illustrates ways parents can confront a teen about drug use (whether it be known or unknown), ways to deal with parental anger, and more.

■ **Read The Full Review Of This Resource On Page 104.**

Parents seeking to clarify their values regarding sexual behavior in teens

Title:	**Teenage Sexuality**
Author:	David L. Bender and Bruno Leone
Overall Rating:	★★★★
Media Type:	Print
Short Description:	The purpose of the *Opposing Viewpoints* series is to present different perspectives on an issue. This 236 page book asks readers to weigh the authors' presentations and consider the following questions: What affects teenagers' attitudes toward sex? What causes teen pregnancy? How can teen pregnancy be reduced? Is sex education necessary? How should teenage homosexuality be treated? A variety of opinions are expressed for each issue.

■ **Read The Full Review Of This Resource On Page 134.**

Pregnant teenagers needing guidance about their options

Title:	**I'm Pregnant, Now What Do I Do?**
Author:	Dr. Robert W. Buckingham, P.H. and Mary P. Derby, R.N., M.P.H.
Overall Rating:	★★★★
Media Type:	Print
Short Description:	This book presents the decision-making process for unplanned teenage pregnancies. Three options are presented for what to do: giving the child up for adoption, terminating the pregnancy through abortion, and continuing with the pregnancy. Three specific case studies are provided which outline three teenagers' decision-making thoughts regarding each of these three options. Numerous teenagers' anecdotes are also included throughout.

■ **Read The Full Review Of This Resource On Page 135.**

Understanding how depression relates to other serious adolescent problems

Title:	**Understanding Your Teenager's Depression**
Author:	Kathleen McCoy, Ph.D.
Overall Rating:	★★★★
Media Type:	Print
Short Description:	The primary focus of this book is that teenage depression should not be taken lightly by parents and other adults. The author presents a lot of information, both in the form of statistics and case studies, that explain her points and support her claims.

■ **Read The Full Review Of This Resource On Page 165.**

Understanding how the father-daughter relationship can affect a teen's eating habits

Title:	**Father Hunger**
Author:	Margo Maine, Ph.D.
Overall Rating:	★★★★
Media Type:	Print
Short Description:	*Father Hunger* touches on a relatively new theory surrounding the etiology of eating disorders—that of emotional craving for a father's attention. It overviews, in 254 pages, the origins of father hunger, its emotional impact, and strategies for overcoming it. Information and advice is provided for fathers, mothers, patients, and professionals. Personal vignettes are interspersed throughout along with documented information.

■ **Read The Full Review Of This Resource On Page 148.**

Understanding how the mother-daughter relationship can encourage eating disorders

Title:	**Like Mother, Like Daughter**
Author:	Debra Waterhouse, M.P.H., R.D.
Overall Rating:	★★★★
Media Type:	Print
Short Description:	This is a 232 page book that aims to help women break the diet and poor body-image trap passed on from mother to daughter. Divided into 8 chapters, the book covers the following topics: recognizing eating patterns in families, understanding the dangers of diets, accepting increased body fat as a needed part of womanhood, reassessing (and modifying) body image, eating well, and creating positive eating behaviors for self and future generations.

■ **Read The Full Review Of This Resource On Page 150.**

INDICES

VII

TITLE INDEX

AUTHOR INDEX

PUBLISHER INDEX

MEDIA INDEX

SUBJECT INDEX
1–4 Stars (4 = Best)

Critical Issues & Concerns: Sexuality & Pregnancy

Critical Issues & Concerns: Eating Disorders

Critical Issues & Concerns: Delinquent Behavior, Gangs

Critical Issues & Concerns: Depression, Suicide

Critical Issues & Concerns: Divorce, Death

Critical Issues & Concerns: General Overview

General Overview Of Raising Teenagers

APPENDICES

INTRODUCTION

Many of the resources we've reviewed include contact information on support groups, associations, and other organizations. On the pages that follow, we've listed a number of these organizations. They are grouped by the principal focus of their work using the four major subject classifications we've used for this guidebook. You'll find that many of these organizations can further refer you to other local, regional, or national organizations that may offer you additional benefits or aspects of support that meet your needs.

The support groups, associations, and other organizations which follow are listed alphabetically within the following topics and subtopics:

HELPFUL ORGANIZATIONS

Understanding Adolescents

American Psychiatric Association

(202) 682-6000

1400 K Street NW
Washington, DC 20005

American Psychological Association

(202) 955-7600

1200 17th Street NW
Washington, DC 20036

National Association Of Social Workers

(301) 565-0333

7981 Eastern Ave.
Silver Spring, MD 20910

National Institute Of Mental Health Public Information Office

(301) 443-4536

5600 Fishers Lane
Rockville, MD 20857

Parent-Teen Relationships

Best Friends

(202) 822-9266

2000 N Street, NW, Suite 201
Washington, D.C. 20036-2336

Big Brothers/Big Sisters, Inc.

(212) 686-2042

223 East 30th Street
New York, NY 10016

Clearinghouse On Family Violence Information

(703) 385-7565

P. O. Box 1182
Washington, DC 20013

Family Resource Coalition

(312) 341-0900

200 South Michigan Ave., Suite 300
Chicago, IL 60604

Family Service America, Inc.

(414) 359-1040

11700 West Lake Park Drive
Milwaukee, WI 53224

National Council On Family Relations

(612) 781-9331

3989 Central Avenue NE, Suite 550
Minneapolis, MN 55421

Students To Offset Peer Pressure (STOPP)

P. O. Box 103, Dept. S
Hudson, NH 03051-0103

Critical Issues & Concerns: Substance Abuse

800-Cocaine

1-800-262-2463

P. O. Box 100
Summit, NJ 07902-0100

Al-Anon/Alateen Family Group Headquarters

1-800-356-9996, 1-800-344-2666, or
1-800-4-ALA-NON

1600 Corporate Landing Parkway
Virginia Beach, VA 23454-5617

Alateen

(212) 302-7240

1372 Broadway
New York, NY 10018-0862

Alcohol & Drug Helpline

1-800-821-4357 or 1-800-252-6465

4578 Highland Drive
Salt Lake City, UT 84117

Alcoholics Anonymous World Services Office

(212) 870-3400

475 Riverside Dr.
New York, NY 10115

http://www.alcoholics-anonymous.org

American Council For Drug Education (ACDE)

1-800-488-DRUG, (301) 294-0600,
or (212) 595-5810 ext.7860

204 Monroe St.
Rockville, MD

American Lung Association

1-800-LUNG-USA, or (212) 315-8700

1740 Broadway
New York, NY 10019

Cocaine Anonymous

(213) 559-5833

6125Washington Blvd., Suite 202
Los Angeles, CA 90230

Cocaine Helpline

1-800-COCAINE (1-800-262-2463),
or 1-800-662-HELP

Community Anti-Drug Coalitions Of America (CADCA)

1-800-54-CADCA

901 North Pitt Street, Suite 300
Alexandria, VA 22314

CSAP National Resource Center Center for Substance Abuse Prevention (CSAP) Center for Substance Abuse Treatment (CSAT)

(703) 218-5700, or 1-800-729-6686

9302 Lee Highway
Fairfax, VA 22031

5600 Fishers Lane, Room 800
Rockville, MD 20857

Do-It-Now Foundation

Box 5115
Phoenix, AZ 85010

Drug Abuse Resistance Education (DARE)

1-800-223-DARE

P. O. Box 2090
Los Angeles, CA 90051

Drugs Anonymous

(212) 874-0700

P. O. Box 473 Ansonia Station
New York, NY 10023

Hazelden

1-800-328-9000

15251 Pleasant Valley Rd.
P. O. Box 176
Center City, MN 55012-0176

Indian Health Services (IHS) Alcohol and Substance Program

(301) 443-4297

5600 Fishers Lane, Room 38
Rockville, MD 20857

Institute On Black Chemical Abuse

(612) 871-7878

2616 Nicollet Ave. S.
Minneapolis, MN 55408

Johnson Institute

1-800-231-5165

7205 Ohms Lane
Minneapolis, MN 55439-2159

"Just Say No" International

1-800-258-2766, or (510) 451-6666

2000 Franklin St., Suite 400
Oakland, CA 94612

youth@justsayno.org

Mothers Against Drunk Driving (MADD)

1-800-GET-MADD, or (214) 744-6233

511 E. John Carpenter Freeway
Suite #700
Irving, TX 75062

Nar-Anon Family Groups

(213) 547-5800, or (310) 547-5800

P. O. Box 2562
Palos Verdes Peninsula, CA 90274

Narcotics Anonymous

(818) 997-3822, (818) 780-3951
or 1-800-622-4672 (Spanish)

P. O. Box 9999 Van Nuys, CA 91409

Or: 19737 Nordhoff Place
Chatsworth, CA 91311

wsoinc@aol.com

National Asian Pacific American Families Against Substance Abuse

(714) 499-3889

31582 Coast Highway, Suite B South
Laguna, CA 92677

National Association For Children Of Alcoholics

(301) 468-0985

11462 Rockville Pike, #100
Rockville, MD 20852

National Association For The Prevention Of Narcotic Abuse

305 E. 79th St.
New York, NY 10021

National Black Alcoholism Council

(202) 296-2696

1629 K St. NW, Suite 802
Washington, D.C. 20006

National Clearinghouse For Alcohol & Drug Information (NCADI)

1-800-729-6686, (301) 468-2600,
or (TDD)1-800-487-4889

P. O. Box 2345
Rockville, MD 20847-2345

Or: 11426 Rockville Pike
Rockville, MD 28052

http://www.health.org

National Clearinghouse On Smoking and Health Centers for Disease Control

1600 Cliften Rd. Building 14
Atlanta, GA 30333

National Clearinghouse/Drug Abuse Information

(301) 443-4273

Parklawn Building
Room 10 A-56 5600 Fishers Lane
Rockville, MD 20852

National Coalition For The Prevention Of Drug & Alcohol Abuse

(614) 587-2800

537 Jones Rd.
Granville, OH 43023

National Council On Alcoholism and Drug Dependence, Inc. (NCADD)

1-800-NCA-CALL, 1-800-475-HOPE,
or (212) 206-6770

12 W. 21st Street, 7th Floor
New York, NY 10010

http://www.ncadd.org

National Drug Abuse Hotline

1-800-622-HELP

National Drug And Alcohol Treatment Referral Service

1-800-662-HELP (1-800-662-4357)

National Families In Action

(404) 934-6364

2296 Henderson Mill Road, Suite 300
Atlanta, GA 30345

http://www.emory.edu/NFIA/

National Family Partnership

(314) 845-1933

11159-B South Town Square
St. Louis, MO 63123

National Federation Of Parents For Drug-Free Youth

(301) 585-5437, (314) 968-1322,
or 1-800-554-KIDS

8730 Georgia Ave., Suite 200
Silver Spring, MD

20910 P. O. Box 3878
St. Louis, MO 63122

National Hispanic Family Against Drugs

(202) 393-5136

1511 K Street, NW
Washington, D.C. 20005

National Institute On Alcohol Abuse & Alcoholism (NIAAA)

(301) 443-3885

6000 Executive Blvd.
Bethesda, MD 20892-7003

National Institute On Drug Abuse (NIDA) National Institutes of Health

(301) 443-1124

5600 Fishers Lane, Room 10A-39
Rockville, MD 20857

http://www.nida.nih.gov

National PTA Drug & Alcohol Abuse Prevention Project

(312) 670-6782

330 N. Wabash Ave., Suite 2100
Chicago, IL 60611-3690

Overcomers

1-800-310-3001

Parents' Resource Institute For Drug Education, Inc. (PRIDE)

1-800-677-7433, or (404) 577-4500

3610 Dekalb Technology Parkway, Suite 105
Atlanta, GA 30430

http://www.prideusa.org

Partnership For A Drug Free America

1-800-853-7867

Pil-Anon Family Program

(212) 744-2020

P. O. Box 120 Gracie Square Station
New York, NY 10028

Pills Anonymous

(212) 375-8872

P. O. Box 473 Ansonia Station
New York, NY 10023

Potsmokers Anonymous

(212) 254-1777

316 East 3rd St.
New York, NY 10009

Resource Center On Substance Abuse Prevention and Disabilities

1-800-628-8442, or (202) 628-8080

1819 L Street NW, Suite 300
Washington, D.C. 20036

Stop Teen-Age Addiction To Tobacco (STAT)

(413) 732-STAT

121 Lyman St., Suite 210
Springfield, MA 01103

Straight, Inc.

(813) 576-8929

3001 Gandy Blvd.
St. Petersburg, FL 33702

Students Against Driving Drunk (SADD)

1-800-521-SADD, or (508) 481-3568

200 Pleasant St.
Marlboro, MA 01752

277 Main St.
Marlboro, MA 01752

Sunburst

1-800-431-1934

101 Castleton St.
Pleasantville, NY 10570-1207

Teen Challenge

1-800-976-6990

Toughlove International

1-800-333-1069

P. O. Box 1069
Doylestown, PA 18901

Critical Issues & Concerns: Sexuality & Pregnancy

AIDS Hotline For Teens

1-800-234-TEEN

Alan Guttmacher Institute

(212) 248-1111, or (212) 254-5656

2010 Massachusetts Ave. NW
Washington, D.C. 20063

American College Health Association

(410) 859-1500

P. O. Box 28937
Baltimore, MD 21240-8937

American College Of Obstetricians And Gynecologists (ACOG)

(202) 638-5577

409 12th Street SW
Washington, D.C. 20024-2188

American Home Economics Program GRADS Program

2010 Massachusetts Ave. NW
Washington, D.C. 20036-1028

American Social Health Association

(919) 361-8425

P. O. Box 13827
Research Triangle Park, NC 27709

Baby Think It Over

(206) 582-BABY

P. O. Box 64184
Tacoma, WA 98466

Center For Adolescent Pregnancy Prevention Family Health Council, Inc.

(412) 288-2130

625 Stanwix Street, Suite 1200
Pittsburgh, PA 15222

Center For Disease Control National AIDS Clearinghouse

1-800-458-5231

P. O. Box 6003
Rockville, MD 20849-6003

Center For Population Options (CPO)

(202) 347-5700

1025 Vermont Ave. NW, Suite 210
Washington, D.C. 20005

Centers For Disease Control & Prevention National Sexual Transmitted Disease Hotline

1-800-227-8922

Focus On The Family

P. O. Box 500
Arcadia, CA 91006-0500

Hetrick-Martin Institute (The)

(212) 633-8920

401 West St.
New York, NY 10014

HIV/AIDS Treatment Information Clearinghouse

1-800-448-0440

March Of Dimes

(914) 997-4792

1275 Mamaroneck Aven
White Plains, NY 10605

Morning Glory Press

(714) 828-1998

6595 S. San Haroldo Way
Bueno Park, CA 90620-3748

National Abortion Federation

1-800-772-9100

1436 U Street NW, Suite 103
Washington, D.C. 20009

National Abortion Rights Action League (NARAL)

1156 15th Street NW, Suite 700
Washington, D.C. 20005

http://www.naral.org

National AIDS Hotline (English and Spanish)

1-800-342-2437,
(Spanish) 1-800-344-7432, or
(hearing-impaired) 1-800-AIDS-TTY

National AIDS Information Clearinghouse

1-800-458-5231

P. O. Box 6003
Rockville, MD 20850

National AIDS Interfaith Network

(202) 546-0807

300 "I" St., NE
Washington, D.C. 20002

National Campaign To Prevent Teen Pregnancy

(202) 857-8655

2100 M Street NW, Suite 300
Washington, D.C. 20037

http://www.teenpregnancy.org

National Gay & Lesbian Task Force

(212) 529-1600

666 Broadway, #410
New York, NY 10012

National Gay Youth Network

P. O. Box 846
San Francisco, CA 94101-0846

National Minority AIDS Council

(202) 544-1076

National Organization On Adolescent Pregnancy, Parenting, and Prevention (NOAPPP)

(202) 783-5770, or (888) 766-2777

1319 F Street NW, Suite 400
Washington, D.C. 20004

NOAPPP@EROLS.COM

Network Publications ETR Associates

1700 Mission St., Suite 203 P. O. Box 8506
Santa Cruz, CA 95061-8506

Parents, Families, & Friends Of Lesbians & Gays (PFLAG)

(202) 638-4200

1101 14th Street, NW, Suite 1030
Washington, D.C. 20005

http://www.pflag.org

Pediatric AIDS Foundation

(213) 395-9051

1311 Colorado Ave.
Santa Monica, CA 90404

Planned Parenthood Federation Of America

1-800-669-0156, or (212) 541-7800

810 Seventh Ave.
New York, NY 10019

http://www.ppfa.org

Program Archive On Sexuality, Health, & Adolescence (PASHA)

(415) 949-3282

Sociometrics Corporation 170 State
Street, Ste. 260
Los Altos, CA 94022-2812

San Francisco AIDS Foundation

(415) 863-AIDS

Sexuality Information And Education Council Of The United States (SEICUS)

(212) 819-9770

130 W. 42nd St., #350
New York, NY 10036

STD National Hotline

1-800-227-8922

Summer Kitchen Press Teen Parents: Reachable/Teachable

1-800-418-5237

314 Chaucer St.
Helena, MT 59601

Wedge Program (The)

(415) 554-9098

1540 Market Street, Suite 435
San Francisco, CA 94102

Critical Issues & Concerns: Eating Disorders

American Anorexia/Bulimia Association (AA/BA)

(212) 891-8686, or (212) 734-1114

293 Central Park West, Suite 1R
New York, NY 10024

American Anorexic/Bulimia Association, Inc.

(201) 501-8351

293 Central Park West, #1R
New York, NY 10024

American Dietetic Association, NCNC - Eating Disorders

1-800-366-1655

216 W. Jackson Blvd.
Chicago, IL 60606

Anorexia Nervosa & Related Eating Disorders, Inc. (ANRED)

(503) 344-1144

P. O. Box 5102
Eugene, OR 97405

Eating Disorder Awareness & Prevention

(206) 382-3587

603 Stewart Street, Suite 803
Seattle, WA 98101

National Academy For Eating Disorders

(718) 920-6781

Montefiore Medical Center Division
of Adolescent Medicine
111 East 210th St.
Bronx, NY 10467

National Anorexic Aid Society (NAAS)

(614) 436-1112

1925 E. Granville Rd.
Columbus, OH

National Association Of Anorexia Nervosa & Associated Disorders (ANAD)

(847) 831-3438, (847) 433-3996,
or (708) 831-3438

1936 Greenbay Rd. Box 7
Highland Park, IL 60035

National Association To Advance Fat Acceptance (NAAFA)

1-800-442-1214, or (916) 558-6880

P. O. Box 188620
Sacramento, CA 95818

National Center For Overcoming Overeating (The)

(212) 875-0442

P. O. Box 1257 Old Chelsea Station
New York, NY 10113

National Eating Disorders Organization (NEDO)

(918) 481-4044, or (614) 436-1112

6655 S. Yale Ave.
Tulsa, OK 74136

445 East Grandille Rd.
Worthington, OH 43085

Overeaters Anonymous World Service Office

(505) 891-2664

P. O. Box 44020
Rio Rancho, NM 87174-4020

Weight Control Information Network National Institutes of Health

1-800-WIN-8098

Critical Issues & Concerns: Delinquent Behavior, Gangs

Adolescent Wellness Program

(617) 534-5196

1010 Massachusetts Ave., 2nd floor
Boston, MA 02118

**Boys & Girls Clubs O...
Gang Prevention...
Outreach**

(404) 815-...

1230...

California Youth Authority Gang Violence Reduction Project

(213) 227-4114

2445 N. Mariondale Ave., Suite 202
Los Angeles, CA 90032

FACES (Family & Community Education Services)

(714) 623-4995

P. O. Box 1781
Pomona, CA 91769

Institute For Intergovernmental Research

(904) 385-0600, ext. 259 or 285

P. O. Box 12729
Tallahassee, FL 32317

Juvenile Justice Clearinghouse

1-800-638-5736

Juveniles Out Of Gangs (JOG)

San Diego City Schools
San Diego, CA 92101-5729

Mothers Against Gangs (MAG)

(847) 934-0105

P. O. Box 392
Palatine, IL 60078

Mothers Against Violence

(212) 255-8484

154 Christopher Street, 2nd Floor
New York, NY 10014

National Association For Mediation in Education (NAME)

(413) 545-2462

205 Hampshire House
Box 33635 University of Massachusetts
Amherst, MA 01003

National Council On Crime and Delinquency

(415) 896-6223

685 Market Street, Suite 620
San Francisco, CA 94105

National Criminal Justice Reference Service Justice Information Center

(301) 251-5500

Box 6000
Rockville, MD 20849-6000

www.ncjrs.org

National Network Of Runaway & Youth Services, Inc.

(202) 783-7949

1400 Eye Street, NW, Suite 330
Washington, DC 20004

National Runaway Switchboard

crisis hotline: 1-800-621-4000,
or (312) 880-9860

3080 North Lincoln Ave.
Chicago, IL 60657

National Youth Gang Center Office of Juvenile Justice and Delinquency Protection

(904) 385-0600

P. O. Box 12729
Tallahassee, FL 32317

National Youth Work Alliance

1346 Connecticut Avenue, N.W.
Washington, D.C. 20036

Paramount Plan: The Alternatives To Gang Membership

(213) 220-2140

City of Paramount 16400 Colorado Avenue
Paramount, CA 90723-5091

Ten Point Coalition

(617) 524-4331

215 Forest Hills St.
JamaicaPlain, MA 02130

Youth Development, Inc.

(505) 873-1604, (619) 292-5683,
or crisis hotline: 1-800-MISS-YOU

1710 Centro Familia SW
Albuquerque, NM 87105

P. O. Box 178408
San Diego, CA 92177-8408

Critical Issues & Concerns: Depression, Suicide

American Association Of Suicidology

(202) 237-2280, or (303) 692-0985

4201 Connecticut Ave. NW, Suite 310
Washington, D.C. 20008

http://www.cyberpsych.org

Depression and Related Affective Disorders Association, Inc.

c/o Johns Hopkins Hospital, Meyer 4-181
1601 N. Wolfe Street
Baltimore, MD 21205

Depression Awareness, Recognition, & Treatment

1-800-421-4211

National Alliance For the Mentally Ill (NAMI)

1-800-950-NAMI

200 N. Glebe Rd., Suite 1015
Arlington, VA 22203

National Committee On Youth Suicide Prevention

(617) 769-5686

825 Washington Street
Norwood, MA 02062

National Depressive And Manic Depressive Association

(312) 642-0049

730 North Franklin, Suite 501
Chicago, IL 60610

National Foundation For Depressive Illness, Inc.

1-800-245-4381, or 1-800-248-4344

P. O. Box 2257
New York, NY 10116

National Institute Mental Health's D/ART (Depression, Awareness, Recognition, Treatment) Program

1-800-421-4211, or (301) 443-4140

Room 10-85, 5600 Fishers Lane
National Institute of Mental Health
Rockville, MD 20857

http://www.nih.gov/publicat/edyprogs/dart.htm

National Mental Health Association (NMHA)

1-800-969-NMHA

1021 Prince Street
Alexandria, VA 22314-2971

Samaritans

(617) 247-0220

500 Commonwealth Ave.
Boston, MA 02215

Suicide Prevention Helpline

1-800-227-8922

Survivors Helping Survivors

(414) 649-4638

St. Lukes Medical Center
2900 West Oklahoma Ave.
Milwaukee, WI 53215

Teen Suicide Prevention Taskforce
(213) 642-6000
P. O. Box 76463
Washington, D.C. 20013

Youth Crisis & Runaway Hotline
1-800-448-4663

Youth Suicide National Center
(415) 347-3961
204 E. 2nd Ave., Suite 203
San Mateo, CA 94401

Youth Suicide Prevention
(617) 738-0700
65 Essex Road
Chestnut Hill, MA 02167

Critical Issues & Concerns: General Overview

American Self-Help Clearinghouse
(201) 625-7101
Denville, NJ 07834

Boys Town National Hotline
1-800-448-3000

Bureau For At-Risk Youth (The)
1-800-99-YOUTH

Crisis Hotline
1-800-421-6353, or 1-800-352-0386 in California

Crisis Prevention Hotline
1-800-9-FRIEND

Families Anonymous
(818) 989-7841
P. O. Box 528
Van Nuys, CA 91408

Girl Power
1-800-729-6686
11426 Rockville Pike, Suite 100
Rockville, MD 20852

Minrith/Meier New Life Clinics
1-800-NEW-LIFE

National Center For Missing and Exploited Children (The)
1-800-843-5678

National Child Abuse Hotline
1-800-422-4453

General Overview

Advocates For Youth
(202) 347-5700
1025 Vermont Ave., Ste. 200
Washington, D.C. 20005

American Academy Of Pediatrics Division of Publications
141 Northwest Point Blvd. P. O. Box 927
Elk Grove, IL 60009-0927

Center For Early Adolescence (The) University of North Carolina
Carr Mill Hall
Carrboro, NC 27510

Child Welfare League Of America
(202) 638-2952
440 First Street NW, Ste. 10
Washington, D.C. 20001

National Adolescent Health Information Center (NAHIC)
(415) 502-4856
1388 Sutter Street, Ste. 605A
San Francisco, CA 94109

National Clearinghouse On Family Support and Children's Mental Health
1-800-628-1696

Parents Anonymous, Inc.
(909) 621-6184
675 West Foothill Blvd., Suite 200
Claremont, CA 91711

Society For Adolescent Medicine
(816) 224-8010
1916 Copper Oaks Circle
Blue Springs, MD 64015
SOCADMED@GVI.NET

RESOURCE PATHWAYS, INC.

For every important issue we face in our lives, there are resources available to us that offer suggestions and help. Unfortunately, we don't always know where to find these sources of information. Often, we don't know very much about their quality, value, or relevance. In addition, we often don't know much about the issue we've encountered, and as a result don't really know where to begin our learning process.

Resource Pathways guidebooks help those doing research on important decisions or facing a challenging life-event by helping them find the information they need to understand the issues they face and make necessary decisions with confidence. Every guidebook we publish includes these important values:

- We review and rate **virtually all quality resources** available in any media (print, the Internet, CD-ROMs, software, and more).

- We define and **explain the different issues** that are typically encountered in dealing with each subject, and **classify each resource** we review according to its primary focus.

- We make a reasoned judgment about the quality of each resource, give it a **rating**, and decide whether or not a resource should be **recommended**. We select only the best as "Recommended" (roughly 1 in 4).

- We provide information on **where to buy or how to access** each resource, including ISBN numbers for print media and URL "addresses" for Internet websites.

- We publish a **new edition of each guidebook frequently**, with updated reviews and recommendations.

Those who turn to Resource Pathways guidebooks will be able to locate the resource they need, saving time, money, and frustration as they research decisions and events having an important impact on their lives.

ABOUT THE EDITOR

John J. Ganz, Ed.D., is a certified School Counselor, adjunct University Professor, community Mental Health Counselor, Trainer and Interventionist, former High School Teacher, Corrections Officer, and Police Officer. John's career includes twenty years of experience in counseling students and their families, teaching high school and university classes, counseling victims of trauma and violence, training school, community and workplace leaders in trauma and disaster intervention, and developing programs for debriefing victims of trauma. Currently, John teaches graduate courses in the Department of Education and Counseling at Seattle University in Seattle, Washington. Since 1986, he has been School Counselor at The Bush School, a K–12 school in Seattle, Washington, where he currently heads the Support Services Department consisting of college counselors, mental health counselors, and academic counselors. He is also the track and cross country running coach at The Bush School. John has been a presenter at regional and national conferences for the American Red Cross, the National Organization of Victim Assistance, the Center for Mental Health Services, the National Association of Independent Schools, and the Pacific Northwest Association of Independent Schools. As past President of Washington Victim Services, a non-profit crime victim advocacy organization that he co-founded, John co-wrote and co-produced two video programs for debriefing groups of victims. He has also worked as a corrections officer in the felony unit of the King County jail in Washington, and then subsequently worked as a patrol officer for the city of Bothell, Washington. John is presently a member of a broad-based coalition of mental health, government, and school officials studying crisis in schools under the direction of the Departments of Education, Justice, and Social and Health Services. In May of 1998, he was the team leader for the NOVA national trauma intervention team following the shooting of high school students in Springfield, Oregon.